TRANSFORMING LEADERSHIP

Equipping Yourself and Coaching Others to Build the Leadership Organization

Second Edition

Terry D. Anderson, Ph.D.

*with Ron Ford and
Marilyn Hamilton, Ph.D. (Cand.)*

St. Lucie Press
Boca Raton   Boston   London   New York   Washington, D.C.

Library of Congress Cataloging-in-Publication Data

Anderson, Terry D.
    Transforming leadership : equipping yourself and coaching others to build
the leadership organization / by Terry Anderson with Ron Ford, and
Marilyn Hamilton. – – 2nd ed.
        p. cm.
    Includes bibliographical references and index.
    ISBN 1-57444-109-4 (alk. paper)
    1. Leadership. 2. Communication in management. 3. Interpersonal
communication. I. Ford, Ron. II. Hamilton, Marilyn. III. Title.
HD57.7.A53 1997
658.4′.092—dc21
for Library of Congress   97-37206
                                                                                    CIP

Leadership Organizations are Headed by Transforming Leaders

"*Transforming Leadership* is for those people who have moved beyond HRD buzzwords and slogans. This book provides the individual manager, consultant, counselor, human resource executive, leadership team, and company a clear insight into the distinct elements that cultivate leadership that develops high quality and performance. Through a straightforward, integrated method, the individual self-evaluates his or her leadership qualities and skills, then commences to enhance them by implementing specific learning actions that are backed by powerful coaching and mentoring support. For anyone eager and serious about developing leadership that equips people for a high performance workplace, this book is an absolute must."

William C. Bean
Chairman, Strategia
Previous Chief Financial Officer, IBM Training

Preface

How the Second Edition is Distinctive from the First

This Second Edition of *Transforming Leadership* is more accessible to a wider range of readers. It is less "academic" but can continue to be used by leadership programs at the university level. The review of leadership theories is still retained: an examination of how leadership development has a truly profound impact on the morale and performance of individuals, teams, and organizations. *Transforming Leadership*'s innovative conceptual contribution to the literature is a focus on how it is necessary to build "a leadership organization" before— and to an extent, while—you move ahead into building a "learning organization."

> **Most major organizational transition efforts fail because leaders do not have the skills to build teams that will accomplish the execution of strategic plans.**

The Second Edition of *Transforming Leadership* addresses this issue squarely, with an emphasis on the importance of the role of executive and leadership coaching and mentoring—in addition to whatever competency-based training may be undertaken—for leadership development.

This Second Edition is front-ended with a self-assessment of skills so the reader can get a snapshot of strengths and areas where there is a self-perceived need for training or coaching. It can be used as a reference book, and can be referred to over and over again during the course of a leader's development. It can be used as a skill prompter in difficult problem situations where forethought and careful consideration are clear advantages. The body of the book is focused entirely on gaining a more in-depth understanding of the fifty-six key leadership skills that are outlined in this book. Other information that focuses on the personal development—rather than skill development—of the leader is now in Part Three, Part Four, and the Appendices of the book.

This new edition is a preparation for the *Policing Edition of Transforming Leadership* to be coauthored by Chief Norm Stamper, Chief of Police of Seattle; his Deputy Chief Nancy McPherson; and Assistant Chief John Welter, San Diego Police Department.

The First Edition of *Transforming Leadership* focused primarily on the development of transformative leadership skills that help build high-performance teams and organizations. This edition, however, is written to accomplish more than the previous one. It is presented to illustrate in more depth and detail how leaders can implement the *Transforming Leadership* process, skills, and principles to develop themselves, their teams, and their organizations. This step is important for leaders to learn to develop high-performance capabilities and high-morale cultures and communities. Therefore, equipping leaders with the knowledge and skills to build a *leadership organization* is the primary theme of the Second Edition.

Transforming Leadership provides a model to integrate other models into a holistic leadership development framework; it provides a map for developing critical leadership skills; and it still has the self-assessment and developmental aspects included in it. This Second Edition, however, amplifies and augments the First Edition in the following ways. Feedback from clients in business, education, and government sectors indicated that the book could more powerfully frame these ideas with a clear understanding of what a healthy, prospering organization could and should look like, with an emphasis on effective ways to build what I am now calling The Leadership Organization.

This new edition aspires to add clarity and perspective to the holistic view of how individual leaders can develop themselves and one another into high-performance team leaders who lead organizations to develop communities of learners. It is my hope that in writing this edition, I will, to some extent, provide a practical and conceptual ladder to assist the reader to reach toward a high ideal—as Kotter wrote, "the highest act of leadership is institutionalizing a leadership development culture."

Who Should Read this Book?

This book is intended for a diverse readership. A generic knowledge and skills focus and a rich composite of competencies are needed by the wide range of professional leaders who will read it. The reader should expect to find examples of various concepts and skills from various working environments including business, education, health, social services, criminal justice, and government.

Transforming Leadership provides the content, structure, and process for the development of those who want to be effective in preparing others to lead more effectively—whether they are managing, consulting, mentoring, training, counseling, or coaching the development of others. An organization that initiates and sustains this kind of development is called a Leadership Organization. This kind of an organization stimulates and realizes what David Dubois calls "high-impact, competency-driven performance improvement."

For centuries, the Japanese have utilized mentors to practice this kind of succession planning and leadership development. The Germans have done so for decades. In North America, formalized coaching and mentoring programs have become established in large corporations such as AT&T, Exxon, Kodak, Pacific Bell, Lytton Guidance and Control Systems, Motorola, Esso Resources, Allegheny Ludlum Steel Corporation, Varian Associates, and many others. William Gray, Ph.D., and Marilynne Miles Gray, M.Sc., principals of The Mentoring Institute of British Columbia, have conducted formalized mentor training programs for the companies mentioned above, utilizing the *Mentoring Style Indicator*, coauthored by Dr. Gray and myself.

Those who are newer to their external or internal consulting and training professions, however, are often lacking in key skills that they must have to be effective. For this reason, they may need to develop in certain areas prior to attempting specific projects. This book will act as a personal and professional development planning guide for these younger professionals, or for those who aspire to be. The book can function as a challenging orientation for those who plan to enter the fields of consulting or training.

Transforming Leadership is also aimed at managers who have had successes in their leadership endeavors but who wish to hone their awareness and skills, or develop skills they lack. Like the 200 managers at GTE who completed a custom-designed version of the *QLEAD* self-management module, many managers have already had some training in self-management skills. They may or may not have had training in interpersonal skills, decision-making, problem-management, change-management, or various other skills. Most lack training in other critical leadership areas, however, such as group and team development, meeting effectiveness, organizational needs and problems assessment, culture-building, or organizational effectiveness optimization. This book will be a catalyst to help individuals begin filling in some of these gaps.

This book is also for those new to the management or leadership arena, who have been timid in their leadership, or who are fearful due to lack of experience. Individuals who feel effective as leaders may want to improve their abilities by reading this book. It is often from lack of knowledge, lack of skill, lack of opportunity, or the presence of fear that many leaders fail to develop the kind of leadership impact they would really like to have.

Transforming Leadership is appropriate reading for those in any positions of leadership in small, medium, and large companies, or in agencies and institutions. It is for managers and supervisors who aspire to be managers. It is for educators, business people, social services professionals, therapists, counselors, health care professionals, and others who deal with the development of people and performance in systems, in organizations, and teams.

Transforming Leadership could also be used by undergraduate and graduate students as a comprehensive introduction to the theory and practice of leadership in any course that has this introductory focus as its goal. For example, business degree programs such as BComm, MBA (*Transforming Leadership* has been adopted by City University's MBA program on a number of campuses), Entrepreneurship, and Organizational Behavior could benefit from a self-assessment and planning program such as this—as well as other change agent programs such as MA programs in Human Resource Development, Organization Development, Counseling, Social Work, and Criminal Justice. The book could be used as an adjunct to existing texts, and to update many university programs still functioning without any kind of comprehensive theory and skills model or competency-based training program. There is an important move afoot in many programs to provide both a liberal arts education and competency-based educational opportunities prior to graduation with even a baccalaureate degree. Employers are demanding a wider range of such skills.

In addition to those in the business and the helping fields, managers in education, health, government, and nonprofit organization sectors could also benefit greatly from completing the self-assessment and planning activities as a matter of course while reading this book.

Last, *Transforming Leadership* is for those who inevitably lead in the family unit and who wish to use this same knowledge and skills to stimulate and encourage the development of their spouses, their children, and themselves. Even though the book focuses primarily on leadership in management-type positions, I have written it in such a way that individuals who are parents will find the book accessible. They, too, are leaders on the grandest scale. Parents can potentially make more impact on our culture and our world than perhaps any other people.

A Desire for Integration and Comprehensiveness

The book grew out of a search lead by me, my students, and my colleagues for an integrative model for developing self, others, and organizations that could be accessible and readily applicable. Attempting to integrate and apply several fields of knowledge normally taught in separate disciplines can be difficult and confusing, especially for people who have received little professional training or formal education. Unfortunately, most people seem to have neither the time nor the opportunity to "put it all together."

Therefore, this book is my effort at integrating several fields of knowledge and practice into one model that is transformable (like a set of "Legos" or modular units), so that later, you can design your own unique version to suit your needs for various situations.

Incomplete understanding of leadership—what it is, and how it works—has resulted in confusion, rigidity, or vagueness in the minds of executives and managers as they attempted to lead people and organizations toward higher achievement and effectiveness. If some of the definitions of leadership are confusing and contradictory, the diverse theories and practices are even more overwhelming. Hopefully, this book will assist you to sort through some of this confusion and inspire you to grasp within yourself some of the "art [of leadership]...that cannot be explained."

The following comparison of traditional management and leadership agendas with transformational leadership illustrates the integration and comprehensiveness of the *Transforming Leadership* model.

	Management	Leadership	Transforming Leadership
Creating an agenda	**Planning and budgeting**—establishing detailed steps and timetables for achieving needed results, and then allocating the resources necessary to make that happen.	**Establishing direction**— developing a vision of the future, and strategies for producing the changes needed to achieve that vision.	**Anticipating future trends**—responding intuitively to change and opportunity, inspiring others to comprehend and rally around the renewed vision of possibilities.
Developing a human network for achieving the agenda	**Organizing and staffing**—establishing some structure for accomplishing plan requirements, staffing that structure with individuals, delegating responsibility and authority for carrying out the plan, providing policies and procedures to help guide people, and creating methods or systems to monitor implementation.	**Aligning people**— communicating the direction by words and deeds to all those whose cooperation may be needed so as to influence the creation of teams and coalitions that understand the vision and strategies, and accept their validity.	**Developing leaders** to support, equip and stimulate the development of people and the competencies, qualities, and attitudes they need to function on high-performance teams in growing organizations.
Execution	**Controlling and problem-solving**—monitoring results vs. plan in some detail, identifying deviations, and then planning and organizing to solve these problems.	**Motivating and inspiring** — energizing people to overcome major political, bureaucratic, and resource barriers to change by satisfying very basic, but often unfulfilled, human needs.	**Assessment, planning and implementation**—organization-wide leadership and self-leadership skills development program.
Outcomes	**Produces a degree of predictability and order**, and has the potential of consistently producing key results expected by various stakeholders (e.g., for customers: always being on time; for stockholders: being on budget).	**Produces change**, often to a dramatic degree, and has the potential of producing extremely useful change (e.g., new products that customers want, new approaches to labor relations that help make a firm more competitive).	**Builds the organization into a community** of challenged and rewarded learners who grow with the organization and have positive impact on their families and communities.

Used by permission. Adapted from Kotter, J., *A Force for Change, How Leadership Differs From Management.*

Phrases like "leading change management," "managing strategic change," "the challenge of change," and "developing change agent skills" are becoming a part of a slang language that has been emerging in the human resource development field for the past decade. In fact, some people are sick of reading and thinking about "change." They are even tired of change itself.

A shift toward a more interdisciplinary approach is already occurring in the fields of communication, counseling, and leadership. It is essential that professionals who educate others to work in human service, health, education, business, industry, the military, and government organizations shift to broader and more integrative educational models—if personal, interpersonal, organizational, and social problems are to be more potently managed and better prevented.

I have had so much feedback from colleagues and other readers since the First Edition of the book was published several years ago that several new developments are included in this updated version. I want to acknowledge the ways I have been inspired by the works of others and how these inspirations have resulted in enhancements and the retitling of *Transforming Leadership*.

The broad "mission" of this book is that individual readers would find opportunity and challenge to self-examine, gain a renewed sense of purpose, clarify their foundational beliefs, and gain a broad spectrum of knowledge and skills. These new skills will ready them to build what I am calling **The Leadership Organization**. In light of this stated purpose, this book seeks to present a positive and hopeful approach: an integrative and innovative self-assessment curriculum—one that I hope can accomplish several objectives.

1. Identify and capitalize on strengths
2. Act as a tool for the assessment of training requirements to pinpoint a manager's (or potential manager's) need to gain critical knowledge and skills to become a better leader of individuals, teams, and organizations
3. Function as an integrated knowledge and theory base that an executive, manager, or supervisor can use as a planning guide for internalizing key knowledge "chunks" in areas that are self-assessed as deficient
3. Provide a metatheoretical base for the development of leaders who will, as they become more adept, be better enabled to develop other leaders through training, coaching, and mentoring activities
4. Provide concentrated focus points for needed and specific "micro" skills training until competency is attained in the areas determined to be necessary for an individual's effective leadership functioning
6. Expand upon the "awareness" and "versatility" skills needed to adapt to fast-changing and demanding environments—role, style, and skill-shifting skills
7. Have this book serve to prepare designated leaders to deliver the Quality Leadership Enhancement and Development program (presently under development)

8. Point the reader toward innovative resources that can act as catalysts to facilitate further individual, group, or organization development. Some of these resources are described by many other authors; some are explored by me.

To my knowledge, this is the only leadership-development book that provides an overarching model for leadership development or a guide for developing curricula that target—specifically and simultaneously—the means for creating the strongest impact on personal, team, and organizational effectiveness.

The need for such a book has become increasingly clear on two fronts—followers need leaders/managers who are simultaneously concerned about effective strategic management and about the human side of enterprise. They hunger for managers who inspire cooperation and creativity in reaching shared goals and dealing with planned and unexpected change. As Kouzes and Posner have pointed out, this rare combination of qualities and aptitudes encourages followers to be optimistic and to perform more effectively.

This book is not written from fear. Nor do I have any intent to cause anxiety to anyone by forecasting difficulty or doom. Rather, it is to assist people to develop into more fully qualified leaders who can help themselves and others become adaptable to change more gracefully and effectively—and remain healthy during the process. It will also assist individuals in their preparation for further clarification and achievement of their sense of purpose in the overall scheme of life. This book anticipates our best response to the exciting challenges we face as we move toward the end of this century and look into the next.

Acknowledgments for the Second Edition

I want to thank Ron Ford for his redesign of the *Leadership Skills Inventory*, for sequencing the chapters of the book, and for the design, graphics, and layout of the text. His encouragement, inspiration, and friendship have made the rewrite of this book an unexpected pleasure.

I appreciate Val Wilson of Val Wilson, Ink, who tirelessly rendered the reading of this book into a less distracting, more comprehensive read.

I want to thank Ken Keis, VP of Marketing for Consulting Resource Group International, Inc. If it weren't for his relentless market research and intuitive sensitivity, in general, certain changes would not have been made in this Second Edition. Ken's capacity to sense needs in others and to stay creatively open to explore options for growth and development at individual and corporate levels is greatly appreciated.

I appreciate the tenacity of Everett Robinson, VP of Training, Consulting Resource Group International, Inc., in pushing me toward further integration and application of the *Transforming Leadership* Theory and Model. Everett's insistence on sequential logic and flow and clarity of presentations challenges me toward excellence.

I appreciate Marilyn Hamilton, President of Consulting Resource Group International, Inc., for the *Transforming Leadership* model and her innovative work in understanding and testing the cutting edge of developing leadership organizations with credit unions, hospitals, and businesses. Her design capabilities, including the fresh, cubic, visual presentation of the model, have made it clearer and more appealing. As a senior partner, Marilyn has demonstrated her leadership in the effective management of our company; her leadership has enabled me to focus more completely on the implementation of *Transforming Leadership* with key clients and on the rewriting of this Second Edition. Marilyn is a true friend and colleague.

I deeply appreciate Bill Bean, past Chief Financial Officer for IBM Training, for teaching me that strategic planning must not only be applied in theory and implemented in practice, but must be accountable in reality for leaders to make significant and meaningful differences in their organizations. Even more important, Bill, thanks for your encouragement and inspiration in leading others toward "Spirit" as the primary issue for personal, professional, and organization development. As a result of your challenges and encouragement, *Deep Structure Strategic Planning* is now developed as a process into a separate chapter as an Appendix in this book. Bill's book, *Strategic Planning That Makes Things Happen*, is a powerfully integrative and practical framework for making best use of a number of theories and practices for strategic planning. Bill, thanks for leading Consulting Resource Group's strategic planning sessions as our external consultant and brother-friend!

I also appreciate Bill Bean for introducing me to a group of professionals who worked with us to deliver a custom-designed version of *Transforming Leadership* to the top 200 executives and managers of GTE North (General Telephone and Electric). Greg Dabicci, Nancy Frauhiger, and Kim Krisco (then, GTE's internal consultants) worked with Everett Robinson and me to get a reading about how a version of the *QLEAD* could work in a larger population of leaders at GTE. Their contribution in the assessment of executive needs, program design, and delivery process was integral to the success of the program. Their feedback since the project ended in 1992 has enriched the revised edition of this book, and has paved the way for improvements in future programs. Thanks, colleagues and friends!

> **To my knowledge, no other single leadership development book provides an overarching model for leadership development.**

I thank Ken Blanchard for his personal support and encouragement of my work in clarifying the issue of spirituality as it relates to personal, professional, and organization development. Ken's concern for the Spirit of people, for the impact Spirit can make in the workplace, and for communicating the importance of this issue has inspired me to focus on it in a separate chapter in this revision, and it is outlined as the first Appendix. Also, Ken inspired me by his example to write another book (in progress), tentatively titled, *The Mystery of Identity: Understanding Your Personal Search*—a book to assist people to understand and move through the steps, stages, and obstacles in their personal search process.

Other Acknowledgments

My deepest gratitude is toward my parents, Don and Hazel Anderson, who through their faithful support and encouragement, have opened opportunities to me I otherwise would never have known. Their moral and personal support played an important role in the completion of this work.

Second, my sons, Aaron and Jordan, sacrificed dearly in their sharing of my vision that this book and the ideas in it will eventually make a positive difference in this wondrous world becoming so fraught with complexity and negativity. They have sacrificed time with me so that I could complete the work of this book. They knew this was a book about love, about the development of people, about our futures. They supported me in good faith with their energy, encouragement, and in providing ideas for examples throughout the book.

I also appreciate Darryl Plecas who has been a model of a transforming leader in many ways. He has had a positive and transforming impact on the individuals and organizations with which he has contact. He also was the source of great encouragement to me when, many times, I wondered if the work of writing the necessary revisions of this book was worth the trouble. A close colleague and friend, he provided a number of fun times, incredible laughter, and stress release when times got tough. His tenacious mental abilities inspired me to stretch for more understanding and more inclusive gestalt as I did more and more research into the field of leadership.

I acknowledge and appreciate Gerard Egan of Loyola University of Chicago, who over eighteen years ago, was the original inspiration for me to write *Transforming Leadership*. In 1978, when I organized his visit to University College of Fraser Valley to give his first "People in Systems" workshop in Canada, I saw a vision for this book.

I also have a deep feeling of gratitude for hundreds of students—in my communication, problem-management, and leadership courses at the University College of Fraser Valley, in leadership courses at Trinity Western University, and in counseling courses at the University of British Columbia—who have given me feedback about the clarity, practicality, or difficulty they had with various parts of the First Edition over a period of several years. I believe they were honest with me. Thanks to them, I discarded one-third of what I normally would have tried to cover in one book, and included some of what I may have never thought of on my own.

Finally, I most deeply appreciate and acknowledge the Spirit of my Christian heritage, the power of which I experience and know to be the driving force behind much of my work and writing.

Terry Anderson
Abbotsford, British Columbia, Canada
September 9th, 1997

Background of the Author

Terry D. Anderson is a results-oriented consultant, executive coach, author and university educator with a Ph.D. (1992) in Administration and Management. His undergraduate work was in English and psychology (B.A., 1967), and his master's level work was in post-secondary education and counseling psychology (M.A., 1973). His undergraduate and master's level academic work was taken at California State University, Chico; and his doctoral studies were with the faculty at the University of Massachusetts School of Management and School of Counseling and Consulting, through Columbia Pacific University in San Rafael, California. His Professional Teacher Education Certification was completed at the University of Victoria, British Columbia, Canada (1971).

As an entrepreneur, he founded and developed a successful publishing and consulting firm, Consulting Resource Group International, Inc. (1979) that is currently flourishing with over 40 publications. He personally authored over a dozen publications, some of which have been translated into Japanese, Dutch, Swedish, Hungarian and French, and are being marketed in eight countries.

As a practical, results-oriented senior consultant and executive coach, he has conducted significant organization and/or executive leadership development projects for General Telephone and Electric, the TORO Company, Irby Construction, Abbotsford Police, New Westminster Police, the Ministry of the Attorney General, the Correctional Service of Canada, Security Resource Group, Inc., Nationwide In Home Services Corp., Denbow Transport, Customs and Excise Canada, and dozens of others over the past 25 years.

As a university level educator, his experience includes teaching more than 5,000 adults over two decades in the areas of communication, problem management and leadership full time at the University College of the Fraser Valley in Abbotsford, British Columbia, Canada. It also includes 10 years part-time teaching the same kinds of courses at Trinity Western University, and part-time teaching at the University of British Columbia. He has also taught the Police Supervisor's Course in Team Development, Strategic Planning and Priority Management at the Justice Institute of British Columbia, and is currently designing a new course (Leadership and the Future, based in part on his research) for managers in the public safety and justice system. This course will be launched in January of 1998.

As a researcher, he has conducted market research for various businesses, curriculum development needs assessment research for business (GTE Executive Leadership Program, 1992), and curriculum development research for the Correctional Service of Canada and the Justice Institute of British Columbia. In nearly every instance, his research has led to the development of innovative curricula in which he has played a significant leadership role—both in the design and in the delivery of the curricula, including the training and development of other educators and trainers. Dr. Anderson's research has resulted in measurably positive leadership development and organization development outcomes.

As an advisor to various organizations, Dr. Anderson currently sits on the Advisory Board for COMDEX (high-tech conference organization), on the Justice Institute's Advisory Committee for the Leadership Degree Program, and serves on the Conference Planning Committee for the Justice Institute of B.C. and the Canadian Police College. In the past he has served as a member and an International Network Director (1993) for the American Society of Training and Development, and was certified as a Professional Consultant by the Academy of Professional Consultants and Advisors (APCA).

Dr. Anderson has two sons, Jordan (18) and Aaron (22), and lives with his wife, Jo-Anne Marie, in New Westminster, British Columbia.

Dedication

This book is dedicated to my wife, Joanne, my sons, Jordan and Aaron, and my mother and father, Don and Hazel Anderson, who—in the course of my life—have believed in me and have:

sacrificed,
contributed,
encouraged,
participated,
inspired,
guided,
loved me when I was exhausted, and
supported me
to accomplish some of our mutual dreams.

Terry Anderson

Table of Contents

Chapter 1

INTRODUCTION: Transforming Leadership that Builds the Leadership Organization

My premise is that leadership is not exceptional (some are born with it), but the natural expression of the fully functional personality. As Warren Bennis put it, "The process of becoming a leader is much the same as becoming an integrated human being."

by John Thompson,
*Corporate Leadership
in the 21st Century*

Transforming Leadership and The Promise of the Leadership Organization

"Institutionalizing a leadership-centered culture is the highest act of leadership."

John Kotter

"Without Vision, the People Perish"

The proverb in this heading reminds us that the vision we have in mind determines the way we respond to challenging conditions. If we have a pessimistic vision, we might tend to stalk the territory like wolves of destruction, seeking only immediate opportunities for gratifying selfish ends. If we have no vision at all, we might wander aimlessly behind others, like sheep lost in a fog of indecision. Or if we have a clear vision of realistic possibilities, we can soar as birds of creative change, rising above the clouds of mediocrity to see new vistas and inspire others to achieve cooperative fulfillment.

Transforming leaders build the leadership organization. They are those who have inwardly decided to grow into being more conscious, developed, skilled, sensitive, and creative participants. They strive to make positive differences in organizations and in the lives of others wherever they go. They climb the heavens, reaching beyond the ordinary, the predictable, the average—charting new territories and possibilities. They reach up for leadership from those who are wiser, and pull others "below" them upward to greater, unseen heights on the way. This is not easy to accomplish, especially in a rapidly changing world where it seems that many cynical people belittle such lofty ideals. With vision and leadership, however, people can live increasingly meaningful and fulfilling lives. This is an important

> **Transforming leaders build the leadership organization. They are those who have inwardly decided to grow into being more conscious, developed, skilled, sensitive, and creative participants.**

foundation to enable teams and organizations to make a serious and positive impact on the communities around them.

This is illustrated in this diagram.

Organization Development Stimulates
Community Development

↑

Team Development Stimulates
Organization Development

↑

Personal Leadership Development Stimulates
Team Development

These are many of the big themes on the horizon that executives and managers must get ready to help the other leaders in their organizations address: Self-Management; Self-Managed High Performance Teams; Beyond Hierarchy; Diversity; Global; Quality; Conformance to Requirements; No-Doubt Contracting; Rapid Response; International Standards; Focused Marketing; The Learning Organization; Continuous Improvement; Customerization; Innovation; Fashion; Entertainment; Multimedia. Family; Credibility; Trust; Competence; Caring; Ethics; Spirit; Transformation. All these themes are important and represent an overwhelming blizzard of change demands on the average decision-maker—demands you can help your people with if you have the skills and the know-how.

Acts of Kindness Are Required

Now, more than at any other time, leaders in your organization need competent and trusted consultants (either internal or external) as associates who can come alongside them and provide the following:
1. A way to gain a visionary view of an encouraging future.
2. A skilled mind at planning, managing and leading fast in unpredictable change environments.
3. An encouraging spirit.
4. Coaching for their own executive and team development.
5. A caring heart, so that they can, in the long term, become their own "consultants" with the skill to act with the same level of competence you have gained over time. In turn then, they will be more able to pass this torch of knowledge and wisdom along to others.

To become this trusted associate, whether you are helping leaders manage a corporate turnaround, a quality programs intervention, or an ISO 9000 series certification process, you must possess the same prerequisite sets of knowledge, qualities, and skills. Although most successful leaders may have the necessary qualities, they are not likely to have developed the full battery of technical and people skills required to lead and empower other leaders to transform their organizations into winners in the globally competitive new millennium.

Critical Leadership Qualities that Managers Want from Consultants and that Employees Want from Managers

All leadership is some form of change management. Fulfilling relationships have the following five qualities that people in your organization and your family seek.

1. Understanding personal and organizational needs, problems, goals, and dreams helps people feel comfortable and optimistic about the relationship.
2. Caring that gets results does inspire people to want to engage you as a trusted leader to help manage necessary change.
3. Respecting people as valuable, unique, imperfect, and developing souls gains their respect.
4. Genuineness is the bottom-line requirement—if we are perceived to be personally phony, or incapable of delivering our claims, we are dead in the water.
5. Specificity in our written and spoken communication—that leaves no doubt in anyone's mind about the intended meaning of words or contract issues—is critical to earning trust and gaining interpersonal and corporate credibility.

All decisions to change, to buy, to repurchase—or even to love—hinge ultimately on the clear content of conversations and the quality of commitments in relationships!

But if we are truly sincere, genuine in our intent to build a leadership organization and the people in it, and if we have the required qualities inside to gain

> **Although most successful leaders may have the necessary qualities, they are not likely to have developed the full battery of technical and people skills required to lead and empower other leaders to transform their organizations into winners in the globally competitive new millennium.**

credibility, that doesn't mean we will have developed the technical knowledge or specific skills to bring our sincerity and compassion forward to meet the people's real needs.

Most Managers Lack Some of the Critical Skill Sets

These are the five skills sets of *Transforming Leadership*:
1. Self-Management
2. Interpersonal Communication
3. Problem-Management
4. Consultative Skills
5. Role, Skills, and Style-Shifting Skills

They are all required for successful intervention as a person or as a professional leader. These skills are more important than the "business," marketing, promotions, sales, analytical, or technical skills you may have because they are central to your gaining credibility with others. They are also required by the mid-managers, supervisors, or people you serve in order for them to manage change, build teams, develop positive culture, and protect themselves and one another from burnout, at the same time.

Our observations suggest that less than one in twenty managers or consultants has all five skill sets required to lead individuals, groups, and organizations effectively. Lacking in any one of the BIG FIVE skill sets causes a breakdown in effectiveness when acting as a person, family leader, consultant, or manager. Also, fewer than one in fifty managers or consultants has developed the *Transforming Leadership* skills to the point where they can teach others these critically important skills. These skills form the foundation of building a *Leadership Organization*.

What is the Leadership Organization?

Definition: The Leadership Organization creates and sustains a leadership-centered culture where leaders are equipped to develop leaders at all levels of the organization—from top down and from the inside out.

To the extent that this is effective, it will result in the development of all people in the organization, who in turn will have developmental impact on their families and communities. This developmental impact occurs because learning occurs. Learning occurs because leaders are competent, caring, creative, and honest.

The Leadership Organization is based on a commitment by visionary leaders to develop people (and organizations) by providing opportunities for on-the-job learning that leads to spiritual, intellectual, interpersonal, physical, career, financial and emotional health, growth, and well-being. The obvious rationale for facilitating this development is that realizing the potentials of people is a worthy endeavor and—from a business point of view—results in higher personal, team, and also organizational performance. The Leadership Organization has at its helm leaders who are developmental change agents—transformation specialists who act as exemplars in the move to lead more fulfilled, service-oriented lives that make a positive difference in the lives of people who will, in turn,

These skills are more important than the "business," marketing, promotions, sales, analytical, or technical skills you may have because they are central to your gaining credibility with others.

affect their organization's success the most. This is the way for organizations to regain the loyalty of so many who have grown distrustful and disloyal due to layoffs, restructuring, re-engineering, and other change initiatives.

Therefore, in a Leadership Organization, those in senior positions are the first to make the commitment to long-term development. With consultative assistance, they assess, plan, develop, and evaluate their own personal and executive team capabilities. They learn how to become better leaders and how to develop other leaders directly through their own mentoring of protégés and/or through the development of organization-wide programs that integrate learning leadership with the management functions of the work itself. After the development of the executive team, there are identifiable steps that a Leadership Organization goes through to effect such a large scale and long-lasting organizational transformation.

1. Shift paradigms from mainly managing the business "status quo" to leading performance teams toward the realization of a preferred future.
2. Develop and communicate an inspiring vision of an ideal future that will motivate individuals and teams. Involve others in creating this vision: People get behind what they help create!
3. Assess the needs, wants, fears, and problems of the organization (including those of the internal and external "customers").
4. Using a systems approach to change management, set realistic, achievable transition goals that, when accomplished, will realize the vision.
5. Strategically plan and implement step-by-step changes, and remove obstacles to realizing the new vision and goals.
6. Prepare, train, coach, and/or mentor the key leaders—those who are willing, ready, and able—to develop self-leadership capabilities in all members of the organization.
7. Research and/or track the outcomes of change initiatives and report progress at regular strategically timed intervals throughout the process so that movement toward the vision can be celebrated and unexpected obstacles can be removed or managed.

8. Engage intentionally in continuous developmental learning that results in ongoing personal, team, organization, family, and community development.

These steps are vital to the long-term health of any organization. Without developed leaders—without a strong team at the helm—the organization will have no vision, no spirit, or will be a house divided against itself and it will not as easily endure the storms of change we are now beginning to face.

How is The Leadership Organization Different from Traditional Organizations?

The Leadership Organization prepares the leaders first, but eventually everyone in the organization learns to work *on* the organization to improve it, as well as work *in* it. People can learn to see their individual contributions in the context of the organization as a whole if they are given feedback about their work unit, how the internal and external customers are influenced by their work, and how their decisions and actions are contributing to or detracting from the financial or service quality of the organization. It is clear that the Leadership Organization is not ordinary and, that even though it is not a quick and simple transition to make, it is necessary to move forward into a preferred future.

> **Without developed leaders—without a strong team at the helm—the organization will have no vision, no spirit, or will be a house divided against itself, and it will not as easily endure the storms of change that we are now beginning to face.**

We compare traditional organizational characteristics with the key attributes of the Leadership Organization on the following page.

The Traditional Organization	The Leadership Organization
Controls Organizational Design	Is Codesigned By Those Who Work in It
Assumes It Knows What is Best	Assumes That What is Best is Always Changing
Delays Change as Long as Possible	Responds to Change Immediately
Clings to Old Paradigms	Anticipates Change in Advance Whenever Possible
A Linear Approach	A Systems Approach
Vertical Command Hierarchies	Collegial Team Relationships
Work is Boring Repetition	Work as Meaningful Self-Expression
People are Cogs In Wheels	People as Collaborators, Team Mates
Focus on Past and Present	Focus on Moving Toward Ideal Future
Sufficiency-Oriented	Continuous Improvement Orientation
Bureaucracy-Oriented	People and Idea-Oriented
Management by Objectives	Strategic, Accountable, Intuitive Leadership
Traditional Gender Roles	Competency is Recognized/ Rewarded
Multiple Levels in Organizational Structure	Cross-Functions: Information Access and Role Clarity
Management by Position-Power	Leadership by Credibility
Problems Get Attacked	Problems Get Prevented
Conformity to Rules	Creative Problem-Solving for Continuous Improvement
Decision-Making out of Consultation	Inter-Team Brainstorming and Decision-Making
Accountability to Boss	Accountability to Team
Self-Interest Orientation	Quality and Customer Service-Orientation
Dollars Top Priority at All Costs	Intelligent, Creative People Produce More Dollars
The Rich Get Richer, Poor Get Poorer	Wealth and Rewards are Distributed by Contribution

Build the Leadership Organization First: Then Build a Learning Organization.

The Leadership Organization provides a foundation of skills for the leader of the Learning Organization. The Leadership Organization development process and *Transforming Leadership* skills provide the process and content to lay the foundation of the learning organization. For example, the five disciplines outlined by Senge—systems thinking, personal mastery, mental models, building shared vision, and team learning—assume that leaders and learners either possess or can quickly develop the requisite competencies to apply these five disciplines.

Our observation during live assessment and training sessions indicates, however, that fewer than one in three trainees who claim to be good communicators can actually demonstrate effective communication skills in a live-video interview where we can assess their competency levels with a high degree of accuracy. Even fewer of those assessed have demonstrated the more complicated and difficult-to-learn counseling, coaching, and consultative skills. Therefore, it is difficult for managers who are unskilled in the foundations of people-leadership skills to lead the transformation toward becoming a learning organization.

Moreover, it is possible to put into place the basics of a learning organization by installing "systems" and still not develop the leaders to the point where they can develop the people who will execute these systems willingly and competently. In a recent conversation with a health care executive, the point was made clear to me that the TQM process that was initiated was being undermined by over 75 percent of the mid-managers in the organization who could not lead teams and could not gain the cooperation of workers to implement the TQM requirements—and morale sagged as never before.

Senge states that the five disciplines of the learning organization, "might just as well be called the *leadership* disciplines as the learning disciplines." He goes on to state:

> These disciplines span the range of conceptual, interpersonal, and creative capacities vital to leadership. But most of all, they underscore the deeply personal nature of leadership. It is impossible to reduce natural leadership to a set of skills or competencies. Ultimately, people follow people who believe in something and have the abilities to achieve results in the service of those beliefs.
> (Senge, The Fifth Discipline)

There is a rising tension for leaders to get themselves ready to build "learning organizations" and high-performance teams because learning organizations promise to deliver increased quality, efficiency, productivity, morale, and profitability as they learn to learn. So do TQM organizations or ISO 9000-certified organizations. There are few, if any, specific training programs, however, to help people get ready to lead or participate in such advanced high-performance organizations. While there are many signs that the future success of organizations lies in their capacity for organization-wide learning, even Senge reservedly states that:

I have yet to experience any organization that comes close to exhibiting the capacities we think of when we think of learning organizations—the ability of everyone to continually challenge prevailing thinking, the ability to think systematically (the ability to see the big picture and to balance the short- and long-term consequences of decisions), and the ability to build shared visions that truly capture people's highest aspirations.

One reason that such organizational capabilities are rare is that they require individual attitudes and skills that are rare. A recent story illustrates the challenges. The "champion" of an ongoing project found herself increasingly challenged by the difficulties of operating in a truly open, noncontrolling manner. She finally confessed, "It is like I have to live in two worlds—the old world of control and domination and the new world of learning. I know that the new world is what is needed, but I am so capable in the old world." Her boss, the CEO, has been a forceful advocate of the new project. But his forceful support continually sends a mixed message: We need to learn "because I say so." As the top management team has begun to actually practice dialogue (one of the core learning disciplines in our work), the CEO has described his experience as "like an 'out of body experience'"— seeing how opposite are my effects on the people around me from my intentions.

Without an unprecedented commitment to select and develop leaders, organizations will have difficulty liberating the innovation, quality, and learning required to successfully weather the storms of the coming years and decades. *Transforming Leadership* can play a critical role in preparing leaders to lead learning organizations because self-leadership is the foundation of individual success, interpersonal development is a prerequisite to team membership and leadership, team leadership is the building block of organization development, and organization development is a critical catalyst for developing healthy communities.

This series of relationships is graphically displayed below.

Effective learning organizations build healthy communities

High-performance teams build successful learning organizations

Effective team leaders build high-performance teams

Personal and interpersonal development builds effective team members and leaders

Self-leadership leads to individual and team success

The issue of leadership skills competencies must be taken seriously or organizations will only go through the motions of developing themselves in mechanical ways. Even the "learning organization" as described by Senge is often interpreted by less experienced managers as a quick way to install feedback systems so they can pump productivity, often without regard to the development of the people who will execute those systems. And, the issue of leadership credibility is also at stake.

People Don't Change for Leaders They Don't Like

In all organizations, the catalyst for high-performing teams, productivity, and quality enhancement is people. Although change agents must understand how to assist leaders to plan for and implement change, if those leaders do not have the skills to be effective with their people, the change effort will likely be perceived as undesirable and will therefore be undermined to some extent— and momentum for positive change can be lost.

Leadership is the primary factor that distinguishes organizations from one another over the long term. I accept this as true when I look at successful organizations and their leaders. Most organizations don't know how to select competent leaders. The fortunate organizations have discovered that by luck, they happened to have had a good leader. But luck isn't good enough for even survival anymore. In our complex and demanding time in history, everyone must become a leader of at least himself or herself to even live effectively. This inner strength forms the foundation of effective leadership of others. Therefore, the successful people and organizations of the future will have taken personal, leadership, and management development seriously. Self-leadership will become a common word and effective leaders will become culture-change leaders. They will engage in what Kotter calls, "the highest act of leadership"—"to institutionalize a leadership-centered culture." In my opinion, this quote expresses the most profound of insights about leadership development and its relationship to organization development.

On the one hand, I agree that it is impossible to reduce natural leadership to a set of skills or competencies. True transformative leadership includes character, spirit, vision, wisdom, and skills. On the other hand, we have observed over and again that many well-intentioned, sincere, committed, honest, inspiring, and even wise leaders often lack self-management, interpersonal communication, coaching and counseling, and consultative skills. These absolutely critical skills deficits can seriously interfere with the leaders' ability to carry out systems thinking, achieve personal mastery, use mental models, build a shared vision, and facilitate team learning.

How many managers have you personally observed who were competent to do the task aspects of the job—often the main reason they were promoted—but who lack even the basic skills to be innovative in designing systems, building relationships, teams, and organizations with credibility? In truth, you have likely seen some of them even be destructive. The worst turns of events that I have seen too often in my consulting work is that people are promoted into supervisory or management positions because of task or technical competencies; they assume that they are competent for the systems design, interpersonal, problem-management, and team-development aspects of their new leadership roles. If they assume they are already competent as managers, what do they do? Stop learning! Manage more! Lead less! Think of people you know who are like this. What problems have they caused you or others? What names or words do you and other people use to describe their incompetence? **Yet, it usually isn't their fault**. They haven't been trained to the level of competence in these critical skills.

In my personal interviews with many managers enrolled in the *Transforming Leadership* courses at the two universities where I have taught it, I have observed they are often full of theories about effective leadership and that they lack many of the practical skills, know-how, and capability to implement them. Without a strong grounding in the skills of leadership, the practices of the learning organization won't get off the ground. Their efforts will be undermined because people won't cooperate with leaders they don't like or don't trust. Providing people with opportunities for assessment and learning of the foundational skills of self-management, communication, counseling, consulting, and versatility will prepare and equip them to be exemplary leaders in their new learning organization.

If Managers Aren't Skilled, It's Probably Not Their Fault

Why are leadership capabilities, as Senge says, so rare among managers? Most managers have not developed the competencies they must have to lead effectively and it's usually not their fault. They haven't been able to find education or training programs that truly equip them with the competencies they need to lead teams toward higher performance and morale. Most of the universities and training programs they have attended have not coached them to develop the critical success skills they must minimally have attained. The reason for this is that the learning they have had has rarely been competency-based, comprehensive, or applied in their lives or workplaces—where it counts the most. Learning often gets lost when it is confined to classrooms or to isolated, off-site training sessions. Usually their program of learning is education about theory—no awareness of skill—or, level two or three on the five-point rating scale we use to assess competency.

> **On the one hand, I agree that it is impossible to reduce natural leadership to a set of skills or competencies. True transformative leadership includes character, spirit, vision, wisdom, and skills.**

Level 1 = Not familiar with skill
Level 2 = Am familiar with skill, but can't perform it very well at all
Level 3 = Can begin to perform skill on my own with conscious effort
Level 4 = Can perform skill naturally in a wide range of situations
Level 5 = Can help others learn the skill

Even most MBA programs are in the past few years beginning to realize how important it is to provide a competency-based curriculum before graduation. Smart employers are demanding that MBA grads present a wide range of demonstrable competencies before they hire them.

Many universities have used the first edition of *Transforming Leadership* to provide a map and a training program for learning the attitudes, qualities, and skills of leadership in their leadership programs. This is in addition to their traditional management curriculum. In addition, more and more companies have formalized mentoring or coaching programs to insure that those who move into management positions are realistically prepared to meet the challenge successfully. In fact, many organizations "throw their new managers into the deep end, see who can swim best, and promote the strong swimmers further." Or they orient them to their new jobs by pairing them up with a "politically correct" but relatively incompetent senior manager who models and passes along the "psychopathology of the average."

But most of all, the job role and skills of leadership (compared to the traditional manager) have been poorly and vaguely defined; therefore, it has been most difficult to formulate a relevant curriculum for leadership development.

Defining Leadership Illiteracy

Many managers are so leadership-illiterate that it is difficult for them to function in the new high-performance learning organizations. Many of them know this intuitively but can't get their finger on exactly what skills they lack so they can get on-track with a specific training and development program. You can use the following examples of illiteracy to compare to yourself, others, or organizations with which you are familiar.

Example of Personal Illiteracy

Here is the story of a business executive who looks back on a time of personal illiteracy: "I began my conscious search for personal clarity when I was nineteen. At that time, I had a psychology professor who was into "consciousness" and the human potential movement. Through my dialogs with him, I realized that I did not know myself at all! Even though I grew up in a good, loving family and went to church, I could not answer the basic questions of life and had most of the recognizable symptoms of the "psychopathology of the average": My religious beliefs were vague and confused; my values were not clear or prioritized; my interests were vague; I had no clear personal or career direction; I lacked a sense of an integrated core of self; I was pessimistic about my own and our planet's future; I was stressed and lacked stress-management knowledge and skills; I

> On the other hand, we have observed over and again that many well-intentioned, sincere, committed, honest, inspiring, and even wise leaders often lack self-management, interpersonal communication, and coaching, counseling, and consultative skills.

lacked learning skills to succeed well at my university in the first year; had no sense of personal purpose; didn't manage time well; was overweight; ate poorly; and was out of shape; depressed; and didn't know it. All I wanted to do was have fun, play music, surf, and avoid responsibility.

Sound like a typical Los Angeles youth in 1964? I was typical of a person who lacked what Senge calls personal mastery skills. I didn't make a high-performance team leader (or even member), except in the band I played music in.

As I realized this, I was horrified! I wanted more! During the following several years, I took my personal search process very seriously: I took courses in philosophy and religion and psychology; attended personal awareness workshops; saw the university counselor once per week for three years; participated in encounter groups and weekend encounter-group marathons; took interest inventories and personality tests; became a health and fitness freak; learned yoga and meditation; sought (and still seek) earnestly for wisdom and truth about the meaning of myself, love, and the ultimate (metaphysical reality). As I began the search process, I found that doors opened and a profound growth process had begun. I was awake to each moment for the first time! Life became richer and had more depth. Clarity did come. A sense of being on the right track came to me even though I didn't know everything I wanted to know. I learned that if I sought and did not stop seeking, I would keep on finding. I haven't stopped searching.

> **Learning often gets lost when it is confined to classrooms or to isolated, off-site training sessions.**

Example of Interpersonal Illiteracy

I worked with two executives who were having difficulty in their marriage. Both of them had experienced painful relationships before, and the pain between the two of them had begun during their courting and engagement period. The premarital counselor advised them: "Whatever you do, communicate! Talk with each other regularly." They agreed that they should do that. Both of them, however, lacked some of the know-how to make their communication times successful.

They didn't know how to develop the inner control to give their undivided attention to one another. They didn't suspend their emotions, judgments, and premature advice—and therefore didn't often listen actively and accurately. They often didn't convey accurate understanding of one another's feelings and ideas. As a consequence, they often were either aggressive or passive in their communications with one another. For the first two years of their marriage, they hurt and disappointed each another many times. Their confrontations were blaming and negative and did not result in getting problems resolved. They talked about separation and divorce. They looked around and saw that most of their relationships with other people had similar problems. They felt inadequate, ignorant, humiliated, and powerless to change.

Then they took a competency-based thirty-five-hour crash course in interpersonal communication skills. This short course equipped them to at least know what they could and should do. As we will see later, just having skills doesn't mean we have an open heart. They had the sincerity and the caring before, but not the competency. After the training, they had competency, but they had to get their hearts opened and fully functioning before they could become really good communicators. They were embarrassed! Those were the days (late 1960s) before competency-based training came to the fore. It wasn't their fault. It wasn't their parents' fault—their parents didn't teach them because they weren't trained by *their* parents. Their lack of skill was typical of most people.

This pervasive interpersonal illiteracy kills intimacy, morale, and performance at work and at home. But, we stumble through our lives in certain areas with blind spots because **we often don't know that we don't know.** Even when people are skilled and their hearts are open, they may sometimes decide for various reasons to "jam out" on their commitments and relationships because they don't at the time "feel love" for their partners. Even those whom you might least expect can be unfaithful or may betray commitments and loyalties in love and in business.

Skill development eliminates a major cause of breakdown and helps to build healthy relationships. Refusing to participate in dysfunctional relationships or partnerships can be healthy when one or more partners are not willing to engage in self-examination and problem-solving. In the final analysis, however, wholeheartedness of commitment and enduring faithfulness must willingly be *given* as a gift so that both parties in a partnership can enjoy the benefits of a steadfast relationship through the tough times. Otherwise, we simply follow our emotions of disappointment or discouragement and dissolve one relationship after another when difficulties present themselves.

Example of Problem Management and Counseling Illiteracy

Several years ago, I was consulting with the managers of a criminal justice organization. Many staff problems and problems with the "clients" were the focus of this agency. Problems were often not faced directly because if anyone had a serious problem, or said that he or she had trouble dealing with problems, this could affect his or her career success with regard to future promotions. Many people pretended that problems didn't exist so that they wouldn't have to be responsible for failing to deal with them effectively. CYA (cover your ass) became the unspoken motto of this organization. Some supervisory staff ignored calls for assistance or delegated the more difficult situations to less experienced staff so that they could avoid stress, danger, political heat, or their own incapabilities. Open truth-telling wasn't the norm in this organization.

One problem, because it was not faced and dealt with immediately and directly, escalated into mass destruction of property that amounted to millions of dollars. People were hurt physically and emotionally. Five staff members came close to being murdered. After an investigation, only a few people "wore" the blame even though most people in the organization were indirectly responsible for participating in the creation of a dysfunctional culture. Some of the senior managers were autocratic and attempted to solve problems by applying arbitrary policies and rules. They lacked the problem-management and counseling skills to confront people head on and engage in problem-solving without delay. They paid the price that many leaders in organizations pay. They were demonstrating the common dysfunction of many organizations: denial and avoidance of personal responsibility. But they did this because they were afraid of failure. At some level, they knew they did not have the skills to do the job and they knew they were in over their heads. It wasn't their fault, either. They hadn't been equipped in these more complex and difficult skills of problem-management and counseling.

They realized that their lack of training and skills was a serious problem and we codesigned a training program that focused on developing the competencies for managing and solving problems, and counseling others to take ownership of their own problem-management processes. This course is still being taught in modified form and the skills are now listed on the job descriptions as requirements of the job. Performance reviews include feedback about how well people engage in proactive problem-prevention and management. People are recognized and rewarded when they spot and "bird dog" a problem early on. To some extent, the leaders were transformed by this experience and they have formed a leadership organization that develops other leaders. It is now expected that to be an officer, you *must* have this skill set. It is recognized as a matter of life or death.

Example of Consultative Skills Illiteracy

An entrepreneur I met started a manufacturing company in 1988. The company manufactured parts of houses to designers' specifications. This entrepreneur was exceptionally successful because of his timing in the marketplace. In 1988, he was the only such manufacturer in our area. But he was lazy. He didn't want to build his organization, understand customers' changing needs, and respond in an innovative way to the opportunities. By 1993, he had three other competitors and was losing significant market share in spite of being in a high-growth area. He had set up an assembly line system for manufacturing that required little expertise or personal involvement of the workers; he paid them low wages and counted on turnover (which had increased from 30 percent per year to 25 percent per month!). To him, people were like computer chips—if it stops working like you want it to, just unplug it and put in another one. I have coined this approach "computer chip management." He failed to count the costs of retraining and time off due to injuries of inexperienced workers. His turnaround time for delivery of goods had decreased and word had spread that this wasn't the place to do business—and that it definitely was not the place to work.

My teenage son was working a summer job in a competitor's firm thirty-five miles away in another town. He liked the way his employer greeted him every day when he came to work, coached him to make continuous improvements and contributions during the assembly process, gave him raises for higher performance, and joked around with him during the lunch hours. To save two hours commuting time and travel expenses, my son applied for a similar position in the dysfunctional firm, which was closer to home, and he was hired. When he came home after his first day, he was very upset, and he said to me:

> *I can't believe the difference between these two places to work! I can't stand this place! I wish I'd never changed from the other place. The owner of this company doesn't know how to build a company. He doesn't know how to treat people. He treats everyone like slaves, not people. When he's not there, people steal things from the inventory, talk about him behind his back, and work as slowly as they can get away with. When someone scraps a part, everyone laughs because they just count it as revenge on the boss for how he treats people. He doesn't even care about his customers. He is often late delivering the goods, lets flaws go through, and tells customers that if they don't like it that they can go somewhere else. I was going to work here part-time while I go to the university in the fall but I'm quitting now and looking for another job. Most of the other workers are doing the same thing.*

We can see how powerful one leader is from this example of the dysfunctional leader. **He only wanted to work *in* his company, not *on* it**. He wanted to see what he could get out of it, not how he could build it. He couldn't play a consultative role and lacked the skills to assess the needs, wants, and problems of his employees and his customers. He lacked the skills to develop programs for change and development, and he is slowly, obliviously, going out of business: even his employees have demoted him by assigning him a new title: "Joke."

Example of Versatility Skills Illiteracy

The image of Popeye comes to mind when we think of style rigidity. His favorite saying was, "I yam wot I yam! I'm Popeye the Sailor Man." His friend, Bluto, was even more rigid and predictable. A certain CEO of a major company was known by his customers as a bureaucratic, arbitrary, and rigid manipulator. This guy was regularly "snarky," continually sought his own benefit—even at others' expense—and engaged in put-downs and guilt-lay-on attempts even while trying to negotiate a contract to his advantage—more like a Bluto than a Popeye. He virtually treated everyone the same. His employees, his wife, and his children, and one friend moved out of town (to get away from him). In the case of one employee who needed support and direction, he criticized her performance and demanded more, calling her a "whiner." When another employee wanted and needed a two-way communication to solve a problem, he just predictably gave his premature advice and demanded conformance to his "solution." When his wife sought consolation in the loss of her mother, he left for a fishing trip, telling her "everyone dies, you'll get over it." He blew up at his kids and yelled at them for over five minutes because their rooms were messy. He lacked the skills and the versatility to become anyone's problem-management facilitator, communicative friend, or consultative colleague. His rationalizations made him even more intractable, as he bragged proudly: "Everyone knows where *I* stand—because *I'm* honest!"

> **They were demonstrating the common dysfunction of many organizations: denial and avoidance of personal responsibility. But they did this because they were afraid of failure—at some level they knew that they did not have the skills to do the job—and they knew that they were in over their heads.**

He engaged in our self-assessment-center process using the *Leadership Skills Inventory (LSI)* and found that he lacked most all of the skills needed to be an effective communicator, coach/counselor, and consultant. Using the "other" version of the *LSI,* he received harsh and "honest" feedback from his employees in an anonymous questionnaire. He realized that if his marriage was to be salvaged, he was going to have to make some major changes. Since he was in his third marriage, he began to take the feedback seriously—especially since he got the same feedback from home as from work. Over a period of two years, he came to be respected as a "jerk-in-process," a person humble enough to admit to everyone that he lacked important skills but who was willing to learn. He did learn most of the skills and came to a new level of self-respect and gained credibility among all those who could forgive the past. His marriage survives to this day, and his kids haven't left home in their teen years. Quite a transition!

Now on to Part One of This Book

Part One of this book will provide an opportunity for you to do a self-assessment of the leadership skills that you have and the ones you need to develop. It will also help you to understand and learn to use the *Transforming Leadership Model* to build a Leadership Organization.

References

Thompson, John, *New Traditions in Business: Spirit and Leadership in the 21st Century.* Berrett-Koehler Publishers, San Francisco, CA, 1992.

Senge, P. F. *The Fifth Discipline: The Art and Practice of the Learning Organization.* Doubleday. New York, 1990.

Senge, P. F. Training and Development. *The Future of Workplace Learning and Performance.* May, 1994.

Part One

Chapter 2

LEADERSHIP SKILLS INVENTORY:
Self-Assessment

Transforming Leadership offers not only the direction and the road map for the leadership development journey, this articulate book gives us the supplies and nourishment to thrive along the way. Terry Anderson knows that leadership development is self-development.

Jim Kouzes

Coauthor of *The Leadership Challenge* and *Credibility*, and President of TPG Learning Systems, a company in the Tom Peters Group

Introduction to Self-Assessment

In this chapter, you will perform a self-assessment using the *Leadership Skills Inventory (LSI)*. The *LSI* examines fifty-six of the skills commonly used by effective leaders, and that account for a significant amount of their success. The results of this self-assessment will provide you with a "road map" for personal and professional development as a leader through the rest of this book.

The logic of this assessment is based upon the following leadership model.

1. The core attribute of an effective leader is his or her ability "to see." Leaders can see where they are and where they are going. They have insight into the current situation and can see the problems and the opportunities. Their decisions and actions are purposeful and intentional because they are able to take advantage of what they see. Without this leadership "sight," they would have nothing to contribute to the life and mission of an organization.

2. Leaders make a difference in the lives of those who follow them. Leaders inspire followers to action and sacrifice. Leaders motivate people and organizations to make changes and tackle challenges. Leaders come in countless varieties and differ from one another in matters of style, personality, and methods. Nevertheless, there is a common, distinguishing characteristic of every leader who is truly effective: leaders have tremendous influence upon the lives and work of others.

3. Finally, the vehicles by which a leader's "sight" is translated into influence are the skills identified and assessed in the *Leadership Skills Inventory.* These skills are central to the leader's ability to function effectively in the context of relationships and organizations.

The diagram on the following page illustrates this dynamic leadership reality.

Directions: Assess your own ability to perform the leadership skills in the following assessment using this scoring system.

This skill is new to me.	I understand the skill	I can perform the skill	I can perform the skill well	I can perform the skill well.
1-2	**3-4**	**5-6**	**7-8**	**9-10**
I cannot do it.	but, I cannot do it.	but not reliably.	in many situations.	I can teach others, too.

For added benefit, space is provided for gathering scores about yourself from two others who know you well enough to assess your skill levels. This will give you a very important reality check by comparing how you see yourself with the way others see you.

I. THE SKILLS OF PERSONAL MASTERY

(For self-control, improved performance, and development as a leader)

These skills have been shown to be the **personal foundation** of leadership and management effectiveness. Without these foundational skills, it is difficult to become proficient in any of the other more complex skills that follow. These skills provide you with the capacity to achieve better balance in life and improved performance in all areas of career and personal life. Your scores on this section will help you evaluate and pinpoint your need for coaching or training in specific skill areas.

		Self	Other 1	Other 2
#1	**Grounding:** I control my attention to focus in the present (not in the past or future).	☐	☐	☐
#2	**Centering:** I maintain clear awareness of self in the context of events going on around me.	☐	☐	☐
#3	**Beliefs Clarification:** I express and live out a clear and consistent set of beliefs.	☐	☐	☐
#4	**Purpose Specification:** I identify and live out a personal statement of purpose for my life.	☐	☐	☐
#5	**Values Identification:** I identify, prioritize, and live out a set of personal values.	☐	☐	☐
#6	**Life Planning:** I formulate an integrated plan and live out an intentional lifestyle.	☐	☐	☐
#7	**Education Goal Setting:** I specify and live a goal-driven plan for lifelong learning.	☐	☐	☐
#8	**Career Goal Setting:** I set and implement motivating and realistic career goals.	☐	☐	☐
#9	**Time Management:** I plan and implement the best prioritized use of time.	☐	☐	☐
#10	**Stress Management:** I apply effective stress-management methods to daily life.	☐	☐	☐
#11	**Health Management:** I get optimum nutrition, exercise, deep relaxation, and restful sleep.	☐	☐	☐
#12	**Positive Mental Attitude:** I control "self-talk" and build my own sense of self-worth.	☐	☐	☐
	Skill Set #1: Total(s):	☐	☐	☐

**Transfer the Total Scores for the Personal Mastery skill set to the *LSI*
Scoring Wheel on page 37.**

For more information on the skills assessed in this portion of the *LSI*, please
turn to Chapter 4 for a detailed discussion and illustrations of these skills in
action.

Chapter 9 provides you with the opportunity to begin developing a personal
plan for growing and sharpening your leadership skills, based on what you
identify in this assessment and in the supportive chapters to follow.

Please note:

> To make this comparison of the *LSI* results even easier, the *LSI* is
> available from Consulting Resource Group in two formats. The *LSI for
> Self* and the *LSI for Others* can be used to achieve a more anonymous
> assessment by providing "others" who are going to assess you with a
> separate assessment instrument to use. To order these tools, call CRG at
> 604-853-0566 or Fax 604-850-3003. Or write CRG at 2760 Trethewey
> Street, Abbotsford, BC Canada V2T 3R1. U.S.A. address: 200 West Third
> Street, Sumas, WA 98295-8000.
> Visit the CRG website at http://www.crgleader.com.

II. THE SKILLS OF INTERPERSONAL COMMUNICATION

(For clear and effective communication with others)

These skills have been shown to be the **interpersonal foundation** of leadership and management effectiveness. The previous skills must be in place in order for these skills to fully develop. These skills provide you with the capacity to achieve clear two-way communication, improved relationships and morale, and more self-confidence as a communicator. Your scores on this section will help you evaluate and pinpoint your need for coaching or training in specific skill areas.

		Self	Other 1	Other 2
#13	**Self-Disclosure:** I reveal my personal thoughts, beliefs, and feelings appropriately to others.	☐	☐	☐
#14	**Image Management:** I positively manage the internal images I create in my mind of myself and of others.	☐	☐	☐
#15	**Impression Management:** I appropriately manage the impression others have of me through my language, dress, and decorum.	☐	☐	☐
#16	**Attending:** I control and focus my undivided attention respectfully toward others.	☐	☐	☐
#17	**Observing:** I objectively check my perceptions and avoid distortions or judgments.	☐	☐	☐
#18	**Suspending:** I wisely withhold emotions, judgments, and premature advice.	☐	☐	☐
#19	**Questioning:** I use (but not overuse) questions to elicit information effectively.	☐	☐	☐
#20	**Listening:** I check for the meaning others intend to convey to avoid prejudgments.	☐	☐	☐
#21	**Responding:** I convey accurate understanding of others' feelings and circumstances.	☐	☐	☐
#22	**Assertiveness:** I speak honestly and kindly and avoid using "put downs."	☐	☐	☐
#23	**Confrontation:** I provide constructive criticism, direction, and positive support.	☐	☐	☐
#24	**Challenging:** I encourage others to capitalize on unrealized potential.	☐	☐	☐
	Skill Set #2: Total(s):	☐	☐	☐

Transfer the Total Scores for the Interpersonal Communication skill set to the *LSI* Scoring Wheel on page 37.

For more information on the skills assessed in this portion of the *LSI*, please turn to Chapter 5 for a detailed discussion and illustrations of these skills in action.

Chapter 9 provides you with the opportunity to begin developing a personal plan for growing and sharpening your leadership skills based on the things you identify in this assessment and in the supportive chapters that follow.

III. THE SKILLS OF COUNSELING AND PROBLEM-MANAGEMENT

(Helping those around you solve and manage problems)

These skills have been shown to be the **problem-solving and decision-making foundation** of leadership and management effectiveness. The previous skills must be in place in order for these skills to fully develop. These skills provide you with the capacity to improve problem-solving and decision-making, decrease stress in relationships, engage in effective conflict-resolution, and enhance your performance management efforts when working with others. Your scores on this section will help you evaluate and pinpoint your need for coaching or training in specific skill areas.

		Self	Other 1	Other 2
#25	**Advanced Empathy:** I show accurate understanding of the deeper feelings and problems of others.	☐	☐	☐
#26	**Problem Exploration:** I explore the implications of internal or external problems with others.	☐	☐	☐
#27	**Problem specification:** I specify the nature, causes, and implications of a problem for others.	☐	☐	☐
#28	**Problem Ownership:** I specify and facilitate appropriate ownership of a problem by others.	☐	☐	☐
#29	**Goal Setting:** I help others identify realistic and motivating scenarios and time lines.	☐	☐	☐
#30	**Goal Ownership:** I specify and facilitate who is to make commitments to take action to resolve problems.	☐	☐	☐
#31	**Action-Planning:** I explore specific pathways and steps for goal achievement.	☐	☐	☐
#32	**Implementing Action Plans:** I increase success rate through follow-up and rewards.	☐	☐	☐
#33	**Confrontation:** I identify and help others and myself to address self-defeating behaviors.	☐	☐	☐
#34	**Self-Sharing:** I help others see problems in a new light by sharing my own story.	☐	☐	☐
#35	**Immediacy:** I point out typical problem behavior in others' present actions.	☐	☐	☐

	Self	Other 1	Other 2

#36 **Referral:** I make an effective referral to a
professional helper.

Skill Set #3: Total(s):

Transfer the Total Scores for the Counseling and Problem-Management skill set to the *LSI* Scoring Wheel on page 37.

For more information on the skills assessed in this portion of the *LSI*, please turn to Chapter 6 for a detailed discussion and illustrations of these skills in action.

Chapter 9 provides you with the opportunity to begin developing a personal plan for growing and sharpening your leadership skills, based on the things you identify in this assessment and in the supportive chapters to follow.

IV. THE SKILLS OF TEAM AND ORGANIZATIONAL DEVELOPMENT

(Building effective teams and organizations)

These skills have been shown to be the **team development and organization development cornerstones** of leadership and management effectiveness. The previous skills must be in place in order for these skills to fully develop. These skills provide you with the capacity to achieve consensus-based problem-solving and decision-making, manage the stress of working in teams, and enhance the team's and the organization's performance. Your scores on this section will help you evaluate and pinpoint your need for coaching or training in specific skill areas.

		Self	Other 1	Other 2
#37	**Informal Assessment:** I assess needs, wants, problems, and fears by one-to-one interaction with people.	☐	☐	☐
#38	**Formal Assessment:** I assess needs, wants, and problems through surveys, research, and info systems.	☐	☐	☐
#39	**Problem-Management Facilitation:** I facilitate effective problem-management meetings that improve performance.	☐	☐	☐
#40	**Needs Clarification:** I clarify the need for change in a language others will understand and accept.	☐	☐	☐
#41	**Readiness Checking:** I explore readiness for change and overcome blocks to constructive change.	☐	☐	☐
#42	**Values Alignment:** I explore and facilitate team spirit and synergy through clarifying and aligning values.	☐	☐	☐
#43	**Vision Consensus Building:** I facilitate consensus about the organization's mission, vision, and purpose.	☐	☐	☐
#44	**Strategy Consensus-Building:** I facilitate consensus regarding objectives, goals, and action plans.	☐	☐	☐
#45	**Program Design:** I design and implement flexible programs to reliably achieve objectives.	☐	☐	☐
#46	**Program and Team Performance Evaluation:** I evaluate and report the impact of action programs and team efforts.	☐	☐	☐

#47 **TQM Leadership:** I lead teams toward continuous improvement of what our organization produces or provides.

#48 **Building Accountability:** I install accountability systems so everyone experiences "no-doubt contracting."

Skill Set #4: Total(s):

Transfer the Total Scores for this skill set to the *LSI* Scoring Wheel on page 37.

For more information on the skills assessed in this portion of the *LSI*, please turn to Chapter 7 for a detailed discussion and illustrations of these skills in action.

Chapter 9 provides you with the opportunity to begin developing a personal plan for growing and sharpening your leadership skills, based on the things you identify in this assessment and in the supportive chapters to follow.

V. THE SKILLS OF VERSATILITY IN STYLE, ROLE, AND SKILL-SHIFTING

(Effectively adjusting to match the individual, group or organization)

These skills have been shown to be the **versatility and flexibility cornerstones** of leadership and management effectiveness. The previous skills must be in place for these skills to fully develop. These skills provide you with the capacity to be more appropriate, flexible, and effective in a wide range of situations, including one-to-one relationships, team relationships, and relationships between teams and in organizations. Your scores on this section will help you evaluate and pinpoint your need for coaching or training in specific skill areas.

		Self	Other 1	Other 2
#49	**Assessment of Styles:** I assess the predominant style tendencies of another person, group, or organization.	☐	☐	☐
#50	**Style Shifting:** I shift into the appropriate style behaviors that match the styles of others.	☐	☐	☐
#51	**Assessment of Roles:** I assess whether the communication, counseling, or consulting role is most appropriate for a given person or situation.	☐	☐	☐
#52	**Role-Shifting:** I shift into the appropriate role that matches the requirements of the situation.	☐	☐	☐
#53	**Assessment of Skills:** I assess which skills would be most appropriate to use in various situations.	☐	☐	☐
#54	**Skill-Shifting:** I shift into appropriate communication, counseling, or consulting skills as required.	☐	☐	☐
#55	**Recognizing an Organization's Development Stages:** I recognize the four stages of group and organization development.	☐	☐	☐

Stage One: Designing, orientation, consensus, and commitment

Stage Two: Making the transition: overcoming resistance and obstacles

Stage Three: Doing the work of the group

Stage Four: Evaluating and celebrating achievements

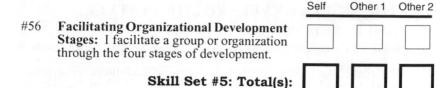

#56 **Facilitating Organizational Development Stages:** I facilitate a group or organization through the four stages of development.

Skill Set #5: Total(s):

Transfer the Total Scores for the Versatility skill set to the *LSI* Scoring Wheel on the following page.

For more information on the skills assessed in this portion of the *LSI*, please turn to Chapter 8 for a detailed discussion and illustrations of these skills in action.

Chapter 9 provides you with the opportunity to begin developing a personal plan for growing and sharpening your leadership skills, based on the things you identify in this assessment and in the supportive chapters to follow.

SUMMARY OF YOUR *LSI* RESULTS

Directions: Graph your scores in each of the five sections of the *LSI* on the scoring wheel below to visualize the results of your self-assessment. Place a "dot" on the line for each skill to correspond to its total score. Then connect all the "dots" with a continuous line. This will give you an overview of the extent to which you have developed each of the five skill sets, an important part of your leadership effectiveness. In addition, ask two other people, who know you well, to complete the *LSI for Others* for you. This will give you a valuable reality check and useful feedback. Graph their scores in different colors to distinguish them from you own self-assessment scores.

LSI Scoring Wheel

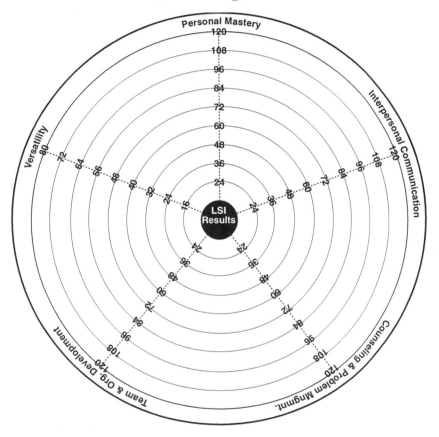

Chapter 3

INTRODUCTION TO TRANSFORMING LEADERSHIP AND THE TL MODEL

...the basic philosophy, spirit, and drive of an organization have far more to do with its relative achievements than do technological or economic resources, organizational structures, innovation, and timing...

T. Watson of IBM

Introduction

In this chapter, we will look into the nature of transformative leadership by examining the following.

1. Examples of *Transforming Leadership*
2. The Emergence of Transformative Leadership
3. The *Transforming Leadership* Model
4. Principles of *Transforming Leadership*
5. Roles and Functions of *Transforming Leadership*
6. Attitudes and Characteristics of Transforming Leaders

Examples of Transforming Leadership

Some examples of leadership that have a transforming effect will help to clarify the important differences between traditional and *Transforming Leadership*.

1. A father and mother mutually decided to plan their lives more carefully, and set goals and priorities. They had family meetings that taught their children how to plan and structure life, and found there was a payoff by the end of the first week. A psychologically closer family ensued, the resolution of some unfinished conflict issues occurred, and two brothers planned to build a car together over the next few years. Traditionally, parents have tended to live more day by day, and deal with opportunities or problems as they arise rather than intentionally build a plan to enrich family life.

2. A teacher of an overcrowded sixth grade class decided to meet with interested parents to train them to work with "underachievers" and "gifted" children in the class. After just a few weeks of the new program, discipline problems diminished significantly, students performed better in class and at home on schoolwork, and at the end of the year, the standardized test scores went up an unexpected 11 percent over the previous year for the underachieving students.

    The more traditional teachers have often considered parents "irresponsible" if they didn't help their kids at home, and tended to just accept classroom overcrowding as a "fact of life" with which they had to cope, at least temporarily.

3. After consultation with her teachers and a local stress and health center director, a principal of a junior high school—where teachers had the highest absenteeism rate in the district—decided to offer health and wellness education programs to teachers, parents, and students. These programs included deep relaxation training, computerized nutrition analysis and diet planning, weight reduction programs, quit-smoking programs, fitness-training opportunities after school, and a team approach to scheduling on-duty time during recesses and lunch hours. She provided a quiet, smoke-free place to practice deep relaxation during the noon hour and held regular staff meetings to air concerns and solve problems. At the end of the second semester, there was a significant drop in absenteeism, a reported increase in morale, and significantly fewer stress symptoms reported among staff.

   Obviously, these results will not occur simply because programs are inserted into the environment—the people involved must accept and utilize such programs, and the programs have to be introduced in such a way that they are perceived as welcome additions.

4. A top-level government executive realized that his management team lacked cohesion and harmony, that their meetings were fraught with tension and competition, and that some of the more important goals of the organization were not being reached because of poor relations among the management "team." He privately surveyed each of his managers, summarized their individual perceptions and concerns, and called them together to present his findings. The main troubles seemed to stem from the fact that the team was thrown together in a hurry during a time of available funding, and no one spent much time discovering others' strengths, clarifying roles, or agreeing upon goals in the organization. They called in a consultant to do a three-day team development session, followed by a three-day strategic planning session, and by the end of that year, the group not only achieved its goals—it surpassed them. Tension levels dropped, job satisfaction increased, and cohesion and creativity developed within the group.

   Traditionally, there would have been no systematic intervention, with the resulting effects of either increased tension and backbiting with lowered performance, or increased turnover, or both.

5. Lee Iacocca had to change the feeling of Chrysler's employees from "losers" to "winners" at a time when Chrysler had a history of irregular performance, and when the workers were suffering from the poor image of having received government money to stay afloat. Iacocca talked personally to the workers at Chrysler, hired back some sharp retirees to lend seasoning to the company, and even made personal appearances in Chrysler's advertising campaign to help change the climate among employees and in the marketplace. The evidence that Iacocca transformed his intentions into reality with new vision, commitment, and follow-through were Chrysler's increased quality, more effective marketing,

increased sales, and government loan pay-back completion. The net result was a transformed Chrysler Corporation, from top echelon executives to frontline assembly workers. With his success, Iacocca transformed and magnified our vision of leadership.

Before Iacocca's leadership, there had already been management and number-crunching attempts to save Chrysler from demise for over five years.

From these examples, you can get a better idea of the essence of *Transforming Leadership* in several different environments. Now, we will turn to the aspects of gaining a better understanding of the foundational theories to *Transforming Leadership*.

Leadership and Management: Interrelated but Different

There are clear differences between management and leadership orientations. As the chart below reveals, however, the integration of the two orientations presents a whole view of what is necessary for effective creation and transformation of an organization and the people in it. Also, the recyclical nature of the *Transforming Leadership* approach illustrated in this chart will give you a sense of the fluidity of the process. Rather than a cycle, perhaps it could be better represented as a spiral moving through time.

Relationship of Management and Leadership Functions

Management: *Task/Result Orientation*
Evaluation, research
Decision-making
Planning systems
Problem-solving
Data-based decisions
Specifying procedures
Administering policy
Day-to-day operations
Present focus to ensure results

Leadership: *People/Process Orientation*
Creatively applying research information
Motivating and rewarding others
Relationship and culture building
Team building and team development
Creative planning and shifting
Envision of end-states process
Personnel selection, orientation, performance management
Future focus for accomplishing a higher purpose

The Leading Manager: Integrating Diverse Orientations

As you look at the steps in the chart, you will see how important each of the tasks and functions are in management and leadership, and how certain functions must be performed prior to others, in a step-by-step but flexible process. It is also useful to think of management and leadership as two separate but interrelated areas because there has been so much confusion about their separate identities and purposes. Without both working together in a balanced manner, each would suffer and be less effective. Without leadership as the foundation of management, management cannot function effectively because it is undermined by a lack of humanity, clarity, focus, adaptability, and creativity. Without management, leadership might never follow through enough to get the results needed for long-term success.

The Nonprofit Society Case Study

A nonprofit society had its origins in the concerns of a group of people for unwed mothers who faced pregnancy, who for religious reasons, did not want to abort the unborn. They formed a society by registering with the appropriate government office.

All the board members were dedicated professionals who were very sincere and very busy, without previous experience in the process of developing a new organization. A rough constitution was written up but not ratified by all members. Staff members were hired, and the operation opened its doors. The staff agreed that the first priority was to conduct counseling sessions with the unwed mothers to assist them to make an independent decision as to whether to keep the child or find parents who wished to adopt the child. Those who chose the adoption route had an opportunity to select the parents to whom their baby would go. In nearly all cases, the adoptive couple was unable to have natural children.

Things went well for a few months, until conflicts began to emerge among staff members. Who should decide which of the qualified applicants on file should be permitted to raise the child: the birth mother, the director of the agency, or the staff person involved in the interviews with the adoptive parents? Should prospective adoptive parents have to reveal whether or not they had ever induced an abortion in the past, used illegal drugs, had a criminal record, etc.? Staff members disagreed and could not resolve their disagreements on these issues.

The board of directors had not specified the extent of the director's authority, even to the director. When the chairman of the board was informed of the conflicts, some arbitrary "management" decisions were passed "down," and the staff felt that their views were not being heard or respected. There wasn't really a team approach, which had been so generously spoken of by everyone, at least in principle.

In the beginning, there was little *Transforming Leadership* to provide clarity of vision, purpose, philosophy, goals, and policies about which people could agree. Therefore, it was very difficult for the board, director, or staff to set forth procedures based on these vague organizational foundations. The moral of this story is: Where there is lack of clarity on issues that require leadership to facilitate a team or organizational consensus, various individuals withdraw their energies or try to overmanage so that at least some decisions get made and action occurs. Had there been clarity established from the beginning on the key organizational issues, many of the problems of the new agency could have been averted.

The chairman of the board eventually exercised leadership influence and acquired the services of an external consultant who understood the social work-oriented goals of the agency, and who was experienced in organization development and team development. He met with the board and the staff members to facilitate the specification of a vision (where the agency wants to be in five years, whom it wants to serve, and in what manner, etc.) and philosophy (beliefs, values, and norms) based on policy statements to which board and staff members could agree. This eliminated power struggles, bonded staff members together around a common purpose and values, and removed confusion and downtime due to disorganization or people working at cross-purposes. The consultative leadership intervention transformed the character and performance of the organization and the people in it for the sake of the parents and children being served. After this leadership intervention, the organization was ready to once again be managed.

> **Without leadership as the foundation of management, management cannot function effectively because it is undermined by a lack of humanity, clarity, focus, adaptability, and creativity. Without management, leadership might never follow through enough to get the results needed for long-term success.**

Leading for a Change

The necessity of integrating management and leadership knowledge and skills within each key decision-maker, or at least on each team, is becoming more critical as world history faces us with increasing complexity, spastic change, and unpredictability. Each manager must lead and each leader must manage in a world where both leadership and management dimensions must be developed in order to respond to constant change and pressures, both internal and external to an organization. Increasing pressures of a technical, interpersonal, and organizational nature are on the horizon.

Change must be envisioned, anticipated, managed, and adapted to by key leaders, and this leadership must be exercised on a global scale. In this way, we can better cope with the acceleration of the rate of change that is happening now, and will likely be occurring in the future. We can influence the direction of events in the future only as we anticipate future trends, formulate alternative responses to these future scenarios, and be prepared to implement alternative action plans. In this way we can continue to correct-course as the winds of change shift direction unpredictably.

Transforming Managers Lead by Serving and Adapting to Change

Brown and Wiener (1984) point out that Japanese managers have not been strategic planners operating by formula management; they have been sensitively accommodating to changes in the environment. They tend to distrust "master strategies" because they can limit a wider vision of changes occurring in clients, technologies, or with the competition.

Upper and middle management in Japan have tended to see that their key task is in responding to important input from "below" (frontline staff and customers), rather than steering the organization from above along a predetermined course. This is closer to leadership than management. A Leading Manager, however, effects a transforming impact by doing both the strategizing and the shifting or adapting simultaneously. Or, alternatively, he or she agrees with another leader that one will play the leader and the other the manager for a specific purpose and period of time.

Naisbitt (1982) outlines major changes in the following chart that we can anticipate in the near future, some of which are occurring even now.

Naisbitt's Ten Megatrends

FROM:	TO:
Industrial Society	Information Society
Forced Technology	High-Tech/High-Touch
National Economy	World Economy
Short-Term	Long-Term
Centralization	Decentralization
Institutional Help	Self-Help
Representative Democracy	Participatory Democracy
Hierarchies	Networking
North	South
Either/Or	Multiple Options

These changes are occurring to various extents in a wide range of environments, but it is clear that with the burgeoning of both technology and information, we are going to need adaptability, innovation, and creative leadership more than ever. An even more recent and revealing expose of the types of changes likely to be advantageous in the future are outlined, and to some extent forecasted, in Naisbitt and Aburdene's book (1986). This book paints a wave of new ideas regarding the transforming of jobs and companies for the new information society. Some of Naisbitt's forecasts include ten considerations for reinventing an organization:

1. The best and brightest people will gravitate toward those corporations that foster personal growth.
2. The manager's new role is that of coach, teacher, and mentor.
3. The best people want ownership—psychic and literal—in a company. The best companies are providing it.
4. Companies will increasingly turn to third-party contractors, shifting from hired labor to contract labor.
5. Authoritarian management is yielding to a networking, people-style of management.
6. Entrepreneurship within the corporations—"intrapreneurship"—is creating new products and new markets, and vitalizing companies from the inside out.
7. Quality will be paramount.
8. Intuition and creativity are challenging the "it's all in the numbers" business-school philosophy.
9. Large corporations are emulating the positive and productive qualities of small businesses.
10. The dawn of the information economy has fostered a massive shift from dependence upon natural resources, transportation, and market proximity to quality of life considerations (such as good climate, good schools, cultural opportunities, etc.).

These evidences of rapid and dramatic changes are important signals for us to heed when we prepare ourselves to meet the leadership challenges that lie ahead, or prepare others to better meet those challenges.

When so many changes are upon us, Naisbitt and Aburdene (1990) outline another list of changes we can expect to see. They call these the "Millennial Megatrends—the gateways to the 21st century."

1. The Booming Global Economy of the 1990s
2. A Renaissance in the Arts
3. The Emergence of Free-Market Socialism
4. Global Lifestyles and Cultural Nationalism
5. The Privatization of the Welfare State
6. The Rise of the Pacific Rim
7. The Decade of Women in Leadership
8. The Age of Biology

9. The Religious Revival of the New Millennium
10. The Triumph of the Individual

These and other trends in our world will force upon us new demands and requirements that we become increasingly able to adapt to and become aware of our own potentials for growth and change, and lead the way with others who will need to undergo the same personal stretching process.

A Time for Vision in an Era of Change

Such a complex and difficult time in human history our planet has likely never seen. For this reason, leaders need to understand the kind of leadership that stimulates positive transformation and breakdown prevention. Egan (1985) most aptly states some basics of a theory of transformative leadership by describing clearly what a transformational leader does.

> *Transformational leaders are shapers of values, creators, interpreters of institutional purpose, exemplars, makers of meanings, pathfinders, and molders of organizational culture. They are persistent and consistent. Their vision is so compelling that they know what they want from every interaction. Their visions don't blind others, but empower them. Such leaders have a deep sense of the purpose for the system and a long-range strategic sense, and these provide a sense of overall direction. They also know what kind of culture, in terms of beliefs, values, and norms, the system must develop if it is to achieve that purpose. By stimulating, modeling, advocating, innovating, and motivating, they mold this culture, to the degree that this is possible, to meet both internal and environmental needs (Egan, p. 204).*

This clear vision of some ways a transformative leader can achieve positive results will assist you to further identify the somewhat elusive nature of *Transforming Leadership*. In addition to clarity of vision, the use of positive power is a necessary aspect of *Transforming Leadership*.

Power for Change

Bennis and Nanus (1985), reintroduce the seemingly lost concept of power as a key to transformational leadership. They observe that many, if not most leaders, have visibly lacked wholehearted commitment to the challenge of leadership, have been overwhelmed by the rapid change and complexity of our era, and have lacked the necessary integrity and credibility to earn the trust and respect of followers. They claim that the kind of leadership needed is transformative leadership and that this leadership power is exemplified by what they call "the Iacocca phenomenon."

> *Power is the basic energy needed to initiate and*
> *sustain action or, to put it another way, the capacity to*
> *translate intention into reality and sustain it.*
> *Leadership is the wise use of this power:*
> *Transformative Leadership. As we view it, effective*
> *leadership can move organizations from current to*
> *future states, create visions of potential opportunities*
> *for organizations, instill within employees commitment*
> *to change, and instill new cultures and strategies in*
> *organizations that mobilize and focus energy and*
> *resources (Bennis and Nanus, p. 17).*

Leaders who are particularly successful in acquiring and sustaining power have a number of things in common. Kotter (1979) observes, in his studies on the use of leadership power, that there are several keys to success for those who are effective in the use of power. They tend to be very sensitive to where power exists in their organizations. They use specific methods to develop power as long as the methods are ethical. They take calculated risks in which they "invest" some of their power in the hope of gaining it back with interest. They recognize that all of their actions can affect their power and they avoid actions that will accidentally decrease it. In their career development, they try to move both up the hierarchy and toward positions where they can control some strategic contingency for their organization.

We can see that it is possible that one of the reasons some people are not very effective in developing leadership effectiveness is that they do not know how to establish their own "power" image in the minds of others. To do this, it is possible to assess the different kinds of power one could possibly have, and set about to develop these different types of power for positive purposes. Image management (managing our own self-images and self-presentations) can have a positive impact on the images others have of us in their minds.

Kanter (1982) found that formal authority was less important to managers attempting an innovation than the power and influence that they exercised beyond the formal mandates of their organizational positions. Clearly, a greater understanding of power, how to develop it, how to keep it, and how to use it effectively is important in *Transforming Leadership*.

The Subtle Nature and Potency of Transforming Leadership

Burns (1978) further clarifies the character of *Transforming Leadership* when he expresses that it is more than mere power-holding, and is the opposite of brute power. He describes the relationship between most leaders and followers as a transactional, favor-for-favor type interchange. He does, however, point us to a view beyond the transactional tit-for-tat relationship of jobs for votes, subsidies for campaign contributions, or raises for more production.

> *Transforming leadership, while more complex, is more potent. The transforming leader recognizes and exploits the existing need or demand of a potential follower. But, beyond that, the transforming leader looks for potential motives in followers, seeks to satisfy higher needs, and engages the full person of the follower. The result of transforming leadership is a relationship of mutual stimulation and elevation that converts followers into leaders and may convert leaders into moral agents of change.*
>
> *...Moral leadership emerges from and always returns to the fundamental wants and needs, aspirations, and values of the followers. I mean the kind of leadership that can produce social change that will satisfy followers' authentic needs.*

Greenleaf (1977) had foresight in predicting the terrain of leadership theory today when he wrote:

> *A fresh look is being taken at the issues of power and authority, and people are beginning to learn, however haltingly, to relate to one another in less coercive and more creatively supporting ways. A new moral principle is emerging that holds that the only authority deserving one's allegiance is that which is freely and knowingly granted by the led to the leader, in response to and in proportion to, the clearly evident servant stature of the leader. Those who choose to follow this principle will not casually accept the authority of existing institutions. Rather, they will freely respond only to individuals who are chosen as leaders because they are proven and trusted as servants. To the extent that this principle prevails in the future, the only truly viable institutions will be those that are predominantly servant-led (Greenleaf, p. 9).*

A more recent view on *Transforming Leadership* is presented by Kanter (1983). She encourages a responsible, balanced leadership in serving the needs of the followers, and the needs of the organization simultaneously through participative leadership.

> *While encouraging participation, innovators still maintain leadership. "Leadership" consists in part of keeping everyone's mind on the shared vision, being explicit about "fixed" areas not up for discussion and the constraints on decisions, watching for uneven participation or group pressure, and keeping time bounded and managed. Then, as events move toward accomplishments, leaders can provide rewards and feedback, tangible signs that the participation mattered (Kanter, pp. 275-277).*

The Qualities Followers Want to See in Leaders

Kouzes and Posner (1987) conducted a most interesting study of over 1,500 managers to discover what positive practices their leaders engaged in. They found four key qualities and ten leadership practices that can be found in the behavior patterns of effective and admired leaders.

Most of us tend to admire leaders who have credibility, those who are:
1. Honest
2. Competent
3. Forward-Looking
4. Inspiring

These credible leaders tend to be committed to consistently implementing ten leadership practices:
1. Search out challenging opportunities to change, grow, innovate, and improve.
2. Experiment, take risks, and learn from the accompanying mistakes.
3. Envision an uplifting and ennobling future.
4. Enlist others in a common vision by appealing to their values, interests, hopes, and dreams.
5. Foster collaboration by promoting cooperative goals and building trust.
6. Strengthen people by sharing information and power and increasing their discretion and visibility.
7. Set the example for others by behaving in ways that are consistent with your stated values.
8. Plan small wins that promote consistent progress and build commitment.
9. Recognize individual contributions to the success of every project.
10. Celebrate team accomplishments regularly.

These ten practices represent central issues important to the understanding of *Transforming Leadership*. *The Leadership Challenge* book is recommended highly as one that has a very practical focus on understanding and integrating these ten most effective leadership practices. We also recommend a more recent work titled, *Credibility*, by Kouzes and Posner, that corroborates their previous findings and outlines critical ways that leaders must develop credibility or fail to have the impact they could.

The Intertwining of Management, Leadership, and Power

Kotter (1990), in *A Force for Change: How Leadership Differs from Management*, outlines how subtly the various successful executives behaved as they artistically intertwined the various aspects of their approaches into a powerful force for positive change.

Specifically, the most effective executives created agendas for themselves—made up of loosely connected sets of short-term plans, medium-term strategies, and long-term visions. They each built resource networks that could accomplish these agendas by staffing and structuring the jobs reporting to them, by communicating their plans and visions to people, and by establishing cooperative relationships with a broad range of individuals whose help they might need. They then actively sought to influence people in those networks when necessary to assure the

> **With the kinds of complex demands placed upon those in positions of leadership, it is not surprising that a wide range of skills should be displayed in the behaviors of those who are most successful.**

achievement of their agendas, and did so in a wide variety of ways, sometimes trying to control people and activities, sometimes attempting to inspire others to new heights of performance. Overall, this behavior was extremely complex and, as has been reported in other in-depth studies of executives at work, did not look much like traditional management.

What these executives were doing, employing the language of this book, was a combination of management, leadership, and still other things (chief among which was the development of sources of power that could help them manage, lead, and get promoted). But all of these various aspects of behavior were highly intertwined. They did not manage for fifteen minutes and then lead for half-an-hour. Instead, in the course of a single, five-minute conversation, they might try to see if some activity was proceeding as planned (a control part of management), gather information relevant to their emerging vision (the direction setting part of leadership), promise to do someone a favor (an aspect of power development), and agree on a series of steps for accomplishing some objective (the planning part of management). As a result, to the observer, what they were doing did not look much like management or any other recognizable activity. The managers themselves even found their own behavior difficult to describe and explain.

> **As a result of learning these skills or developing such qualities, it is easier to bring forward into reality not only competencies, but some sense of the "art" or charismatic (character) power involved in *Transforming Leadership.***

With the kinds of complex demands placed upon those in positions of leadership, it is not surprising that a wide range of skills should be displayed in the behaviors of those who are most successful. A model that can capture the components of this complexity and render them transferable to others is needed. Such a model will provide guidance for self-assessment, planning for training, and for evaluating the effectiveness of your own or others' leadership behavior. *Transforming Leadership* provides a model that is an attempt at this integration of the various complex parts of the effective leadership behaviors exhibited by the executives Kotter studied—where their leadership helped turn around NCR, P&G, and Kodak, and stimulated business growth at American Express, PepsiCo, and ARCO.

The Transforming Leadership Model

In developing this model, an interdisciplinary approach was taken to capture philosophy, theory, and scientific investigative results, which have a range of practical applications. The following theory and practice bases should be recognized as being important in the formation of a more integrative and comprehensive model such as *Transforming Leadership*.

1. Interpersonal Communication
2. Counseling and Problem-Solving
3. Human Development
4. Human Resource Development
5. Organization Development
6. *Transforming Leadership* Theory and Principles

From the above bodies of research and theoretical formulations have emerged "chunks" of applicable knowledge or sets of easily learned and teachable qualities and skills. As a result of learning these skills or developing such qualities, it is easier to bring forward into reality not only competencies, but some sense of the "art" or charismatic (character) power involved in *Transforming Leadership.*

A model is an approximate map of what reality could look like, and it is clear enough to give us a reference point for evaluation of our own effectiveness when we try a particular leadership intervention. With this clarified reference point and increased evaluative ability, we are able to make the necessary shifts to fine-tune our responses to people and organizations so that we can have more positive and potent impacts.

Transforming Leadership: A Research and Philosophy-Based Model

There are so many theories and philosophical assumptions about what one should do to become more effective that it is difficult to trust just anyone spouting off about another panacea, wonderful training, or action-oriented program. The concepts in the model are based on applicable theory in communication, counseling, and consulting (OD and HRD). Philosophers and practitioners often attempt to simply convince others that their one school of thought is the correct one. I am not doing such a thing with the *Transforming Leadership* Model. What I am doing is providing dozens of practical examples of how each skill in the Model can be applied in concert with other skills to form a comprehsive approach to the development of people, teams, organizations, and communities. A visual overview of the *Transforming Leadership* Model is presented on the next page.

An explanation of the details of each section of this model is contained in the text of each chapter. For example, in Chapter 4 the Self-Management skills, will be explained; in Chapter 5 the Interpersonal Communication skills will be the focus; in Chapter 6 the Counseling and Problem-Management skills will be defined and illustrated, and so on. The meaning and application of the model will become clearer as you read through this book.

> **It is important to understand that in reality, *Transforming Leadership* is not a rigid, linear, step-by-step process, even though a series of steps can be outlined to assist in understanding how the process can work.**

Leaders who utilize the five *Transforming Leadership* skill sets and knowledge areas in the Model have greater potential to shape an organizational climate and the interpersonal environment to achieve the desired results. Except for the management functions, these skills and knowledge areas will be discussed in greater detail in Chapters Four through Eight. It is not the purpose of this book to introduce the reader to the knowledge and skills of effective management because there are a wealth of good books that accomplish this goal more than adequately. First, it is important to understand that, in reality, *Transforming Leadership* is not a rigid, linear, step-by-step process, even though a series of steps can be outlined to assist in understanding how the process can work.

Transforming Leadership Principles

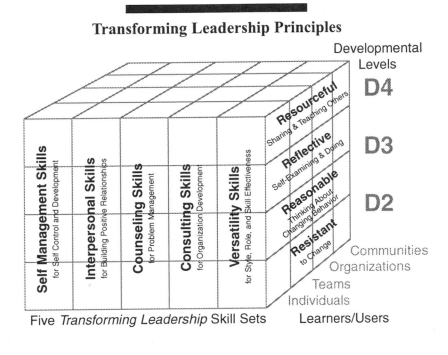

Five *Transforming Leadership* Skill Sets

Steps in the Transforming Leadership Process

We can see leadership as a complex process involving a fluid series of steps (which may overlap or reverse into one another, depending upon the circumstances). When this process is understood, it can assist leaders to develop people and to bring a vision of human and organizational transformation into reality. Without a compelling and clearly communicated vision, the status quo often remains, and innovation and development are arrested.

Learning to use the steps in the *Transforming Leadership* process model can increase your leadership behavior appropriateness "score."

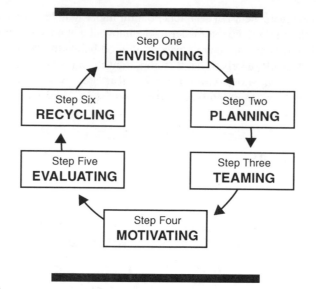

A further delineation of what is entailed in each of these steps is presented below.

1. **Envisioning**: This first step requires imagination, creativity, and an understanding of the history of a group or organization so that what is possible in the future can be more accurately and realistically specified and articulated. For most people, this is the most difficult of all the steps because it requires originality and stepping out of the ordinary ways of thinking and doing things. Since habits are strong and new ideas are accepted slowly, there is more risk involved than many people are willing to take. It is the critical step, however, because innovation and improvements usually happen because some person conceived of a better way to work or a better way to live. Envisioning must also be based upon the specifying and meeting of some kind of human need, or there will be no market for the new service or product being offered by a person or an organization.

2. **Planning**: Once a vision is captured (with or without dialog with others), it can be built upon through carefully specifying just how, where, and when a thing can best be done, and by whom it might best be done. This may involve family or committee meetings, brainstorming sessions, team development sessions, conflict resolutions, and negotiations. As the plan develops, if it is to succeed, there must be enough acceptance of the plan, and enough enthusiasm about the plan and the vision for it to be truly shared by all involved. Otherwise, the likelihood of its succeeding can be seriously diminished. When those involved have an opportunity for involvement that challenges them personally, they are more likely to invest themselves at a deeper level in making it work. Finally, this planning

process must include highly specific and concrete goals, objectives, and program steps for the timely accomplishment of worthy and realistic aims.

3. **Teaming**: Selectively giving responsibility to others involves building harmonious and productive teams by placing people in appropriate groupings that they see as desirable (whenever possible), giving them tasks appropriate to their strengths and interests, and supporting them emotionally and physically in the process of their taking on responsibility. This ensures that they will more likely meet the challenges they hopefully chose to meet. Matching the nature of a person with the nature of the job and matching people with people is an effective way of exercising leadership discernment.

4. **Motivating to Action**: Once some acceptance is established, motivation must develop inside of people (for internal or external reasons) on a continuing basis, or the plan will not be realized to the level of quality originally envisioned, or within the time allotted. A system of rewards must be established and valued so that motivation can be kept at a challenging and yet comfortable peak. People won't work hard when they feel that what they give is a great deal more than what they get—they find it demoralizing. Many things act as rewards, and identifying people's "hot" buttons—a whole range of them—and giving them reasonable rewards and opportunities that encourage them to stay motivated are key factors in transforming people and organizations. Motivation leads to the most important aspect of organizational life: Action. Higher levels of motivation and achievement can be accomplished by meeting the deeper needs of people: needs of recognition, accomplishment, challenge, belonging, meaning, and purpose. To do this is not manipulation, but rather respect for people to have a sense of need for both internal and external rewards in return for the sweat of their lives.

5. **Evaluating**: Evaluation of the results of a change effort is tricky but necessary business. It is important in terms of making improvements on the plan and in being able to jointly celebrate a specific level of success. The more carefully specified the plan is in terms of identified accomplishments to be reached, the easier the evaluation of the results. In designing the plan, evaluation criteria should be made a part of the plan. They should be realistic, desirable, concretely defined in terms of accomplishments, and measurable.

6. **Recycling the Process Through Evaluation**: Periodically, after a time of evaluation, all the steps in this process need to be repeated so that false assumptions are not made about how events are going, or how they should best go. Rethinking the vision, reformulating and renegotiating the plans, finding new motivators, regrouping for greater harmony and productivity, and reevaluation all keep people and organizations alive to what is real, and to what has positive change potential.

Using the skills and understanding in the *Transforming Leadership* Model and these process steps as a backdrop, we can now examine the twelve principles that lie at the heart of *Transforming Leadership*.

Twelve Principles of Transforming Leadership

As a part of this summary of *Transforming Leadership*, an outline of principles involved in the model are important. Principles of *Transforming Leadership* are general operating guidelines that can be applied in a wide variety of situations. These principles are listed below.

1. Every person in every situation is having an impact, for better or worse, on the people and the situations that are present.
2. Learning to observe this impact alerts us to the reality of positive or negative leadership opportunities and events. Increasing our level of awareness of people and events can be fruitful for everyone.
3. Every person can choose to try and make a positive difference in each moment with each other person, and at least within that immediate sphere of influence, can likely exert some positive, and therefore *Transforming, Leadership*.
4. The use of positive and respectful power and influence is necessary for leadership to have enough impact to be effective. Knowing one's own strengths, gaining strategic position power, developing a power network of like-minded people, and communicating your personal and position power in a positive way to others will assist you to reach higher goals.
5. Everything begins with the initiative of each individual. Privately, inwardly, individuals determine within themselves what to do, how to act, and how to treat people. If we are each clear within about our own beliefs, purpose, goals, and objectives, we will much more likely achieve them from this solid and well-defined center within ourselves.
6. Leadership, in its deepest sense, is the understanding and meeting of the deeper needs of the people being led/served. Even when achieving goals of increased innovation or productivity, our meeting of the deeper human needs of worth, recognition, reward, accomplishment, and personal development of others are cornerstones of motivation and satisfaction.
7. *Transforming Leadership* has a moral component centrally important to all other aspects of leadership, because few people will trust a leader who has lied, one who has embezzled, one who hurts others.
8. *Transforming Leadership* understands and involves others, so that they can gain a critical sense of belonging and experience the mutual sense of respect and trust that follow. Personal ownership in any venture can potentially increase motivation, morale, creativity, energy, and productivity.

9. There is opportunity for leadership in every environment, in every interaction, in every situation, in every moment. Leadership is intentionally making a positive difference in the development of organizations and individuals for a specific purpose. Being awake to these opportunities and seizing them increases our personal meaning and impact in life and work.

10. *Transforming Leadership* looks for long-term impact and long-term development, rather than just immediate results. Satisfaction increases when we can see a continuing positive development over longer periods of time, rather than just short-term successes.

11. *Transforming Leadership* begins deep within a person's belief and value structures, and a solid sense of purpose or mission in life is necessary for leadership effectiveness to be sustained. Have a well-defined, achievable sense of purpose that "sets you on fire" and that distinguishes you from the herd of people who follow along with a more vague purpose of some relatively unknown leader-heroes (such as political, sports, scientific heroes, etc.).

12. *Transforming Leadership* is open to the potential that there could always be another, higher, or deeper understanding of reality beyond what is presently comprehended. An attitude of humility not "puffed up with pride" characterizes a transforming leader. The splitting of the atom, radio, TV, and radar are practical examples of how what used to be hidden is now revealed.

I believe that these principles, when internalized and implemented in a leader's life, will result in greater leadership impact in the wide range of roles leaders must play. These roles will be examined further in the next section of this chapter.

Comparing Traditional and Transformational Functions and Roles of Leadership

Classical theories as outlined by Stogdill (1974) in his monumental review of leadership theory and research suggest that the primary functions of a leader are planning, organizing, and controlling. Various theorists have added coordinating, supervising, motivating, and others to the list. Functions that have been identified by behavioral theorists and researchers include:

1. Defining objectives and maintaining goal direction
2. Facilitating team task performance
3. Facilitating team action and interaction
4. Maintaining team cohesiveness and member satisfaction
5. Providing and maintaining team structure
6. Providing means for goal attainment

Functions of *Transforming Leadership* are necessary for greater impact to be made on the development of individuals and the organizations in which they live and work. These are:

1. Creating and communicating vision and purpose
2. Doing strategic and versatile thinking and planning
3. Facilitating peer, subordinate, and team development
4. Facilitating the development of the organization
5. Protecting individuals from destructive forces
6. Protecting the organization from destructive forces
7. Seeking and communicating consensus between teams
8. Specifying philosophy and values and creating culture
9. Creating insight
10. Motivating people to action

Traditionally, the roles of leadership have been divided into three main categories (Mintzberg, 1973). These are interpersonal, informational, and decisional roles. *Transforming Leadership* Theory asserts that the informational and decisional roles are primarily management functions, even though they can be handled creatively from a leadership as well as from a "hard line" management perspective. Therefore, these three traditional roles exclude some important dimensions that can make a critical difference to leadership effectiveness and potency. The important roles that encompass some of the traditional roles and introduce some new ones form the structures and avenues for the effective execution of *Transforming Leadership*. These roles are graphically introduced and expanded upon in the graphic illustration on the next page.

Although these roles and functions are not exhaustive, they capture some of the essence of what is believed to produce a transforming effect on individuals, groups, and organizations. It should be remembered also that effective management practices form the solid platform from which these additional functions can be carried forward.

Now that we have reviewed the roles and functions central to *Transforming Leadership*, we can examine the critical attitudes and characteristics of transforming leaders.

Attitudes and Characteristics of Transforming Leaders

This part of the chapter can be used as a way for you to look at yourself in relation to what has been discovered to be effective attitudes and characteristics of transforming leaders. In doing this self-examination, you can discover areas that are in need of development, and you can devise a short-term and long-term plan for your development as a leader. Highlight or underline parts of the following that you think will help you to formulate such a plan.

Roles and Functions of Transforming Leadership

Role	Function
Communicator	Get to know others Manage personal image Communicate corporate image Understand others accurately Communicate concern Recognize others' achievements Suspend judgements and emotions Resolve interpersonal conflicts Build effective, enjoyable relationships Build self-worth in others Empower and encourage others Confront others effectively
Counselor	Help others define and own their problems Help others to set achievable goals Help others explore and evaluate plans Motivate others to take action Sustain and support others to achieve plans Reward and recognize achievement Confront resistant or stuck people Make referrals effectively Share your experience at the right time Coach people to reach goals Mentor people to prepare for new roles Evaluate performance and give feedback
Consultant	Act as PR person for the organization Apply the consulting process Develop corporate values and culture Delegate to achieve goals through others Legitimize your leadership Facilitate group and team development Clarify norms, values, and beliefs Communicate vision and purpose Assess organizational needs and problems Deal with distracting members Research and report important information Plan and coordinate HRD and hiring

A Portrait of the Transforming Leader

General Characteristics The transforming leader is critically involved in envisioning, communicating, and creating an improved future for self, any other person, group, or organization. The transforming leader has clear personal beliefs: without clarity about one's own life stance on life's major questions, an individual can be easily swayed by situations—which are becoming increasingly complex, unstable, and unpredictable.

The transforming leader also has a well-defined sense of mission, purpose, values, goals, and strategies based upon a deep understanding of the people and aims being served, and a clear understanding of the cultural, political, and economic environment surrounding the change endeavor being attempted. The transforming leader is able to arouse a sense of excitement about the significance of the organization's contribution to society or the group's contribution to the organization. The transforming leader has working knowledge and skills in the areas of human development, organization development, interpersonal communication, counseling, consulting, and problem-management/solving.

> **Without clarity about one's own life stance on life's major questions, an individual can be easily swayed by situations that are becoming increasingly complex, unstable, and unpredictable.**

Transforming Leaders Need Exceptional Physical Health To be in leadership positions often requires an ability to deal with stress and difficult situations with some degree of resilience. The fitness required to sustain higher levels of energy and performance is described and prescribed very clearly by Schafer (1987). The energy to achieve higher levels of performance must also come from the nutrition program appropriate for you. You can find a wide range of books on fitness and nutrition to assist you to develop your understanding in these two key areas.

Transforming Leaders Are Peak Performers Garfield (1986) has, for the past two decades, researched top achievers through all strata of business, science, and the professions. He provides an illuminating profile of those people he calls peak performers: They are individuals motivated by a personal sense of mission; they possess the twin capacities of self-management and team mastery; they have the ability to correct course and manage change. These qualities are similar to the findings of other theorists mentioned above, except Garfield has gone to great lengths to specify some of his findings.

Summarized below are some of these findings about peak performers—that are similar to others' findings about transforming leaders.

Exercise Self-Management Through Self-mastery

1. **Self-Confidence**: Being willing to go out, hear "no," and move on to focus on the next opportunity.
2. **Bimodal Thinking**: Combining macro and micro forms of attention. Analyzing a problem situation within a company requires the overall macro view.
3. **Mental Rehearsal**: Preparing for action so that both the mind and the emotions are conditioned positively for the upcoming events.

Use Course Correction

4. **Mental Agility**: Having the flexibility to change perspective and do the creative thinking necessary to deal with challenges.
5. **Concentration**: Consisting of the stamina to work long hours, adaptability to change, and the hardiness that could also be called resilience under stress.
6. **Learning From Mistakes**: Taking appropriate actions based upon updated information.

Have a Results Orientation

7. **As Individuals**: Envisioning and communicating a clear mission, following up with a plan of action that includes specific goals, complete with benchmarks necessary for assessing timing, quality, and quantity of results.
8. **As Collaborators**: Using a "magnet mentality" to draw in what they need from other people.
9. **As Innovators**: Understanding that there is no guaranteed path from A to Z, and being prepared to make new paths in the service of results.

Cultivate Necessary Skills

10. **Develop New Skills**: Assessing what new skills are needed and then developing those skills though readings, courses, workshops, and tapes. Then asking for and getting feedback.
11. **Use Leverage**: Maximizing opportunities to use the skills they already have so they stay in their "peak performance" zone.

Develop Teams to Accomplish Results

12. **Delegate to Empower Others**: Empowering (releasing power in and from) others by giving them tasks and assignments that they do best, and never doing themselves what others can do better.
13. **Stretch the Abilities of Others**: Challenging others to develop to their potentials and offering opportunities and projects for them to do so (with the necessary support to succeed).
14. **Encourage Educated Risk-taking**: Encouraging others to take higher payoff risks if there is reasonable chance for success.

15. **Are Students Forever**: Seeking lifelong learning opportunities, which means there is a willingness to admit sequential ignorance, that a degree is not the end of the game.
16. **Expect to Succeed**: Having confidence and the ability to visualize at least one way in each moment that things can work.
17. **Map Alternative Futures**: Having alternate game-plans to shift into if the present one does not materialize as expected.
18. **Update the Mission**: Having an open mind to restating the mission—or critical paths to it—can be a necessary ability in times of spastic change.

Refined Self-Awareness and a Broad Base of Self-Development

The transforming leader has a refined self-awareness; is able to acknowledge and compensate for limitations; has ability to use self as an instrument for change; has developed good interpersonal communication skills, counseling skills, problem-solving and problem-management skills; and has an optimistic attitude in general.

The transforming leader takes initiative in transforming all parts of an organization where there is opportunity for positive change. Ideally, the person who has been placed "in charge" of any family, group, department, or organization would facilitate development at the personal, interpersonal, and organizational levels. All too often, traditional leaders attempt only one level of impact, or at best two, and fail to comprehend the breadth of influence they could have (Egan, 1985).

Consciousness: An Openness to New Perspectives

The transforming leader values increasing consciousness of self and others without overloading awareness with clutter and detail. It is important to have an ability to see patterns in the past and project them into the future to sense new directions. The transforming leader understands that a personal commitment to become a more conscious, clear-minded, and intentional person results in important personal growth that attracts others and wins their trust. Some call this personal "presence," presence of mind, alertness, or expanded awareness (beyond the average).

Caring: The Critical Factor

Most of all, the transforming leader cares deeply about self and others and is committed to the higher goals of developing both the inner lives and affirming the worth of individuals. The transforming leader is committed to developing positive organizational climates that result in high morale and increased quality and productivity. The transforming leader knows that increased morale, in general, means increased productivity, and that to an extent, increasing productivity and quality of products or services can boost morale. Facilitating the personal development of people as individuals adds depth and character to an organization over the long term, and workers are more likely to have a positive self-image, which often results in improved performance in producing quality goods or delivering quality services. The transforming leader builds a learning organization capable of continuous improvement.

> **Posner and Kouzes claim that love is the secret of leadership success. I agree.**

Bennis (1985) quotes Irwin Federman, president and CEO of Monolithic Memories, one of the most successful of the high-tech companies in Silicon Valley:

> *If you think about it, people love others not for who they are, but for how they make others feel. We willingly follow others for much the same reason. It makes us feel good to do so. Now, we also follow platoon sergeants, self-centered geniuses, demanding spouses, bosses of various persuasions, and others as well, for a variety of reasons. But none of those reasons involves that person's leadership qualities. To willingly accept the direction of another individual, it must feel good to do so. This business of making another person feel good in the unspectacular course of his daily comings and goings is, in my view, the very essence of leadership.*

Caring about the well-being and development of others is a quality that is not only necessary—but when absent from an otherwise good leader—most of us feel a sense of having being deceived, or at least having been let down, or sadly disappointed, as is exemplified in the extreme by such leaders as Napoleon, Hitler, and Nixon. It would seem that the tragic flaws of deceptiveness, lovelessness, and the insane tragedy of destructiveness are, to most of us, unacceptable, no matter what the promises or other accomplishments of a leader are.

The Secret of Leadership Success

Posner and Kouzes (1987) claim that love is the secret of leadership success. I agree. They define love as encouragement, loyalty, teamwork, commitment, respect of others' dignity and worth, and claim it is an affair of the heart and not of the head. If any one thing will cause people to be distrustful of a leader, it is when they sense that the leader does not care. In contrast, Kouzes and Posner write, "When we encourage others, we give them heart. And when we give heart to others, we give love." To further explain what is meant by love, I think of an ancient wisdom on this point and find it worthy of quoting: "Love never gives up. Love cares more for others than for self. Love doesn't want what it doesn't have. Love doesn't strut; doesn't have a swelled head; doesn't force itself on others; isn't always "me first"; doesn't fly off the handle; doesn't keep score of the wrongs of others; doesn't revel when others grovel; takes pleasure in the flowering of truth; puts up with anything; trusts God always; always looks for the best; never looks back; but keeps going to the end." (Quote from, *The Message*, p. 424-425). This quote summarizes some of the underlying assumptions of this book, but the following section will assess the extent to which you really "buy into" the principles of *Transforming Leadership*.

Assessment: Identifying Your Own Position in Relation to Transforming Leadership Principles

Rate the extent of your agreement with the twelve Principles of *Transforming Leadership*. This will give you an opportunity to discover the extent to which you "buy into" these basic "beliefs" of *Transforming Leadership*. Doing this assessment will assist you to identify how much you are committed to the idea of seeing yourself more and more as an agent of positive change. You can rate each of the twelve principles from 1 to 5 to indicate your acceptance of these principles into your value structure.

1 = rejection
2 = avoidance
3 = neutrality
4 = general acceptance
5 = complete acceptance and agreement

Score:

1. Every person in every situation is having an impact, for better or worse, on the people and the situations that are present.
2. Learning to observe this impact alerts us to the reality of positive or negative leadership opportunities and events. Increasing our level of awareness of people and events can be fruitful for everyone.

3. Every person can choose to try and make a positive difference in each moment with each other person, and at least within that immediate sphere of influence, can likely exert some positive, and therefore *Transforming, Leadership.*

4. The use of positive and respectful power and influence is necessary for leadership to have enough impact to be effective. Knowing one's own strengths, gaining strategic position power, developing a power network of like-minded people, and communicating your personal and position power in a positive way to others will assist you to reach higher goals.

5. Everything begins with the initiative of each individual. Privately, inwardly, individuals determine in themselves what to do, how to act, and how to treat people. If we are each clear within about our own beliefs, purpose, goals, and objectives, we will much more likely achieve them from this solid and well-defined center within ourselves.

6. Leadership, in its deepest sense, is the understanding and meeting of the deeper needs of the people being led/served. Even when achieving goals of increased innovation or productivity, our meeting of the deeper human needs of worth, recognition, reward, accomplishment, and personal development of others are cornerstones of motivation and satisfaction.

7. *Transforming Leadership* has a moral component centrally important to all other aspects of leadership, because few people will trust a leader who has lied, one who has embezzled, one who hurts others.

8. *Transforming Leadership* understands and involves others so that they can gain a critical sense of belonging, and experience the mutual sense of respect and trust that follow. Personal ownership in any venture can potentially increase motivation, morale, creativity, energy, and productivity.

9. There is opportunity for leadership in every environment, in every interaction, in every situation, in every moment. Leadership is intentionally making a positive difference in the development of organizations and individuals for a specific purpose. Being awake to these opportunities and seizing them increases our personal meaning and impact in life and work.

10. *Transforming Leadership* looks for long-term impact and long-term development, rather than just immediate results. Satisfaction increases when we can see a continuing positive development over longer periods of time, rather than just short-term successes.

11. *Transforming Leadership* begins deep within a person's belief and value structures, and a solid sense of purpose or mission in life is necessary for leadership effectiveness to be sustained. Have a well-defined, achievable sense of purpose that "sets you on fire" and distinguishes you from the herd of people who follow along with a more vague purpose of some relatively unknown leader-heroes (such as political, sports, scientific heroes, etc.).

12. *Transforming Leadership* is open to the potential that there could always be another higher or deeper understanding of reality beyond what is presently comprehended. An attitude of humility that is not "puffed up with pride" characterizes a transforming leader.

Total Score :

Interpretation of Scores: If you scored between 52 to 60, you have a high degree of agreement with the underlying principles of *Transforming Leadership* and are likely willing to move ahead with further development of the skills. If you scored between 44 to 51, you have a moderate degree of agreement with the principles of *Transforming Leadership* and you may have some reservations about proceeding with further development of the skills. If you scored below 43, you likely have serious reservations about the underlying assumptions of *Transforming Leadership* and will likely not proceed with further training.

References

C. **Hickman** and M. **Silva**, *Creating Excellence: Managing Corporate Culture, Strategy, and Change in the New Age.* (New York: New American Library, 1984).

C. **Hickman**, *Mind of a Manager, Soul of a Leader.* (New York: John Wiley & Sons, 1990).

A. **Brown** and E. **Wiener**, *Supermanaging: How to Harness Change for Personal and Organizational Success.* (New York: Mentor Books, 1985).

J. **Naisbitt**, *Megatrends.* (New York: Warner, 1982).

J. **Naisbitt** and P. **Aburdene**, *Re-Inventing the Corporation.* (New York: Warner Books, 1986).

J. **Naisbitt** and P. **Aburdene**, *Megatrends 2000.* Ten New Direction for the 1990's. (New York: William Morrow and Company, 1990), 13.

G. **Egan**, *Change Agent Skills.* (Monterey, California: Brooks/Cole Publishing Co., 1985).

W. **Bennis** and B. **Nanus**, *Leaders: The Strategies for Taking Charge.* (New York: Harper and Row, 1985), 66-67.

J. **Kotter**, *Power in Management.* (New York: AMACOM, 1979).

B. **Schlenker**, *Impression Management.* (Monterey, California: Brooks/Cole Publishing Company, 1980).

R. **Kanter**, *Power and Entrepreneurship in Action: Corporate Middle Managers. Varieties of Work* (Beverly Hills: Sage, 1982).

J. **Burns**, *Leadership.* (New York: Harper and Row, 1978), 4.

R. **Greenleaf**, *Servant Leadership, A Journey into the Nature of Legitimate Power and Greatness.* (New York: Paulist Press, 1977).

R.M. **Kanter**, *The Change Masters.* (New York: Simon and Schuster, 1983).

J. **Kouzes**, and B. **Posner**, *The Leadership Challenge, How to Get Extraordinary Things Done in Organizations.* (San Francisco: Jossey-Bass, 1987).

J. **Kotter**, *A Force for Change: How Leadership Differs from Management.* (New York: The Free Press, 1990), 103-104.

H. **Mintzberg**, *The Nature of Managerial Work.* (New York: Harper and Row, 1973).

W. **Schafer**, *Stress Management for Wellness.* (New York: Holt, Rinehart and Winston, 1987).

C. **Garfield**, *Peak Performers: The New Heroes of American Business.* (New York: William Morrow and Company, 1986).

G. **Egan**, *Change Agent Skills.* (Monterey, California: Brooks/Cole Publishing Co., 1985), 204.

W. **Bennis**, and B. **Nanus**, *Leaders: The Strategies for Taking Charge.* (New York: Harper and Row, 1985), 17, 66-67.

J. **Kouzes** and J. **Posner**, *Credibility.* (San Francisco: Jossey-Bass, 1992).

Part Two

Chapter 4

THE SKILLS OF PERSONAL MASTERY

I knew who I was this morning, but I think I must have been changed several times since then.

Alice, in
Through the Looking Glass

Introduction

In this chapter, you will gain a more in-depth understanding of the skills you will need to have greater positive impact as a leader while you are in the process of developing yourself and others. The *Transforming Leadership* skills that will be discussed in this chapter include the following.

You may want to pay special attention to those skills in which you felt stronger and weaker when you took the *Transforming Leadership* Skills Assessment in Chapter 2.

In the future, when you see a workshop or course outline you think may be relevant for your development, you will be able to evaluate immediately whether or not that particular professional development opportunity fits your individual learning needs in this foundational area of personal and professional development.

The Need for Identity, Clarity of Beliefs, Vision, and Purpose in the Face of Chaotic Change

As we approach the end of this millennium, we face changes of a magnitude never faced by people before. In the next ten years, nearly one and a half billion babies will be born. The world's population will be tilted toward the Pacific Rim, with 60 percent of it living within two thousand miles of Singapore. Vast cities, with all their problems, will prevail on the planet. More than twenty-two mega-cities will be populated with more than ten million people each. The health of our environment is seriously threatened. There is more than a slim chance that a terrorist group will attack an area on the planet with nuclear weapons. Disease, wars, and crime are on the increase globally. Information is exploding at a rate faster than the average person's ability to process and use it. National economies are rising and falling with international consequences. The whole business environment is rapidly transforming, but no one is certain where it will end.

Technological Changes Overshadow Our Ability to Manage Their Effects on People

We have created a technologically advanced environment that outstrips our ability to integrate and manage it! In addition, the knowledge and skills on the people side of managing change are falling behind the demands to cope with the new technologies. "Inner" technologies are lagging behind the demands of "outer" technologies. Many fear that we can't keep up with what we're creating. "Future Management" will have to become a new skill!

The Competencies Needed to Adapt to Profound Change, and Help Others Adapt

The competencies needed to be an effective leader in the face of this rate of change are many and complex, but it is possible to learn them. Are executives and managers ready to lead the way? Do they have the inner clarity and grounding to avoid losing their balance as the "top" spins faster and faster?

Of all the areas of awareness and skill in focus for this book, the most difficult are those of beliefs and values. Many of the people I have taught in university and college classes have given up, to some degree, on the hope of achieving inner clarity and resolution regarding personal beliefs or life stance. They have become somewhat numbed to the challenge of tackling life's most difficult of questions. Many have even consciously resorted to a kind of waning scientific materialism they also describe as lacking in vitality and inspiration. Srivastva and Cooperider (1990) have so aptly described the precipice near which so many stand.

*While the voices sometimes clash and the arguments
reel in complexity, there is one powerful consensus
that reverberates throughout: the scientific
materialism that so confidently dominated the
postindustrial era and so thoroughly insinuated itself
into virtually every aspect of institutional life is now a
dying orthodoxy. While there is little agreement as to
exactly what we are moving toward, there is no
question that the shift now taking place in society's
dominant metaphysic—Who are we? What kind of
universe are we in? What is ultimately important?—
will have a transforming effect on all our institutions.*

With this ominous prospect of huge paradigm shifts in the minds and belief
positions of large numbers of people, we turn to the process of self-assessment
that will trigger a beginning of a new, careful, and conscious clarification
within.

In this book, we are providing you with an opportunity to begin your
search for clarity and resolution. If you have not consciously begun your search,
you can do so with the assistance of some structure and process provided in
the pages to follow. If you have already intentionally begun your search process,
you can more easily monitor your clarity and progress.

Values are perhaps the next most perplexing area of life to clarify and
resolve so that a sense of inner peace and integrity is in place within each
person. Since there are so many criteria for judging which values are more
correct or appropriate, which criteria shall we trust? Our inner sense of what
should be our priorities? Evidence from history regarding the consequences
of certain values being implemented? Are there any absolute values? Or should
we adjust our values to the situation? Or, are some values situational in nature
and others absolute? These questions, and others are very difficult for most
people to answer to their own satisfaction. Even so, the need for clarification
and regeneration of values is nevertheless greatly needed. As pointed out by
Gardner (1990):

*The truth is that disintegration of the value framework
is always going on—but so are regenerative
processes. Some people see little hope that such
processes can be effective, believing that we have lost
the capacity to generate a new vision. A still gloomier
view is that we may have lost the capacity to tolerate
a new vision. The debunking reflex is powerful today.
We are sick of past hypocrisies. We have seen the fine
words of morality used as a screen for greed, for
bigotry, for power-seeking. Granted. But to let that
estrange us from all attempts to regenerate the moral*

framework would be petulant and self-defeating. Creating value systems is something that the human species does. "It's our thing," as the recently popular saying goes, and without that irrepressible impulse, civilization would not have survived. Destroy every vestige of lay and morality, demolish every community, level the temples of justice, erase even the memory of custom, and one would see—in the midst of chaos, savagery, and pillage—an awesome sight: the sight of men and women, bereft of all guiding memory, beginning to forge anew the rudiments of order and justice and law, acting out of the mysterious community-building impulse of the species.

If it is true, and I agree with John Gardner that it is—that we by instinct seek order, peace, and benevolent control—then let's get on with the task of clarification and teach others to do the same.

Inner Skills of Self-Mastery for the Transforming Leader

TL Skill # 1. The Skill of Grounding: *Focusing Awareness in the Present*

This awareness skill of *grounding* involves your taking responsibility for placing your attention in each present moment, and not in memory about past events or in fantasy about future events. When you focus your attention in the "here and now," you are grounded in the present, fully available for interaction with self, the environment, and people in each passing moment. Individuals who are grounded have more personal presence, and people who are focused in fantasy or memory seem to be "spaced-out," somewhere else, or in some ways "out of it."

Example of Grounding: You can probably think of a person who is very spaced-out most of the time, and another person who is grounded most of the time. I know a person who has done a history of drug abuse in his lifetime and this has caused him to become inwardly distracted, lacking in memory power. He is, as a result, socially dulled. He is wrapped up in himself and his nervous system is so stressed that it is very difficult for him to be grounded in the present with others. I have seen a number of inmates in prisons who are in a similar state because of lifelong stress accumulation. I have observed the same with workaholic executives who just cannot inwardly get their attention focused to "be here, now." I have also observed those who have decided to be grounded and live a life that is grounded. Their "command presence" is visually and psychologically evident. I know one police chief who, when he walks into the room, is so conscious that others come to attention more because of this conscious attitude than because of his position as chief.

This skill, and the commitment to strengthen it, is the foundation of all other skills, for if we are psychologically unavailable to present events, our interactions with ourself and others will be interrupted or blocked.

TL Skill # 2. The Skill of Centering: *Including Self in the Context of Events*

Centering is an important prerequisite for being a conscious, alert, and intentional person, especially when exercising leadership. It is an awareness skill that enables you to intentionally be conscious of your own presence as a person with your specific beliefs, biases, creative ideas, intuitions, revelations, emotions, physical experiences, and judgments in each moment. This awareness level is distinct from your awareness of external events. This deeper self-awareness can develop more quickly through self-conscious effort and through the practice of being very still (deep relaxation, meditation, or prayer states). Centering is the opposite of selfishness because this part of yourself that can be more aware of you is the same part of yourself that can be more receptive, sensitive, and giving to others.

Examples: You have probably observed a person who is easily "knocked off center." I recall the example of most of my classmates in my first public speaking class in university. Most of us forgot what we wanted to say and became overly "self" conscious to the extent that we lost the capacity to inwardly keep track of the task at hand, which was to focus the self and speak clearly and articulately. How embarrassing it was to be unable to think and speak clearly in front of others! Some people feel this way all the time! They are so shaky in the self-worth department that their sense of being connected to themselves is blown—they become "beside" themselves and lose control. In contrast, you have seen those who are smooth-performing musicians, athletes, or speakers. They are on dead center with their inner strengths, talents, and have the practiced confidence that enables them to bring forward their message, music, or athletic performance with ease and grace.

TL Skill # 3. The Skill of Beliefs Clarification and Resolution: *Taking a Stance on Life's Basic Issues*

This awareness skill area will be the longest one because of its importance, and the most difficult to explain because of its complexity. This area of skill or "wisdom" in discerning the nature of things is the primary cornerstone for the development of the other skills to come. If, when a person looks inside there is fog or "mush," there is too vague or soft a foundation to build on. We all could benefit from further clarification or a deepening of understanding of our operating assumptions about life. This skill focus will help you move ahead toward enhanced clarity of your beliefs.

Science defines and explains the "what and how" of observable life, and in the last 100 years, has delved more into the powers of the previously unseen forces—radio, electronic, and atomic. Beliefs—philosophy and religion—deal with the questions of "who and why." These questions are much more difficult to answer but they are, at the same time, more essential to our integrity because the answers we give to key questions determine our whole approach to our lives, to others, and to life itself.

What is Beliefs Clarity?

This awareness "skill" is developed by examining carefully the main questions of existence and, over time, searching and discovering workable answers to them, and validating or invalidating their authenticity or "truth." If we are, however, to have any confidence in our answers, they must have their validation in at least some of the following ways of knowing (epistemology): through empirical investigation (science), historical evidence, personal experience (phenomenology), archeology, intuition (psychological), revelation (spiritual), etc. Otherwise, we have little confidence that our assumptions about the nature of life are grounded in any kind of reality that is substantial and, therefore, believable. That we should be able to validate our positions at all of the levels listed above may also be of critical importance. If there is historical evidence to support the validity of our belief position, but no other evidence (or conflicting evidence), we should be suspect! Perhaps our beliefs should be true at every level, or are they only partly true?

> Science defines and explains the "what and how" of observable life, and in the last 100 years, has delved more into the powers of the previously unseen forces—radio, electronic, and atomic. Beliefs—philosophy and religion—deal with the questions of "who and why?"

For example, most people in the free world believe absolutely in the sanctity of life, that murder is wrong, and that the only justification for the use of force is to stop unjust, immoral, or illegal killing (but only with the appropriate and necessary amount of police or military use of force). Evidence that murder for self-gain has negative consequences can be supported by historical documentation, empirical investigation, archeological findings, intuition, and possibly revelation (depending upon the belief system of the investigator). Therefore, we assert for the sake of discussion that premeditated murder of an innocent child, for example, is truly and absolutely wrong because under no circumstances does it have positive consequences that can be validated in the long term—it only has negative consequences. Some questions are not so easily answered, however, as we shall see.

Some people maintain that addressing the most difficult of life's "belief" questions is irrelevant to a meaningful existence in the here and now, and that mere values and goals are adequate for living (Ellis, 1976). Values and goals are very important, but the presumption that it is irrational for us to expect to clarify metaphysical issues and arrive at resolute beliefs does nothing for those of us who want to grasp some further essence of life, to go beyond what is visible, to comprehend life in new and deeper ways.

The Personal Nature of Beliefs Clarity

Beliefs are by their nature intensely personal. They are our operating assumptions about life, love, safety, happiness, leadership, management, etc. If we want to know a person intimately, we might first ask what he or she believes to be most real, true, good, unreal, false, or bad. Then we will begin to get a picture of their position on some of the basic issues of life, which are really the 20 major questions in life. In an annual survey (over four years) of college and university students, twenty of "life's most unanswered problem questions" were identified in their order of estimated difficulty to answer.

1. What is really happening here on this planet? What is the purpose of matter and existence, if any?
2. Is it really possible to know at all, or should I just skip it as an issue I can't resolve?
3. What criteria do I use to discern what is true from what is not true, good from bad, real from unreal?
4. How can I know whether these criteria are reliable and true, and what are the sources of these criteria?
5. Who am I: in relation to others, the world, the universe, God, etc.?
6. What should I do with my life: a purpose for living, goals to accomplish, a career or "life calling" (vocation)?
7. What is truth? What is my definition of truth, where did I get it, and how do I know it is true?
8. What is the nature of human beings? Good? Evil? Neutral? Where did I get my belief? How did this human nature I believe in get to be the way it is: creation, the environment, the "fall into original sin," conditioning, parents, all of the above, etc.?
9. Is there a supreme being or ultimate cause, or did everything just evolve from nothing, and how do I know?
10. Where did matter come from? Creation by some conscious designer, or statistical happenstance, evolution?
11. Is everything absurd, or is there underlying and inherent purpose in life and in the universe?

12. Are there any absolutes (truths that are immovable) or is "reality" relative to each person's perspective?
13. What is the source(s) or cause(s) of negativity ("evil") and positivity ("good") in life? Are there many sources, one, none?
14. Is there life after death? If so, what kind, where, and with whom? If not, what happens, and how do I know this?
15. Is it possible to communicate with a higher being(s)? If so, how? If not, what difference does that make in my life?
16. What should I value? What is most important in life and what are my priorities?
17. Whom should I join up with in life: to marry, live with, work with, etc.? What criteria should I use to choose these people with whom I ally myself?
18. Where (geographically) on this planet do I want to live and why?
19. How do I prepare myself to fulfill my purpose and goals?
20. How do I know if I am doing OK in life?

> **Beliefs are, by their nature, intensely personal. They are our operating assumptions about life, love, safety, happiness, leadership, management, etc. If we want to know a person intimately, we might first ask what he or she believes to be most real, true, good, unreal, false, or bad.**

These questions are among many critical questions people ask, attempt to answer, or attempt to avoid answering. The fact that different people come up with clashing answers to these questions accounts for much of the discord, misunderstanding, and conflict in relationships, in organizations, and even between nations.

Why Some People Give Up on Gaining Clarity of Beliefs

For most people, getting to the bottom of the above kinds of questions is a meaningful task (or quest, depending upon their view of the issue). When I asked over 600 students over the past twelve years how many of them had generally either given up on answering these kinds of questions or found them to be irrelevant, approximately 32 percent said "yes." These were the reasons they gave for giving up trying to answer the difficult questions of life.
1. Confusion, or a feeling of being overwhelmed by the complexity of both the questions and the diversity of answers
2. Lack of satisfying criteria for validating what is true or good
3. Lack of interest in the issue of clarification

4. Lack of understanding of the benefits of being more clear
5. Lack of information and knowledge about alternatives
6. Laziness or fear

About 30 percent of these 600 students reported that they were determined to "crack the code" to some kind of "higher reality." They said that they had already had some experiences that had led them to believe there was a discernible reality beyond what they could see with the eye. One person explained that if radio and television waves aren't hard to believe in, then why should other "waves" of communication be so hard to fathom?

Another 32 percent of the 600 claimed to have satisfying answers to these and other more difficult-to-answer questions. They seemed to have some kind of clear frame of reference, stance, faith, or belief about the questions of death, a supreme being, the nature of humans, why we are here, who we are, and where we are going. Some of these students admitted that their beliefs were not really examined by them, or searched for, but simply accepted because of their family and cultural upbringing. Approximately 6 percent decided not to respond to the questions put to them.

The Advantage of Beliefs Clarity

It would seem in one way that those who have more clarity of beliefs enjoy an advantage over those who haven't dealt with these questions. There is research (a good starting place is David Larson's article in the *American Journal of Psychiatry* (1992) that summarizes twelve years of psychiatric literature) to suggest that people with clear belief systems have less anxiety, more success, lower divorce rates, and lower stress-related illness rates. In a state of conscious awareness, they act on specific assumptions and are more likely aware of the consequences of taking action based on each specific belief position. This enables them to gain feedback from their environments about the validity and workability of their assumptions. Contrast this clarity of mind with the person who is unsure and unresolved, or who wavers from situation to situation and gets mixed feedback.

Some of those who claim to know specific answers were criticized by others for not having ever really searched and opened their minds in the first place, because they may have simply "swallowed" what was "fed" to them when they were children. This is a good point. Someone said that the unexamined life is not worth living.

It would appear from this informal study that the issue of beliefs is a highly charged and intensely personal one to most people. When challenged to rate the importance of this issue of beliefs clarity on a scale from 1 to 10, the average person gave the issue an 8.6 out of 10 (with a range of 4 to 10).

The Process of Developing Beliefs Clarity

It is for this reason that I developed a self-guided process for clarification of beliefs. The process is clearly a developmental one—usually there is not a sudden flash of blinding light on the road to Damascus as St. Paul is reported to have had, although slightly over one-third of those who claimed to have achieved some clarity of beliefs said there was a definite time that an internal "light went on."

Before outlining what we call steps in the search process, we will refer you to a summary of the developmental stages delineated by Fowler (1981). These are longer and are located at the end of this book in Appendix A, titled, *Stages in the Development of a Personal Faith Position.* I have also developed a systematic way for you to explore these critical issues of life and build a personal life plan—this process is called *Deep Structure Strategic Planning*, and is located in Appendix B.

Steps in the Process of Clarification of Your Belief Stance

The process of clarifying your beliefs is very complex and often happens—without your intention—because of significant events in your life. If you want to embark on a conscious search, however, that can involve a series of steps. By following these steps, your own belief stance will become more clear as time passes. The steps for clarifying beliefs can be done yourself, or you can help an individual or group of people gain resolution by coaching them through the following steps.

1. As best as you can, specify in writing your present answers to life's major questions, which were outlined above, or attempt to answer your own problem questions.
2. Search out where you got your beliefs and write what you can remember about these sources for later comparison.
3. Examine your criteria for accepting these beliefs as true, and write down the various validations for your beliefs that you accept.
4. Write a clear and concise position paper about your stance on life's 20 major questions and issues.
5. Read this paper over once a week while you consistently attempt to take on this position in a real way, living it out on a daily basis as congruently as you are able.
6. Review your position statements every three to six months, and examine how your position helps you to deal with problems or better appreciate the joys of life.
7. Note any "holes" or inconsistencies in your belief position that you think may be invalid, incomplete, or problematic.

8. Examine other differing belief positions (ones you think are incomplete or false, if any) that validate for you how true your position is. Or, note how there are parts of other positions that seem to have truth in them on the premise that "truth is truth wherever it is found" in a course on world religions or through additional reading.

To assist you to get started with this last step, I would suggest you consider reading Chapter 9 in Naisbitt and Aburdene's book, *Megatrends 2000*. This book will give you an overview of what is occurring in the world of beliefs. Using this chapter as an introduction, you could move ahead with a more thorough study of each of the various philosophical or religious belief positions.

Students who have generally followed this series of steps in our courses on self-awareness and interpersonal communication have reported in the course evaluations at the end of term that this exercise was the most challenging and meaningful of their semester; some of them even reported it was the most important step in their whole lives. The process outlined above, however, is a structure for cognitively oriented people. Some people don't learn well this way, following steps. Some students have told me they have had better results by simply asking, as though they will get an answer through circumstances, from thoughts coming into their minds, dreams, etc., from a source they don't fully understand—they are convinced of the "magic" of simply asking to know, like a child would ask his or her father an innocent question and not give up asking until satisfied that he or she got an answer. This childlike approach, oddly enough, is the approach I have found to be even more powerful than the cognitive approach because I have tried both.

If you would like to read the story of my own personal search, you may request one by phoning 1-604-852-0566, emailing me at terry@crgleader.com, or faxing me at 1-604-850-3003. My story will be mailed, faxed, or emailed to you.

The Downside of Failing to Clarify Beliefs

People who avoid this whole issue of belief clarification, or give up on its resolution, perhaps are less deeply "rooted" in a life position. They may be more easily influenced to move in a number of directions, depending upon which way a personal, social, political, or economic "wind" is blowing at the time. They often claim that this "flexible" tendency is a strength, that they are open-minded, and willing to change with the times. They also often say, however, that they have little inner peace, that decision-making is difficult without a clear reference point, and that their relationships suffer because they often clash with individuals who have clear beliefs and they don't really align well with people who do not have clear assumptions.

Those who have a metaphysical understanding of and an orientation to life (answers to the "why" questions) have a distinct advantage, even if their orientation may be ultimately incorrect in the end. They are more "solid," act more consistently, can get feedback from the environment as to the validity and workability of their assumptions (because they have a position as a reference point), and, many times, are better able to understand others' positions—a "tolerance" skill important when leading people. Some people who are "clear" are not tolerant, however. Some people are narrow, intolerant, have to be "right" about everything, are not very compassionate of others' struggle for clarity, and just want others to "swallow" their truth. But not all of these people who claim to be "sure" are "fundamentalist fanatics" who would negatively judge you for not being clear or for not wanting to agree with their positions. Some people really are clear, truly peaceful, kind, patient, and caring people who just quietly "know." You likely know at least a few people like this. Ask them what they believe and listen to their stories.

Beliefs form the solid foundation of a clear purpose in life, and a clear set of values are structures upon which to build goals, strategies, and actions. With only values to live by, the "why" of life is not addressed, explored, or resolved in the least. Beliefs address the "why" and "what" questions of life directly. The hierarchical relationship between beliefs, purpose, values, goals, strategies, and actions is illustrated as follows.

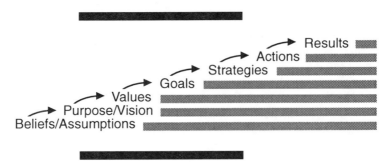

When people can share some basic beliefs, they are more likely to join together to create something productive. This is true for marriage partners or any other type of endeavor in business, health, education, community development, the military, or human services—where team effort is required.

Furthermore, if you understand others' beliefs, you are more likely to comprehend why they have given their "hearts" to them, why they feel they need them, why they need to keep their own beliefs, and you can then be even more tolerant.

TL Skill # 4. The Skill of Specifying Your Personal Purpose/Vision: *A Critical Life Skill*

A **purpose** is a reason to do anything; a reason to get up in the morning. A vision is clear picture of a preferred future where you can picture yourself accomplishing this purpose. As you gain a greater sense of clarity about what you believe or assume to be real and true, it is easier to move ahead to specify a keener sense of purpose and vision in your life that is in harmony with your beliefs. If your beliefs are fuzzy or unresolved, you will have more difficulty specifying a definite purpose or vision. A desire for clarification and a belief that it is possible are good requisites for making progress in this area.

> **A vision is a clear picture of a preferred future where you can picture yourself accomplishing a clear purpose.**

Finding or developing a clear sense of personal purpose and vision is not an easy task. One of the authors tried for a number of years to state, on paper, his purpose for living. He did not have a sense that he had actually captured the essence of it. His life was less focused and organized because of this. He found himself saying "yes" to things others wanted him to do and things he couldn't see a good reason to say "no" to, and as a result, his life became filled with tasks, goals, and even obligations that didn't "click way down deep." He would get up in the morning and say to himself, "What am I *really* up to today, anyway?"

In the French language, the phrase that roughly translates as "purpose" is *raison d'etre*: specifically, it translates as "reason for BEING." Why should you and I even bother to BE at all? If we can answer that question so that we have a burning sense of mission or purpose that we are passionate about, then we will be internally motivated, we will be able to better clarify and set priorities, and better able to specify high-drive goals that match our strengths and abilities.

My personal purpose statement reads as follows:

> *"My purpose in life is to increasingly become a transformative leader, facilitating the spiritual, mental, emotional, physical, and interpersonal development of others who can become transformative leaders in the lives of others, and in organizations, for the purpose of making positive impact on the life of communities."*

So, I am an author, encourager, facilitator, helper, knowledge resource, consultant, and supporter of other leaders (or leaders-to-be) who have, as their purpose, to impact human and organization development for positive ends. I include my family in this purpose; my two boys are leaders in some ways and becoming better at it. My identity is steeped in this purpose. I plan my days around this purpose, set my priorities and goals around this purpose, and encourage and assist, willing others to do the same. I have also learned to have fun and enjoy each moment—thanks to my precious wife—in the midst of all of this endeavoring, something many people forget to do when they become too goal-oriented.

I feel fulfilled with this purpose and get a charge of excitement when I see it realized. It is highly motivating to me. You may want to write your own purpose statement in the space provided.

Your First Draft: Personal Purpose Statement

My purpose in life is to . . .

Your First Draft: Personal Vision Statement

In five and ten years, my spiritual, financial, interpersonal, health, and lifestyle will look like . . .

It is challenging for anyone to complete the above sentences. Therefore, additional help is provided for defining and writing your personal purpose and vision statements in Appendix B, *Developing a Personal Faith Position*. If you are having difficulty specifying your sense of purpose, a course in career and life planning, a workshop in personal life planning, or counseling can be a very worthwhile investment. Readings in this area could also be useful.

TL Skill # 5. The Skill of Identifying Your Values: *Setting Priorities in Life*

The more clear your purpose is, the greater ease you will have in identifying what is important to you. Confusion rules when our sense of purpose is vague. Clarifying and identifying values (personally important or of high priority) is a somewhat difficult matter of prioritizing various things in our lives, such as spirituality, family, career, education, money, geographic location, etc. When we know what we find to be most important—more valuable in relation to other values—it becomes easier to set goals.

As you gain clarity of purpose and identify your values in order of priority, you will be able to clearly and more easily set motivating goals in specific areas of your life, development, and career.

I have, as my highest value, human life and human development. I value the quality of the inner life of myself and others more highly than anything else. Developing a quality inner life and learning to express high quality to others through caring and the use of knowledge and skills is very important to me. I value high-impact activities where the payoff is primarily human development. It is because of these values that this book was written.

An example of an organization where people often have conflicting values is a prison. In one prison I visited, not only were the inmates pitted against one another with conflicting values, the staff were as well. Some staff valued respecting and trying to rehabilitate inmates, and other staff wanted nothing to do with "the slugs." Some staff didn't care one way or the other, but just wanted to collect their paycheck and get their retirement at the end of the road. This conflict of values is like a house divided, unable to stand the stresses and strains of longer-term oppression from some of the inmates. The negativity was triggered one Christmas Eve when a manager ordered a cell search, found alcohol fruit-juice brew in a number of cells, confiscated it, and precipitated a million-dollar riot. Those people who had clear values, no matter what they were, believed they were right—no matter what happened. Staff who suffered the greatest stress were the ones caught in between, with little or no clarity of their values. Because they stood for nothing, they had no reason to stay in such a high-stress environment and many of them chose to leave their jobs. Those who had clear and positive values were the ones who chose to stay on after the riot and help rebuild a better culture where both the keeper and the kept must live together, hopefully in greater peace.

Another way to get at our values, especially in relation to work, is to assess our patterns of interest in relation to others. Testing in this area with interest inventories is available in most counseling centers at colleges and universities, for free.

If you wanted to go through a more complete values preference prioritization exercise, you could obtain a copy of Robinson's (1990) *Values Preference Inventory*.

As you gain clarity of purpose and identify your values in order of priority, you will be able to more easily and clearly set motivating goals in specific areas of your life, development, and career. Effective goals are based upon clear beliefs and assumptions, a deep sense of purpose, and clear values. They must be desirable, concretely defined, realistically achievable within the time you have available, measurable so you know when you have reached them, owned or chosen by yourself instead of imposed on you by others, and celebrated when achieved. The following three skills focus on this proactive approach to these three key areas of your life.

> **We can sell our souls for success, money, security, sex, pleasure, laziness, or whatever. Designing and living an intentional life plan can help prevent the various ways that we live an imbalanced life.**

TL Skill # 6. The Rare Skill of Life Planning: *Setting Motivating Goals*

Someone said that we spend more time planning our vacations than we do our lives. One study of over 600 students found this to be true. Is it for you? This area of living skill is so often overlooked that up until the last twenty years, few courses were available on life planning. Until fairly recently, it was not something for which you ask a professional counselor for assistance. I just did a search on the Internet for "life planning" and found a number of resources that weren't available in years past. Life planning is not a skill that our children are regularly being taught in school. The earliest we see this skill being taught systematically is in a student success course in the freshman year of university.

But leaders—or prospective leaders—need this skill perhaps more than most people. The one great hazard of leaders is that they tend to overload their lives and their work to the point of being addicted to the adrenal high of workaholism, life-aholism, or love of money. This is due to lack of focus on a higher sense of purpose and vision, and, therefore, a leader tries to accomplish too much—thus the addiction to accomplishment or success overtakes his or her life. One accomplishment leads to the next, until there is not time left to enjoy the moment, to do things like take a walk for no purpose, to enjoy just BEING.

We can sell our souls for success, money, security, sex, pleasure, laziness, or whatever. Designing and living an intentional life plan can help prevent our living an imbalanced life. Planning too much and robotically living our lives can kill risk-taking and spontaneity. We recommend that the "balance" area of the skill be taken seriously and developed. Balance and joy in life are perhaps more important in the long run than we might think at first. The scope of this book does not cover this area in depth. You may want to look further into the resources that are available from Strategic Resources and coauthored by Ron Ford, such as the workbook, *Living On Purpose*, or others you can find through library or Internet research.

TL Skill # 7. The Skill of Educational Planning: *Setting Motivating Goals*

Today we must have a learning plan because our fast-changing environment will leave us behind unless we are plugged into relevant, meaningful, and targeted learning opportunities. We have to know what our beliefs, values, career, and life goals are, however, or it will be difficult to develop an educational plan. Hopefully our learning plan will be based on our life plan and not just on our career goals. Otherwise, you could become like many people who have good careers and hollow or wrecked lives.

Most people don't consider what their true interests and passions are when they choose a career and then decide how long they need to attend school and what courses to take there. In the past thirty or so years, most people enrolled in courses that struck their fancy at the time, or that their uncle or aunt or mom or dad took. Before that, most people enrolled in the standard career programs, of which there were relatively few. Now there are so many learning choices available that you really must focus and prioritize on who you really are and what you really want—or you could go to school forever and never accomplish anything else! Many of us have become professional students to a certain extent. But that can be a trap, too! Richard Bolles, in his annually updated book, *What Color is Your Parachute?*, asserts there are three "boxes" of life in which we can get caught: school, career, and leisure. If we spend too much time in any one day or week on any one of these things, we can feel boxed in by that activity. But if we balance our lives with learning, working, and leisure each day—so we continue to stay abreast of changing knowledge and skills, engage in meaningful work, and enjoy life—we will be much happier and more productive overall. This seems to me to be wise! In summary, a good learning plan should be based on a good life plan, and should be linked to a solid and clear career plan.

TL Skill # 8. The Skill of Career Planning: *Setting Motivating Goals*

"To thine own self be true and thou can'st not then be false to any man." This saying by Shakespeare is worthy of consideration when it comes to career planning and setting wise career goals. Most people tend to choose a career goal and then revolve their lives around this one goal. It controls their daily schedule (especially for those involved in shift work); it controls the environment in which they work, often the location of where they live, their daily stress level, their economic future, and their overall destiny to some extent.

Leaders need to be especially sure that what they are doing is connected directly to their strengths, gifts, talents, interests, and life goals—otherwise people will tend to look at the leaders' lives to see how integrated they are and if they see problems, that can hurt the leaders' credibility. People will see that the leaders talk the talk but have a difficult time walking the walk. This is why life planning as a skill is listed before career planning: it is better that our careers are based on our life plans that include how we want to live, where we want to live, how we want to spend our waking hours, with whom we want to spend them. Our careers are, at best, vehicles to get us to the destination we want to reach in life, not just in a job or career in isolation from the rest of life.

> **A life plan, learning plan, and career plan truly go together to form an integrated approach to living an intentional life.**

It is especially important for leaders to have a career path plan or succession plan so they can see how their current role is a preparation for the next level of promotion or development they want to achieve. It is important that they find and develop mentors and coaches (such as counselors and career coaches at colleges and universities) to help them optimize their real job and career skills. That will help them avoid running headlong into the Peter Principle: being promoted to their level of incompetence and staying there. This is another reason why a life plan, a learning plan, and career plan truly go together to form an integrated approach to living an intentional life. We recommend that if you haven't already done so, you invest in these three areas lavishly as the foundation of building your vision for your future and preferred life here on planet Earth.

TL Skill # 9. The Skill of Time Management

After teaching this skill for years, I estimate that few people actually want to practice time management skills to increase their own productivity and balance in life. Most of us tend to just live from day to day, get done what we can, and avoid what we can avoid in terms of stress. Many people become discouraged when they start to plan their personal and work lives. At first, they aren't very realistic; their plans don't work out as expected; they often try to do too much in too short a time; they find that time management is an additional hassle and distraction. They experience some "burnout," and give up on any kind of systematic approach to planning and living. This is unfortunate because it *is* possible to find a more comfortable and productive way of becoming more effective with the use of time. I have discovered a very practical approach to dealing with the complexities we face in our work and personal lives. I create three "bins" into which each task gets placed.

Priority 1:   Must be dealt with today
Priority 2:   Would like to do today if there is time for it
Priority 3:   Will get to it if I can, someday

As time goes by, various tasks can be moved up into a higher priority "bin." If everything just keeps piling up, then, of course, we have to ask ourselves if we really want to live or work in that way!

Another important way to manage time is to "chunk" out time blocks by the type of task: all phone calls returned between 9 am and 10 am, all letters written between 10 am and 11 am, etc. For some people, this approach is very effective and eliminates distraction and complexity that can interfere with effective performance.

When your beliefs, purpose, values, and goals are clear, it is much easier to decide in which of the three piles things belong. My experience is that I become better at managing time as I do it over and over. It is an art as well as a logical planning activity. Sometimes I allot a block of time that is not structured or goal oriented, except that my goal during that "loose" time is to get loose from any regimen. There are fine workshops in time management, good resources to read, and excellent time management systems for you to purchase and use. But it is necessary that as a leader, you find your own style of managing time. You will continue to get better at it as you go along, and when we manage our time, what we are really managing is our lives.

TL Skill # 10. The Skill of Stress Management

This skill is often learned after we get so stressed, we have to find a way to unwind stress. In the course of time, we haphazardly find stress management techniques that work well, and others that work well but have undesirable side effects (such as the use or overuse of anything that temporarily relieves stress—drugs, food, sex, work, exercise, leisure, etc.). An upstream approach to the prevention of stress accumulation is more desirable. The very best stress prevention method is a well-designed and well-lived life that is not overloaded—one that is balanced and enjoyed. The two most powerful tools we have for stress management, to knock down the stress that we do accumulate, are a regular, daily program of cardiovascular exercise and deep relaxation. Twenty minutes a day of exercise and deep relaxation can do an incredible job of reducing pent-up stresses in the body and preventing the accumulation of stress. Talking through problems to resolution can release emotional tension and promote a sense of well-being. People who are good self-managers and have developed the skills outlined in this chapter will likely have lower stress levels, look younger, be healthier, and enjoy life more. If you want to look into this area in more depth and learn more, refer to Walt

Schafer's book, *Stress Management for Wellness*. If you want to do a self-assessment, you could complete *the Stress Indicator and Health Planner*, coauthored by Terry Anderson and Gwen Faulkner. Another way to look at stress management is to look at each leader's life as an energy system. The next section will provide that useful perspective.

TL Skill # 11. The Skill of Energy Management for Improved Health and Performance

Energy management is the preventive approach to managing stress. If you can get the "jump" on stress accumulation in your mind and body by nourishing, strengthening, and resting yourself physically, then you will have a much greater reserve of energy to cope resourcefully with more difficult or demanding situations. In addition to avoiding harmful substances such as tobacco, alcohol in moderate to large quantities, and various medical and nonmedical drugs, there are four areas where increased knowledge and development can result in a greater resilience and hardiness.

The Four Lifestyle Management Keys to Increased Energy and Performance: Optimum Nutrition, Exercise, Deep Relaxation, and Restful Sleep

The wide range of opinions about what makes up the optimum amounts and best types of nutrition, exercise, deep relaxation, and sleep is overwhelming and confusing for most people. Just what sources or experts should one rely on when attempting to establish an appropriate balance in these four energy resource foundations? After reviewing the literature in the four resource areas that has been published in the last twenty years, the following basic learnings and guidelines become evident.

1. There is little disagreement among various experts in the fields about things one might best do in general to increase baseline energy and performance levels.
2. Individual differences between people are significant enough that a generic prescription for any one person may not be appropriate. Therefore, a health care specialist should be consulted before any major changes are made.
3. Assessments of a particular individual's unique physiology, needs, and style are prerequisites to any appropriate health and fitness program design for that person.
4. Monitoring of progress on any program is necessary if you are to know if, in fact, that changes made in diet, exercise, relaxation practices, or sleep patterns make any worthwhile difference.
5. Lifestyle changes (clarity of purpose, values, goals, plans, and activities) often accompany increased control and balance of energy resources, which

result in higher performance and vitality. These lifestyle changes need to be protected and supported if the programs are to promote sustained higher energy and performance.

6. Once new and more effective habit patterns have been well established—more preferable than the old patterns—there are side benefits of increased self-awareness, self-esteem, and, therefore, self-confidence.

7. A combination of professional medical advice and personal experimentation with various programs yields the results of improved health, wellness, increased performance, and well-being.

It is not the purpose of this book to look in depth at this area, but to introduce you to the importance of learning to manage this part of life well. The benefits of healthful practices are obvious, and the limitations that can occur when we allow stress to overtake us are also obvious.

Two books that could be beneficial reading in this area are by Schafer (1987) and Roglieri (1980).

TL Skill # 12. Positive Mental Attitude: The Inner Skill of the Winner

In his studies of professional athletes, Waitley (1979) found there were specifically identifiable patterns of thought and action that distinguished winners from losers. The major differences were found in mental attitude, and other less significant differences were found in physical ability. He studied winners from many fields and found similar success patterns.

The ability to face an apparent problem and see it as a positive challenge is one internal ability winners have. They inwardly control their reactions to an event and assign it the weight of importance appropriate to the situation, rather than assess the situation by the intensity or depth of their emotions at the moment.

Winners take failure and use it to improve their next performance. Their rationale is, "The more times I fail, the more practice I get, the better I get." Because they practice more often without presuming they cannot achieve a particular goal, they succeed more often.

References

T. **Anderson** and G. **Faulkner**, *The Stress Indicator and Health Planner.* (Abbotsford, Consulting Resource Group, 1990).

W. **Schafer**, *Stress Management for Wellness.* (New York: Holt, Rinehart and Winston, 1991.

E. **Robinson**, *Values Preference Inventory*. (Abbotsford, Consulting Resource Group, 1990).

J. L. **Roglieri**, *Odds on Your Life.* (New York: Seaview, 1980).

D. **Waitley**, *The Psychology of Winning.* (New York: The Berkeley Publishing Company, 1979).

Chapter 5

THE SKILLS OF INTERPERSONAL COMMUNICATION

In order to wholly be with another person, I have to first be inwardly connected with myself—then I am in a position to be awake to others, to see them, hear them, and understand them. Then, and only then will I gain their trust and the cooperation that is required for us to reach together toward deeper friendship, higher achievement, and service.

Terry Anderson

Introduction

This chapter continues the in-depth exploration of the skills involved in being a Transforming Leader. If we manage ourselves and our lives well, as indicated in the previous chapter, we will be in a better position to be fully present, whole, and influential in our relationships with others. Even one serious deficit of a skill area in these foundational skills of self-management and communication can undermine our leadership credibility, diminish our influence with others, and result in our not being as effective as we could be. This is especially true when it comes to our learning the more complex skills of counseling, coaching, and consulting that are expanded in the chapters that follow.

We have all seen how few people around us are really consistently good self-managers and communicators! Most of us seem to have a blind spot or undeveloped skill (or two) that continues to frustrate others and that interferes with our gaining credibility or resolving interpersonal difficulties. This has been demonstrated in my unpublished research studies that indicate that others see us as less effective than we see ourselves (on a 10-point scale, the average person rates him or herself about 7.5 ("good"), and "others" rate him or her at 6.0 (and 6.0 = "minimally acceptable"). In addition, when people come into our university-level courses in interpersonal communication and do a first videotaped assessment, they exhibit typical communication problems regardless of their educational background or level of professional experience. In other words, most of us have blind spots that can be quite easily correctable with competency-based training or coaching. Also, most of us can learn quickly to avoid doing some things that undermine our effectiveness when we become

> **Even one serious deficit of a skill area in these foundational skills of self-management and communication can undermine our leadership credibility, diminish our influence with others, and result in our not being as effective as we could be.**

aware of what we are doing. When the skills are presented as "microskills," they are more transferable, more easily learned, and certainly easier to understand.

The *Transforming Leadership* skills that will be focused on in this chapter include the following:

TL Skill #13	Self-Disclosure	Page 100
TL Skill #14	Image Management	Page 101
TL Skill #15	Impression Management	Page 102
TL Skill #16	Attending	Page 104
TL Skill #17	Observing	Page 105
TL Skill #18	Suspending	Page 106
TL Skill #19	Questioning	Page 108
TL Skill #20	Listening	Page 109
TL Skill #21	Responding	Page 110
TL Skill #22	Assertiveness	Page 111
TL Skill #23	Confrontation	Page 113
TL Skill #24	Challenging	Page 118

You may want to pay special attention to those skills in which you felt strongest and weakest when you took the *Transforming Leadership* Skills Assessment in Chapter 2.

What Are Interpersonal Communication Skills?

Interpersonal communication skills are the vehicles by which all interactions between you and other people are made clear. Much of the communication that occurs between people is one-way, without either party truly hearing the other and accurately understanding the feelings, thoughts, or reasons for these feelings or thoughts. In fact, if you think about it, our modern culture— especially in cities—teaches many people not to have two-way communication because it is too personal and imposing, or too time consuming

Have you ever taken a course where you were trained in interpersonal communication skills so it was confirmed you had competencies, not just knowledge? Where do people go to get such training? There aren't very many places: not at most schools, not in most families, not at most churches, not even in most business schools, medical schools, or law schools. Schools of social work, education, and counseling often have such courses as a required part of their programs, but few of us get the opportunity to gain confirmed competency in the use of these all-important foundational skills.

Serious Problems Can Be Traced to Communication Skill Deficits

I recently bought my son a three-month trial membership in a gym as a birthday gift. Unfortunately, at the time, he was working so many hours per week that he couldn't use the membership. We decided to cancel it and get a refund. After the owner finished a twenty-minute phone call—she knew I was waiting to see her—I explained the circumstances. She briskly and efficiently pulled out the contract and told me that I would lose the money I had paid. She took this position even though the staff person who sold me the contract had previously told me that if my son didn't want the membership, my money would be refunded. The owner acted in an officious manner, using the contract for justification, and seemed only to see the situation from her perspective. She expressed no understanding of, or empathy toward, my feelings or my views.

> **Have you ever had a course where you were trained in interpersonal communication skills so that it was confirmed that you had competencies, not just knowledge?**

In handling the situation that way, she followed the letter of the contract rather than the spirit of the agreement. I didn't want to become a return customer at this point. Then, when I further explained that my son had not used the membership at all, she said, "I don't know that he hasn't been here. We don't keep records." In making that statement, she expressed distrust in me, the customer.

As you might have guessed by now, I was becoming less and less comfortable as this interchange progressed. In an effort to help her understand, I explained it seemed only fair that I receive a partial refund because my son did not decide to buy the membership but received it as a gift, and had in fact not been to the gym even once.

She said, "I don't think a refund is necessary."

I said, "Do you want to create a satisfied customer or a dissatisfied customer?"

She said, "It's up to you whether you are satisfied or not." I left her my business card and told her that if she thought about it, she might change her mind, and if she did, she could give me a call. She looked away. I left the gym feeling unfairly treated not only about the money but mostly because I was treated in such an officious and distrusting manner.

Will I recommend that gym to others? No.

Will I go out of my way to caution others from doing business there: yes, but not vindictively. She simply did not gain my respect for her operation. She "won." I lost. Adept communication skills could have made the whole difference in this situation. (She went out of business six months later.)

Exploring the Skills of Communication

The practice of good communication skills results in two-way communication that builds intimate relationships or solves practical problems, whichever is the intent. This chapter will assist you to review and self-assess the extent to which you have the skills that have been researched as critical to the development of effective interpersonal communication in any setting (Carkhuff, 1971).

TL Skill #13: Self-Disclosure: *Appropriately Sharing Yourself With Others*

Self-disclosure refers to the ability to appropriately reveal deeper and deeper levels of self to others, as the other person in the relationship earns trust, which warrants such deeper and more genuine disclosure. This skill is critical in the development of both your self-concept and your relationships with others.

It seems that we earn trust and intimacy to the extent that we can be genuine, from the heart. Being open, but not unwisely risking too much information too soon, promotes this

> **It seems that we earn trust and intimacy to the extent that we can be genuine, from the heart.**

type of trust, and can even encourage the development of intimacy. If no one knows you very well, you will likely not feel much of a connection to others. Perhaps a sense of belonging and being connected with others is one deep need we all have, and if that need is frustrated, some people experience the pain of loneliness and emotional difficulties. If you are shy—fearful that others will use any knowledge they have about you against you—you will likely have difficulty with this skill of appropriately sharing yourself with others. If you are outgoing—can easily share your feelings with others—you may find that this tendency of yours makes more introverted people uncomfortable. Therefore, self-disclosure appropriate to the level of familiarity with the style of the other person is an important factor to consider.

Self-disclosure, to be most effective, must be well timed, not too deep or too shallow for the purpose of improving the relationship, and be shared in confidence and trust. An example of how truth-telling in relationships is healthy is when a special friend recently said to me:

> *My wife and I have had relational problems develop*

over the years that we sort of ignored and adjusted to without really realizing it. But the romance and closeness grew faint as the years passed and we became distant to one another. She has wanted to work on facing these things but I have avoided it for years. It was just too humiliating that a professional like me would have to admit failure in this area of life when I teach communication to people as a profession! But in the past few months, I made a commitment to really listen to her and tell her the truth about what I am feeling in the relationship. We asked each other two questions: 1) Where is our marriage from your point of view on a 10-point scale, and why? and 2) What could I do to make it a 10 for you? Wow! Did that ever open up the communication on both our parts! The truth hurt, but we didn't hurt one another! As a result, we are closer than ever, the romance is back in a new and deeper way, and this is in spite of the fact we are both busier than ever in our careers. I can't tell you how important this is to my overall happiness and optimism for the future. And our kids are getting the bonus of seeing us be joyful and playful together as they grow up!

TL Skill #14: Image Management Skills: *Taking Responsibility for How You See Yourself*

Image Management: This skill refers to your ability to be conscious of how you are seeing your own self. This means that you self-monitor any negative images or internal "voices" that would undermine your effectiveness as a person or leader, and manage these in a number of ways to ensure that you remain positively focused, no matter what external circumstances occur. This critical skill area is often neglected by many people. It is mainly a skill activated by awareness and by carefully choosing and affirming a positive self-image. Also, it is important to live congruently (with integrity) to that image so that it can develop as a part of the very fabric of your being. No one enjoys the tension of being divided internally and presenting him or herself as "duplicitous" to others. Studies of successful people reveal that this inner capacity and strength of managing self-image and inner integrity is an important contributor to success in career and life (Glasser, 1984, and Waitley, 1983).

An example of this skill is a client of mine who is quite cognitive in his orientation to life, and who wants assurances of control and order in every area of life. He tends toward being constantly anxious about the gap between his ideal world of how things "should" be and how they really are. He can't relax and just enjoy being alive! He sees himself as imperfectly able to tackle the challenges of a constantly changing world, feels overwhelmed too often, and has a hard time enjoying himself, his friends, or family members. He seems to communicate to others the attitude of "the glass is half-empty and what is in it is evaporating." His internal self-talk goes like this: "I'll never earn enough money; there's no way out of this rat race; I'm not good enough to cut the mustard." My coaching to him has been rather impatient and blunt—"give up stinking-thinking."

He has had to make a conscious decision to focus on himself as a person able to achieve what is possible, not what is unlikely. The truth is that his cup is at least half-full of his good talents, skills, and qualities, and he has many ways to fill it up the rest of the way, and have it spill over to others—but only if

> **If I believe I can climb the mountain, I will get at least part way to the top! If I believe it is useless to even try, I won't attempt it. I'll stay where I am.**

he gets control of how he manages his own thoughts (and, therefore, the emotions that follow from these thoughts).

If I believe that I can climb the mountain, then I will get at least part way to the top! If I believe it is useless to even try, I won't attempt it. I'll stay where I am. Failing to perceive and to take advantage of opportunities is just another kind of failure. My seeing just one way that things can work out well produces some success for me. I don't have to be perfect or exceptionally successful to enjoy life and be a respectable person. Even when I fail, I can treat myself like I would treat my best friend when he is suffering from a failure of some kind, with compassion and understanding.

TL Skill #15 Impression Management Skills: *Taking Responsibility for How Others See You*

Impression Management: This skill involves awareness of the impact of your behavior, appearance, and mannerisms on other people. It is also choosing your behavior intentionally to alter this impact in a desired manner. It is related to the foregoing skill in that it involves the bringing forward of the positive images of self that have been created or discovered. The skill includes the following:

1. Learning to dress appropriately for various social situations
2. Learning to speak effectively and articulately
3. Expressing strong, effective, and pleasant nonverbal messages to others
4. Creating the image in others' minds that you desire them to have of you
5. Avoiding being "pigeonholed" by others' limited perceptions of you

This brief story will illustrate how impression management works. For twenty-one years, I have trained university students to get ready to go out into the real world and find a job that fits their newly acquired skills and qualifications. Most of them struggle with anxiety when preparing for the first job interview. Most of the students haven't had validation and confirmation that they are perceived as competitive and desirable prospective employees. Many have severe self-doubts even though the track record of the program they are graduating from is that over 90 percent of the graduates find employment in their area of interest. What we do to get them ready is to "grill" them as though we were the interview panel. We know in general what questions they will be asked. We know what the employers are looking for in terms of personal appearance, conceptual understanding, and specific kinds of answers to questions.

When we finish with students after about one to two hours, they report feeling a large relief from anxiety and a much greater confidence. Many of them have said that the experience is like a "rite of passage." They know what to do to capitalize on their strengths and what to stop doing to minimize their weaknesses. Here is a top ten list of many of the main things they learn in their "grilling" session.

1. Dress the way the interviewers dress. Find out ahead of time what this code is and match it.

2. Eliminate "uh" and "um" and such phrases as "and stuff like that" and "you know what I mean" from your vocabulary.

3. Match the strength of the handshake, if you are offered a handshake. Don't give either an overpowering grip or a "gentle flower" handshake to the interviewer.

4. Dress business-like, not fashionable; looking professional, not masculine or feminine.

5. Talk about your strengths without an apologetic tone, and let the interviewers know how you really believe you have demonstrated job-related skills in your training and field work experiences. Be specific and tell short stories about how you made a difference.

> **Being a leader is like preparing for a whole range of interviews in varying environments. You need to be appropriately flexible, yet genuine in how you present yourself.**

6. Give consistent eye contact without staring in order to maintain an image of poise, confidence, and receptivity to the interviewers.

7. Remember that interviewers are not comfortable making you uncomfortable. Acknowledge your understandable nervousness and move on to answering the questions with energy and specific examples.

8. Don't take the situation too seriously, as though the outcome of it is a measurement of your worth. Treat the interview like a practice session at which you will get better as you do it. You will get a job. You are qualified. You have been trained for this career and specifically for this interview. Some interviewers will likely prefer you over the competition. The average student has to go to eight interviews to land the job he or she wants.
9. Laugh at yourself and inject humor into the situation whenever it is natural to do so, but be careful you aren't seen as trying to be funny to win the interview. Your response must be natural.
10. Hold your head and body up! Don't stoop or slump. Would you want to hire someone who has poor posture? It's often a sign of low self-esteem to have poor posture.

This list gives you an idea of how we help students manage the image they are projecting of themselves when they are getting ready for an interview. Being a leader is like preparing for a whole range of interviews in varying environments. You need to be appropriately flexible, yet genuine in how you present yourself. You want to earn respect, credibility, and the right to influence people in positive ways through the trust you gain with them. Learning to be intentional about understanding what "images" and "languages" (both verbal and nonverbal) people are comfortable with and shifting into them will have a bearing on your success as a leader.

TL Skill #16 Attending: *Giving Undivided Attention to Others*

Attending involves both your appearing to be attentive to others and your actually (inwardly) giving your undivided attention. Attending behaviors that give you the appearance of being interested in others are: facing the other person; squaring your shoulders; making appropriate eye contact; having an open and relaxed posture; leaning into the relationship (instead of leaning back); observing appropriate distancing (usually three to six feet in North American culture, farther away in Asian cultures, and often closer in Mediterranean, some European, and South American cultures).

> **Focused attention from the heart is what most people want and expect from one another, but receive all too seldom.**

Genuinely giving attention to others is something that others can sense as well as observe. Focused attention from the heart is what most people want and expect from one another, but receive all too seldom. Attending forms the basis for observing another person accurately, and is a prerequisite skill for observing without distorting your perceptions. Make a review of your attending behaviors and your ability to inwardly direct your attention where you want it to go on a continuing basis.

By way of illustration, you have probably experienced what it is like to go into a bank where the teller or loans officer is so busy with the task part of the job that he or she forgets the relationship part. You stand there waiting to get his or her attention, and you don't get it. You find yourself becoming impatient because the teller is there to serve you and you are waiting. The same experience can occur in a restaurant, in a doctor's office, or in a law office. Most of us just don't have the "time of day" for people who don't have it for us. People who won't even look at us are communicating some form of preoccupation, lack of availability or caring, and we never know which it is unless they tell us. If you are busy and preoccupied, then say so. Tell the other person when you will be able to give him or her your undivided attention. This is better than not giving attention at all.

The giving of attention is so powerful that it is the foundation of expressed love. You have seen lovers in a restaurant, eyes like big "love crumbs." They are looking goo-goo-eyed at one another. This is what we enjoyed as babies when our parents tossed us up in the air and held us on their laps. In our Western culture, eye contact is what we appreciate

> **The giving of attention is so powerful that it is the foundation of expressed love.**

from others, especially when we seek it or want it for various reasons. Those who cannot give steady, comfortable, pleasant eye contact are often not trusted, are suspected of perhaps being devious, or are seen as weak or withdrawn.

Giving eye contact can be nourishing, encouraging of communication, welcoming, and can put others at ease, especially if you are a genuinely kind person seeking to serve or to make things better for everyone. If you aren't genuinely kind or really don't care that much about people, it may show up in how you fail to give contact with your eyes.

One employee who worked for a leader I was coaching told me somewhat humorously about her frustration with her boss's inattentiveness. She felt so discounted and undervalued that she said to me, "The next time I go into his office and he keeps shuffling his papers and won't look at me, I am going to tell him that he had better look at me or I will set his desk on fire. Maybe that will get his attention!"

TL Skill #17 Observing: Simply Seeing Another Person Without Distorting or Judging

Observing skills involve your consciously receiving information about another person from all visible sources: a person's physical tension and energy levels; facial expressions; skin flushes; body posture; manner of dress; expressive mannerisms; hand movements; gestures; and the sum total of all other body language. When you can just simply look and see what another person is doing, and keep those observations separate from any judgments you might be having, then you are being more objective in your understanding of others.

Using the skills of observing prevents the development of assumptions and alerts us to judgmental tendencies we all seem to have at times. Observing is the prerequisite skill for effectively and temporarily suspending your own frame of reference (judgment or value system). Consider the effectiveness of your ability to observe accurately and keep your personal reactions separate from what you see as you read this chapter.

This skill is the one that connects you with the world of another person. If you want to motivate that individual to learn, perform better, engage in problem-solving with you, trust you, and find you credible, then it will help if you demonstrate that you are sensitive and observant. Noticing how people feel and processing that as a part of your communication with them is a more subtle and advanced way of developing credibility and influence with others. If I want to understand the extent to which someone is motivated to wrok on a project, it helps to notice his or her face and eyes. Women naturally seem to notice these nonverbal cues more keenly and immediately than men. This may be one of the major causes of the "battle of the sexes." Men often complain to women, "You're too sensitive!" and women often complain to men, "You're so insensitive!" To resolve the differences that may be accounted for by temperament and by gender, we need to be conscious that different people have differing capabilities in their ability to be sensitive to others in their environment. If I tend to be less observant, then I need to even more consciously decide to focus, observe, and note what is going on with others nonverbally. If we assume we are never perfectly accurate in our perceptions, we are in a position to reserve judgment and check for their accuracy, thus saving much grief and misunderstanding in relationships.

> **Noticing how people feel and processing that as a part of your communication with them is a more subtle and advanced way of developing credibility and influence with others. If I want to understand the extent to which someone is motivated to work on a project, it helps to notice his or her face and eyes.**

TL Skill #18 Suspending Frame of Reference: *The Key to the Golden Rule*

The skill of temporarily suspending your frame of reference is perhaps the most critical and important of all skills in that your credibility and effectiveness can, at times, rest solely on your performance of this skill. Your frame of reference is made up of your beliefs, assumptions, values, feelings, judgments, emotions, advice, moods, thoughts, perceptions, and stress levels at any given moment. Because our frame of reference is so personal and deeply imbedded in each of us, it is very difficult to practice suspending it on a regular basis. Most interpersonal, counseling, and leadership problems stem from this difficulty we all seem to have of needing to interpret reality from our own vantage point, and reacting in a self-oriented manner. It is very important that we learn to react in such a way that we take into consideration others' points of view and feelings, as well as our own.

This skill, simply put, is inner strength for self-control of emotions, judgments, and premature advice. Practicing this suspending skill involves putting others first before self, checking things out before jumping to conclusions or reacting emotionally, and giving others the benefit of any doubts we might have about them. Making snap judgments, reacting emotionally to a situation before we really understand it, "writing a person off" before we give him or her a fair chance, or assuming that something is true before we check it out, are all signs of not suspending.

Suspending is especially appropriate when others need to be understood so that their tension or stress can to be defused. In this way, we can help them become ready to hear our own thoughts, feelings, or points of view and, from a leadership point of view, help them get into action on a project that is important. Suspending, which is based on the facts of accurate observation, is the foundation of patience, gentleness, kindness, respect, and effectiveness in all leadership, counseling, and communication situations.

> **This skill, simply put, is inner strength for self-control of emotions, judgments, and premature advice.**

I did some executive coaching with a client, Bill, the new VP of sales and marketing for a wholesale distribution company. Bill came into the company as a graduate of an Ivy League school with an MBA and was commissioned by the President to accelerate the effectiveness of the marketing and sales functions. When he joined the firm, it had over thirty locations with over 240 salespeople, and no one was attending to marketing issues at all. Bill was brazen and proud in his approach, presuming that he, based on his MBA qualifications and his previous track record of building his own company, was the most qualified to decide what needed to be done. He used his own frame of reference almost entirely to assess the current state of affairs in the sales area and wrote a prescription for disaster by diagnosing the sales team's weaknesses and taking a remedial "Mr. Fix-it-and-get-all-the-credit" approach to "making change happen." He thought he had to do that to please the President and justify his salary.

Most of the salespeople had been there a long time and had enjoyed a successful track record of getting the company to the level of 180 million dollars in sales that it currently enjoyed. The sales team was operating at perhaps a 70 percent efficiency, and Bill treated the staff and the sales managers as though they needed his expert advice and he needed none of theirs. As a result, they rejected him. Within the first year of Bill's arrival, over 15 percent of the salespeople quit the organization (over half were higher performers) because, as one sales manager explained, they refused to deal with such a "condescending bastard." Sales plummeted and the organization lost 35 million that year! Bill rationalized that the drop in sales was due to his having to get rid of the "dead wood" on the sales team and would more than make up for the loss with outstanding progress the following year. The President believed him. Further loss in sales occurred the following year. No one asked the people who quit why they quit until we did follow-up interviews with them.

This is a classic case of "know-it-all-ish" managers trying to work "on" a team of salespeople to get "desired results" instead of working "with" them to make things happen for the better, for everyone. Bill—and the President— were presumptuous, domineering, unreceptive, inattentive, and did not suspend their frames of references enough to even listen to what their people were saying. They paid a dear price.

TL Skill #19 Questioning: *Appropriate Gathering of Information*

Questioning is a much overused skill that often puts others on the defensive. An appropriate and effective leadership behavior is to use open questions like "What do you think about that?" when we want a person to expand on a particular topic without influencing the direction of his or her talk. As we will see, however, active listening and checking for what people intend to convey to us is often more effective than questioning. Questioning makes us seem that we are the ones controlling the situation, much like interrogations during a police interview. Closed questions like "How many times did you beat your wife?" leave little room for discussion and force a person into the answer we hope to hear.

Questioning is used effectively when we need to gather information

> **In general, questions are less personal than active listening, and should be reserved for less personal interchanges, when correctness or completeness of information is the main focus.**

about a person's address, what he or she thinks about a specific issue, or when we want directions to get to a particular place. In general, questions are less personal than active listening, and should be reserved for less personal interchanges, when correctness or completeness of information is the main focus. Questions are risky to use on a habitual basis because when we question others, we are often taking the ball from them, leading the direction of the conversation—usually unconsciously—in the direction we think it should go (and thereby we fail to suspend frame of reference and truly listen).

Though it is possible to be effective and appropriate in the use of questions, more often than not, questions can interfere with good communication because they can be misused and overused so easily. We have hundreds of video tapes of leadership interviews where most often, when questions are being overused (and therefore not much listening is going on), and find that an accusatory, blaming, or suspicious tone of voice is evident while the interrogation is being conducted.

> **A person who listens well actively checks for the intended meaning from the sender's point of view.**

If you have a style of interacting with others where questions are the main theme, consider achieving more of a balance between listening, sharing, and questioning. This will increase the amount and quality of two-way communication that leads to problem-solving and conflict resolution in your personal relationships; and will lead to performance improvement when you are leading others.

TL Skill #20 Listening: *Checking for What Others Intend to Mean*

A person who listens well actively checks for the intended meaning from the message sender's point of view. A good listener is grounded; centered; gives undivided attention; temporarily suspends emotions, advice, and judgments; uses questions in a limited and appropriate manner; and checks with the sender to see if there is mutually understood meaning.

The skill of active listening also involves letting others finish, even when you feel like "butting in" to make your point. Helping others to feel heard and get finished with what they are saying only increases the chances that the door of their perceptual system will be open when you do send a message to them from your own frame of reference.

To some people, letting others finish talking, and then checking for accurate understanding so that they feel understood (and say so) seems to be a phony way to interact (because they are holding themselves back), and they are uncomfortable with it as a skill. Perhaps it can be seen that way, but nevertheless, careful listening works to clarify confusing messages and defuse tensions that are often at the root of conflicts or misunderstandings in all kinds of relationships. Here are some language formats that can be used for active listening.

"You mean, _____?"

"Maybe you're saying, _____?"

"What I hear you saying is _____. Is that right?"

"Could it be that you mean _____?"

"Can you clarify that for me?"

Notice that all of the above formats suggest a tentative, not a presumptuous, approach to checking with the other person to see if we are grasping a good part of the meaning that he or she intends to send to us. Also, notice the questioning tone at the end of each format. By asking the other person if you are understanding accurately, you are stating that you have an open mind and can learn more. You are showing interest and respect. Here is a way you can ask questions all you want and it won't make the other person so uncomfortable!

TL Skill #21 Responding With Understanding: *Getting on the Inside*

The skill of responding with understanding is a more powerful, personal, and intimate skill that can require the other person's permission for use. To carefully understand what someone is feeling, all of the foregoing skills discussed in this chapter must be applied first. Many people will resist or even resent your responding to their feelings directly. Many others will experience relief or satisfaction when you show understanding of their feelings in a specific way. Yet, one of the most frequent complaints we hear from employees, spouses, children, and relatives is that "he/she doesn't even understand how I feel." The most important point here is that this particular skill is best used when others want us to use it with them.

> **One of the most frequent complaints we hear from employees, spouses, children, and relatives is that "he/she doesn't even understand how I feel."**

Otherwise we might be accused of being like "phony bleeding-heart social workers."

The use of this skill requires more expertise and sensitivity than any of the other skills reviewed to this point because careful observation of nonverbal cues is required, and this is how responding gets you inside another person's emotional world. Responding with accurate understanding also enables you to see and feel things from others' points of view.

That is why this skill is the foundation of the quality called empathy. Empathy is defined as communicated understanding, so that you can prove to other people you understand what they feel and think and why they feel and think the way they do. This is one language format that can be used for conveying empathy.

"You seem to feel (feeling word) because (reason)."
"Maybe you're feeling (feeling word) because (reason)."

Formats are just general guidelines and may be changed to fit the situation or person, but must contain a direct and accurate response to a person's feeling state and the reason why he or she feels a particular emotion. Empathy training is available as a part of most communication skills training courses or workshops. Understanding others' feelings (until they **tell** us we understand) is an important cornerstone of building leadership credibility and trust in the minds and hearts of those with whom we work.

TL Skill #22 Assertiveness: *Speaking Honestly and Kindly with Self-Control*

Practicing the skill of being assertive means that you send a part of your frame of reference to others in a respectful manner, letting them know your feelings, ideas, opinions, reactions, beliefs, judgments, or points of view. If you want leadership credibility, it is important for you to be genuine and "up front"—without being overly pushy—to avoid getting walked on by others' behaviors, false expectations and assumptions about you. Assertiveness involves speaking the truth about yourself to others in a patient, kind, and understanding manner, thus giving others the opportunity and the right to do the same thing. If you want to make the communication and relationship even better, then model putting the other person first! Being assertive also involves not getting your frame of reference "hooked" and then overreacting emotionally in anger— which can add fuel to an already blazing fire.

> **Combining assertiveness with responding skills prevents your communications with others from seeming aggressive, or passive, and promotes two-way completed communication that can result in problems getting solved.**

Combining assertiveness with responding skills prevents your communications with others from seeming aggressive or passive and promotes two-way completed communication that can result in problems getting solved. Therefore, if you are angry with someone because of her or his behavior, you might use a format such as this.

> **"When you (describe behavior), I end up feeling (one word), and then (describe what else tangibly happens to you)."**

If the other person is having difficulty receiving your message, you could respond in an empathic way, "You seem upset when I tell you how I feel;" and help the other person to process your message. Combining the skills of assertiveness and responding enables you to manage your half of the communication and gives every opportunity for two-way communication to take place. Your taking this responsibility can more often than not result in problems being solved and relationships developed. Some people, however, may choose not to enter into two-way communication for a number of reasons. If this occurs, at least you can know that you have done your part well.

Self-Control: A Worthwhile Responsibility

A major goal of personal development and the key to effective assertiveness is self-control. It only makes sense that the more self-control people have, the better they will be able to use the abilities and skills that are at their disposal.

Control is achieved through knowledge, practice, and maturity. For an individual to develop tennis skills, he/she needs to exercise control over her/his body on the tennis court. The same is true for personal relationships in that those individuals who have solid relationships usually also have self-control and interpersonal skills.

A very important part of controlling self is self-discipline. Egan (1977) states, "Discipline means, at least in part, self-control. A person is disciplined if he or she makes whatever sacrifice is necessary in order to achieve a goal. Thus, discipline often involves some kind of hardship—doing things that aren't pleasant and giving up things that are."

This kind of self-control and self-sacrifice is an essential ingredient for personal satisfaction and successful relationships. Individuals who lack control over their frames of reference become more self-centered and tend to have shallow relationships with others. As a result, they can be lonely people who are neither giving nor receiving much love in their lives.

People who behave assertively, rather than aggressively or passively, tend to be more in control of self. This occurs because these individuals accept both their rights and their responsibilities. They do not aggressively take what belongs to others or passively let others blame them for what is not their responsibility. Assertive individuals think of others as having equal value and attempt to treat them as they would like to be treated.

> **Individuals who lack control over their frames of reference become more self-centered and tend to have shallow relationships with others.**

On the other hand, people who are aggressive are usually not in control of their thoughts, feelings, and behaviors. They either cannot or will not take charge of their frames of references. Therefore, they have trouble controlling their actions, and others suffer as a result. They suffer, too. These types of individuals are labeled aggressive or "hot heads" because they attempt to take others' rights away from them so that they themselves can have more control to get what they want. They also attempt to make others assume their responsibilities so that they will not have to do so. These individuals often put themselves before and above others.

People who are passive tend to go to the other extreme in that they often overcontrol their frames of reference to the point of self-suppression. They place others before themselves even if they (or others) have to suffer for doing so. While this sounds noble, often it is for selfish reasons. Passive individuals, like those who are aggressive, are most worried about their needs first, and others second. Notice some of the qualities, behaviors, and skills of the three style characteristics in the chart of interpersonal style characteristics on the following page.

In the gym membership story, the owner treated me in an aggressive manner and did not use even basic communication skills. Had she been assertive, a "double-win" situation could have been achieved.

> **You have to earn the right to confront by proving ahead of time to others that you care about their development as persons, that you are seeking to develop a relationship with them, that you are attempting to build rather than tear down.**

TL Skill #23 Confrontation: *Telling People the Truth about Unacceptable Behavior*

Assertiveness is mainly concerned with presenting yourself honestly and realistically in tight social situations. Confrontational communication, on the other hand, is more focused on other people's problem behaviors or attitudes, and your need for them to change in order for them to be more effective with you, in their job role, in their own lives, or with others.

Sometimes it is important or even necessary (in the case of performance reviews) to give critical feedback to others about how their behavior is ineffective, stressful, or inappropriate. This is a difficult skill to perform effectively because it is required that a certain level of trust is developed in the relationship before others will receive your feedback in a positive manner, and, therefore, engage in positive change. In a sense, you have to earn the right to confront by proving ahead of time to others that you care about their development as persons, that you are seeking to develop a relationship with them, that you are attempting to build rather than tear down, and that you are willing to accept confrontational feedback as well as dish it out.

It is possible to get agreements in advance with others that your relationship with them will be characterized by genuineness and honesty for the purpose of mutual personal development, and for the purpose of your

Interpersonal Style Characteristics

	AGGRESSIVE	ASSERTIVE	PASSIVE
Qualities	Insecure	Secure	Insecure
	Insensitive	Sensitive	Oversensitive
	Domineering	Respectful	Submissive
	Impatient	Patient	Patient
	Self-oriented	People-oriented	Other-oriented
	Win-lose attitude	Negotiable Attitude	No-win attitude
	Dishonest	Honest	Dishonest
	Decision-maker	Decision-maker	Indecisive
	Unreliable	Reliable	Reliable
Behaviors	Verbal/Physical Abuse	Respectful Communication	Manipulative Negative messages
	Lies by distorting	Truthful	Lies by omission
	Power-oriented	Respect-oriented	Escape-oriented
Skills	Physical Verbal	Centered	Attends
		Attends	Observes
		Observes	Gives
		Listens	LIstens
		Understands	
		Communicates	
		Challenges	
		Solves Problems	

developing your work or personal relationship with them. With this advance permission, giving difficult feedback can be easier and more effective. The predominant culture in an organization can be honesty about difficult things

and the resolve to deal with them quickly. Also, using confrontation and responding with understanding skills can assist others to process your confrontational feedback to them. This can be helpful to defuse the stress and tension often involved in giving and receiving feedback.

This skill is the most risky of all communication skills, and is actually least likely to succeed. If the maturity or personal security of the person you are confronting is marginal, he or she will likely not handle your confrontation very well. In these cases, it is advisable not to confront but to use challenging skills, if possible (the next and last skill in this chapter). Sometimes it is necessary to confront people with the ultimatum that they must either perform up to expected standards or they will have to be fired, or, if it is in a personal relationship, then sometimes it is better for the relationship to end if it is a destructive one, without hope for restoration.

In a small company, there were five executive-level managers who worked together quite well in most ways. One of the managers, however, was very critical of how the CEO was performing and would sometimes lash out at him without any seeming justification at that moment. Small things would trigger his near-rage reaction! As an external consultant, I was asked by the CEO to confront this person about the negative impact of his behavior. In my first conversation with this angry executive, I was told all the reasons the manager had to feel justifiably angry at the CEO. I listened until he felt secure that I understood his point of view and then I asked him if I could confront him about something I saw in him with which he was having difficulty. Note here that I respected his boundary, his right to say "no." He consented and I told him that even though he may have justification for feeling angry, venting on the CEO in an executive team meeting was not considered responsible or effective behavior on his part.

I told him simply that his approach did not work to build a better relationship with the CEO and did not help to solve the problems for which the CEO may, in fact, be responsible. I told him that his behavior alienated the CEO, poisoned the team atmosphere with negativity, and wasn't matched with two-way communication and problem-solving behavior. When I stated it this bluntly, and in a kind and patient tone of voice, he said, "Wow, you're right. How stupid of me to think that I was doing anything constructive!" We then explored alternative behaviors for him to apply to the situation and he decided to confront the CEO directly for the first time, and tell the truth to the CEO in the same way that I had told the manager the truth about his behavior. He asked me to come along and facilitate, which I did, and because of the willingness and maturity of the CEO, this became the turning point in the relationship between them. The team morale was no longer in jeopardy in future meetings and the performance of the team was enhanced by the new problem-solving capabilities released in the new relationship between the VP and the CEO.

> **Confrontation is the most risky of all communication skills, and is actually least likely to succeed. If the maturity or personal security of the person you are confronting is marginal, he or she will likely not handle your confrontation very well.**

Another clear example of a confrontation occurred when a new police chief came into office and discovered that a "good ol' boys" network of several sergeants was demoralizing many of the younger recruits. They justified their treatment of the younger officers as "that's they way *we* were initiated into this organization." As the new chief interviewed some of the subordinate officers, he found that the sergeants were awarding overtime hours to their longtime friends, treating the younger officers with disdain, and giving them the more dangerous and difficult assignments without adequate supervision or back-up.

When the Chief corroborated that these practices were typical with about 20 percent of the sergeants, he called them into his office one-by-one in the presence of his Deputy Chief as a witness. He confronted them with the unacceptable behaviors, asked them to own up to or deny the allegations, and made it clear to them that they would be fired if the behavior continued. Over a period of one year, the Chief fired several sergeants for continuing these dangerous and morale-destroying actions. The other sergeants confronted for their behavior changed their approach and engaged at least satisfactorily in upholding the new values of treating all employees with dignity, respect, and equity.

The Four-to-One Law:

For people to receive "bad news" and internalize it, take ownership of it, and change their behavior, they do need to know that they are seen as having "worth" as persons and that their worth is a separate issue from their value to the organization.

> In order for people to get "bad news," internalize it, take ownership of it, and change their behavior, they do need to know that they are seen as having worth as persons and that their worth as a person is a separate issue from their value to the organization.

In our experience in giving confrontational feedback, we found these results were true for the average person.

1. He or she can process fairly well one negative confrontational statement if it is prefaced with four positive statements about how positive past behavior is valued.
2. He or she can tolerate two negatives when they are prefaced with three positive statements.
3. He or she can barely process three negatives when they are prefaced with two positive statements.
4. He or she cannot process four negative statements when they are prefaced with only one positive statement.

This "Four-to-One Law" is supported by research but it is really common sense when we think about how we feel when receiving negative feedback ourselves. Perhaps, this is where the "golden rule" applies very strongly, that we would treat others the way we would like to be treated if we were being confronted by them, especially if they have position power over us!

Last, our leadership in this delicate situation can be positive if the person, regardless of past behavior, is told in various ways that he or she has worth, and that we are willing to work with them to increase their value to the organization. As soon as we communicate verbally or nonverbally that they have little or no value or worth, it is unlikely that the confrontation will produce positive results in the short or long term. Shaking the head from side to side, frowning at the corners of the mouth, rolling the eyes back are all nonverbal signals to many people (especially insecure people in high-pressure situations) that you are writing them off as having little or no worth!

> **As soon as we communicate verbally or nonverbally that they have little or no value or worth, it is likely that the confrontation will fail to produce positive results in the short or long term.**

Example formats for the language of this skill are listed below as guidelines for assisting you to plan your next confrontation with someone.

> **"Here are (specify behaviors) that we appreciate you for doing well."**
> **"Here are (specify behaviors) that we appreciate you for doing well."**
> **"Here are (specify behaviors) that we appreciate you for doing well."**
> **"Here are (specify behaviors) that we appreciate you for doing well."**
> **"You have been observed doing (specify unacceptable behaviors)."**
> **"Of which, if any, of these alleged behaviors do you take ownership?"**
> **"If you continue to do (unacceptable behaviors), the consequences will be (specify reasonable consequences)."**

These formats are guidelines to assist you in formulating statements that are factual and nonblaming in their tone. They help you focus on the issue of the confrontee taking ownership of behavior, get the message across that the behavior is not acceptable, and provide clear understanding of the consequences of continuing the unacceptable behavior. Of course, the consequences must be in line with labor laws and personnel policies and procedures in your workplace, and cannot be arbitrarily assigned by you if you are in a formal business or organizational environment. If you are using this skill in the context of a personal, marital, or parental relationship, you can decide what your boundaries are, what is acceptable and not acceptable, and can often enforce those boundaries by saying "no" to unacceptable behavior and making the reasonable consequences happen.

Keep in mind the mutual quality of the interpersonal communication role and skills in this chapter. Even the police chief invited critical feedback of his performance from his subordinates by sending around an anonymous questionnaire. He also had an open door policy, managed by "walking around talking with people," and rewarded people for speaking their truth to him even when he disagreed with them.

TL Skill #24: The Skill of Challenging: *Helping Others to See Strengths and Opportunities, and Move Toward Positive Change*

Challenging is a skill that is especially reserved for encouraging people to look at unused opportunities or personal strengths, and spurring them to take positive action. This skill is different from confrontation (which confronts smokescreens, blind spots, performance deficits, weakness, or discrepancies) because it is focused more on the positive potential of other people and the hidden or unseen creative opportunities that exist within their current relationships or environments. This skill is also less risky and easier to handle by those on the receiving end.

An example of this skill in action is that of the same Police Chief who also met one-on-one with all the other sixty supervisory officers in his policing organization. His Deputy Chief was also present in these very positive interviews. The Chief's goal was to recognize the worth of each dedicated officer, acknowledge specifically his or her value to the organization, and to make it known to each officer that he personally appreciated the individual's good work, support, and continuing commitment. In each of these interviews, personnel files were reviewed beforehand and specific, positive feedback was given for all past achievements, length of service, heroic behavior, and loyalty to the force and the community. Later in the year, plaques were given to all officers in leadership positions for their exemplary service, including the officers who had been given formal warnings. Career-path planning sessions were held during the Chief's second year to give encouragement and feedback to all those seeking promotions in the organization. The officers were given opportunities to plan for further training that would prepare them to compete more effectively for promotional opportunities.

This team of police leaders moved on to build one of the world's most effective community policing forces. As you know, the exceptional leadership that was exercised here is not typical of every organization. You can also see how using this challenging skill can have a positive impact on the future of an organization and the community it serves.

Conflict Management: Putting the Communication Skills Together

When managing an interpersonal conflict, all the skills we have examined above must be utilized to the fullest to have as positive an impact as possible. Conflict management involves managing your own frame of reference, your feelings, words, wants and needs, and assisting the other person to feel respected and yet understand your position at the same time. This is why the conflict management process is the most difficult of all applications of the interpersonal skills: often you have to manage your half and the other person's half at the same time. This is the case because most people do not have well-developed interpersonal skills.

Research on conflict management (Burke, 1977) has produced a general list used in managing conflict. These methods, which form parts of the interpersonal conflict management process, are outlined as follows.

1. **Forcing**: using power to cause the other person to accept a position; each party tries to figure out how to get the upper hand and cause the other person to lose.
2. **Withdrawal**: retreating from the argument.
3. **Smoothing**: playing down the conflict (differences) and emphasizing the positive (common interests), or avoiding issues that might cause hard feelings.
4. **Compromise**: looking for a position in which each gives and gets a little, splitting the difference, if possible; no winners and no losers.
5. **Confrontation and/or problem solving**: directing energies toward defeating the problem and not the other person; encouraging the open exchange of information; discovering the best solution for all. The situation is defined, the parties try to reach a mutually beneficial solution, and the situation is developed as "win-win."

A problem-solving approach to conflict management is an ideal one to implement when attempting to resolve a conflict. It should be your first choice. Then, if it doesn't work, back off to method number 4, compromise, and so on.

In the problem-solving approach, it is best for you to begin your communication this way.

1. Make a date to communicate with the person with whom you are having a conflict. Set a mutually convenient time instead of dumping your tension and demanding that the problem be solved now.
2. Then, whenever possible, take into consideration your personal style and the other person's style, and get ready to shift styles, if necessary, to encourage the other person to engage in two-way communication and problem-solving with you.

3. Agree together on a clear definition of the problem by redefining it several times from one another's points of view, using listening and understanding skills. Express your own points of view when the other person is able and willing to listen, or the session will turn into a power struggle (a lose-lose position).

4. Then agree on mutually satisfactory goals for your session. State and come to consensus about what you hope to achieve at the onset of your session so no expectation gaps are present that can lead to disillusionment or bitterness.

5. Take turns sharing honestly, not in a blaming tone, each person's views, needs, wants, etc.

6. Explore alternative solutions to the problem that could potentially be satisfactory to both parties. Consider the consequences of each alternative, both short and long term.

7. Implement the agreed-upon solution(s) by deciding together who will do what, when, where, etc. Set a date to review how things are going and to see if any adjustments need to be made for the plan to work better in the future.

8. When you cannot agree or come to a plan that is satisfying to both parties, it is acceptable to negotiate time for reevaluation and then plan another meeting.

9. After a time of further exploration, if a solution is not forthcoming, then withdrawal from the situation, putting the conflict into others' hands for management, or proceeding in your own direction may be the only alternatives possible.

10. There are always consequences to pay when you decide to walk away, get help from a mediator or person in a position of authority, or just take your own course of action without compromise. Weigh the consequences carefully before acting. You want to be as constructive as possible without giving up your own sense of integrity.

Conclusion

In this chapter, we have examined interpersonal communication skills particularly from the point of view of establishing a base of mutuality, respect, and openness in personal and work relationships. The most-respected leaders are those who are honest without putting others down, are willing to solve a problem so that as many people are respected as possible, and who show caring about other people without being manipulated—the "bleeding-heart" syndrome.

In the next chapter, we will examine the skills of counseling and problem management. These skills and the counseling/coaching role are different in character in that quite often, it is difficult to maintain the predominantly mutual quality in the relationship. In counseling and problem management, the transforming leader is exercising a more direct influence and accepting even more of the responsibility for facilitating the communication and the problem-solving process.

References

R. R. **Carkhuff**, *The Development of Human Resources.* (New York: Holt, Rinehart & Winston, 1971).

W. **Glasser**, *Taking Effective Control of Your Life.* (New York: Harper and Row, 1984).

D. **Waitley**, *Seeds of Greatness.* (Old Tappan, New Jersey: Fleming H. Revell Company, 1983).

G. **Egan**, *The Skilled Helper.* 2nd ed. (Monterey, CA: Brooks/Cole, 1977).

R. **Burke**, "Methods of Resolving Superior-Subordinate Conflict: The Constructive Use of Subordinate Differences and Disagreements." In *Readings in Interpersonal and Organizational Communication*, eds. R. C. Huseman, C. M. Logue, and D. L. Freshley, 3rd ed. (Boston: Holbrook Press, 1977).

Chapter 6

THE SKILLS OF COUNSELING AND PROBLEM-MANAGEMENT

Leaders are effective at problem management to the degree that the people they work with are better equipped to manage their problem situations.

Terry Anderson

Introduction

We have used the term problem-management skills to clarify what many people mean by the word counseling. In counseling, coaching, and mentoring relationships, the same generic problem-management skills are used to help people become more effective at learning to work through change and solve various types of problems. The skills can be used with yourself, other individuals, teams, organizations, and communities. They are important aspects of the practice of *Transforming Leadership* because these skills can help to move people you lead toward greater self-understanding, self-responsibility, and performance. Each leader needs to develop these skills for personal use and to encourage others to develop and perform at their full potential.

Personal applications include self-examination and problem-solving (counseling one's self), and assisting family members to gain self-understanding and to solve problems they may encounter in everyday life. These skills can also be used with peers in organizations so that people in these settings may become more effective and enjoy a greater sense of well being. Corporate applications may include counseling, coaching, and mentoring others who may need assistance in overcoming blocks to performance, help in dealing with personal or work-related crises, or guidance in career planning. Problem-management skills are necessary prerequisites to effectively coaching others' performances and mentoring to facilitate their development.

> **In counseling, coaching, and mentoring relationships, the same generic problem-management skills are used to help people become more effective at learning to work through change and solve various types of problems.**

There has been great confusion about the differences between counseling and coaching and mentoring. As we have said above, it is simple and clear to think that all three of these unique types of relationships require the same generic set of problem-management skills. Another feature that these roles have in common is that they occur in the context of a formal or informal agreement with another person with whom it is your role to engage in solving problems in a specific way. Counseling, coaching, and mentoring to many people are just different words to describe the same thing. This is confusing, and often causes problems with conflicting expectations between leaders and their team members, bosses and employees, parents and children, etc.

Therefore, we present the following definitions of counseling, coaching, and mentoring. In examining these definitions, you will see how the problem-management skills apply to all three of these distinctive ways of helping others to self-examine, remove obstacles to change or growth, and move ahead into greater learning and performance.

Definition of Counseling Relationship: Counseling is often personal in nature. The counseling relationship is one often based on the role you have agreed to play in your organization. You are engaging in some kind of counseling relationship if you are a supervisor or manager and it is an expectation in your job description that you engage people you lead in conversations of a personal nature that will help them resolve personal or family problems to improve their job performance. This is especially true of small businesses where any counseling done in the workplace is done by coworkers, supervisors, or owners. This is often true when the nature of the problem is not perceived to be the employee's fault, such as a tragic loss in the family or when a marriage partner is abandoned.

Counseling relationships in larger companies and organizations can often occur in the context of employee assistance programs, or when an employee goes to visit a psychologist during a time of distress. It is possible for a wide range of people to provide good, skilled counseling even though they have not had formal training to be a counselor. It is nearly always better to have been trained as a professional counselor if longer-term counseling is what is required. It is possible, however, to learn the effective short-term counseling skills outlined in this chapter.

Definition of the Coaching Relationship: Coaching is most often job-performance related. Supervisors do performance coaching of their subordinates orient and coach their performance up to speed on certain tasks. Again, if it is the supervisor's job to coach, there should be an agreement between the employee and the supervisor for coaching to take place. The relationship may shift into counseling at times, but primarily is focused on coaching for improved performance.

I do executive coaching with CEOs, presidents, and other leaders. We have agreed that this is the relationship we will have. We set up a list of things we want to work on in each session on the phone or in person, and I provide the coaching relationship so the leader can develop and apply specific skills to deal with identified personal, team, or organizational problems.

Sometimes, we agree that counseling of a more personal nature is needed and I shift into providing this more focused service.

Definition of Mentoring Relationship: Mentoring can be both formal and informal. Perhaps some of the best learning experiences people can have is when, at the right time in their lives, a mentor appears and helps them learn exactly what they need to know to succeed. This happens by Providence or by chance. More often and more preferably, formalized mentoring programs can be built into an organization's strategic plan so it becomes a part of the culture that people, especially leaders or potential leaders, be mentored. Mentoring programs identify those who would be the best mentors and pair them up with those most in need of mentoring. Specific goals are set for the protégé's development. Often the mentor and protégé make a commitment to work together for a year or more. The relationship is free of any formal job-performance evaluation.

Counseling, coaching, and mentoring can happen in the context of the same relationship, but often it is helpful to be clear with the other person about what it is you are agreeing to do with and for the individual. If you are doing coaching and it appears it would be beneficial to shift into a counseling relationship for a period of time, it is helpful to get agreement with the other person for you to do so.

How This Chapter is Organized

This chapter is divided into two sections. First we will take a careful look at each of the twelve *Transforming Leadership* skills included in this problem-management skill set. You may want to pay special attention to those skills in which you felt strongest and weakest when you took the *Transforming Leadership* Skills Assessment in Chapter 2.

The second part of the chapter will explore the larger steps and processes involved in problem management when using these twelve skills.

The *Transforming Leadership* skills to be discussed in this chapter include the following.

Section One: Understanding the Twelve Problem-Management Skills

These skills are presented with the idea that it is possible to be proactive in our approach to managing and preventing further problems. It is also possible to divide the skills into specific language and observable behaviors that can be demonstrated, modeled, practiced, learned, and passed on to others. This approach to learning skills has been described as the microskills approach. Learning skills in this micro fashion, however, can make the whole process seem mechanical or robotic. Therefore, when you practice or apply a particular skill, keep in mind that each skill flows into another—I have listed the skills (below) in logical, progressive order—but the process of problem management is fluid.

Therefore, you may find yourself moving from one skill, then back to another, based on what the other person needs. Genuineness on your part is more important than perfectly performing each step of the process in order!

It is the same when you learn any new skill—you will feel awkward at first because it may

> **When you learn the skill and see it work, you will then enjoy the power and ease with which you can assist yourself and others in the problem-management process. It can become enjoyable!**

be different than the way you have done things before. When you learn the skill and see it work, you will then enjoy the power and ease with which you can assist yourself and others in the problem-management process. It can become enjoyable!

TL Skill #25 Advanced Empathy

Sharing your hunches with others about their experiences, behaviors, or feelings can help them move beyond blind spots and develop the new perspectives they must have for breakthrough thinking to emerge. In using the skills of advanced empathy, you can help others express what they are implying; help them to identify themes in their stories; assist them to connect islands of experiences, behaviors, or feelings; and help them to draw conclusions. This skill is critical to facilitating deeper understanding in others, but must be approached with caution and respect because of the powerful and intensely personal nature of the material likely to emerge.

As an example of how this skill can work, I was recently doing executive coaching with a CEO who continued to complain about personal and work overload. He couldn't keep up with all the demands, phone messages, e-mail messages, pager messages, meetings, and family obligations, and complained he had no time of his own. He was having difficulty sleeping, was losing weight, and was experiencing the beginning symptoms of depression. I responded with deeper understanding to what this exhausted man was saying with his whole being when I said, "You seem overwhelmed to the point of losing hope because you realize you are caught in a pattern of overextending yourself that you can't stop." His response was a deep sigh, and a big, "YES! That's it! I say yes to everything but I don't know why and I can't stop it! I am really making myself miserable living this way." When I said what I did to him, the situation came together for him like pieces of a puzzle, and a light of truth went on. That truth set him free to make significant changes.

A language format for this skill can be: **"You feel (one feeling word) because you realize that you are (accountable in some way for the consequences you now face)."**

This personal realization of a blind spot helped him to later change his relationship with his wife, children, partners, and community. During the next few weeks, he clarified his personal purpose statement, dropped out of his over-enrollment in too many committees that did not fit his purpose, got his wife and kids back into high priority in his daily planner, and even booked in some time for himself to regenerate and relax. After twenty-six years of living a compulsively driven life without a clear vision or purpose, all this change was precipitated by one turning point realization during our coaching interview.

TL Skill #26 Problem Exploration: *Exploring External and Internal Problems*

This skill requires that you follow other people through their own understandings of their problem situations first. Then, if they are ready or developed enough, assist them to see the personal *internal* problems they are having with those external problems. This step is best done prior to setting goals, exploring alternative courses of action, and before you give any advice from your perspective. Understand the specific problem first—and its causes—then offer advice when the other person's own ideas are exhausted.

The facilitative process of helping others see and take ownership of problems is much like the quarterback leading the runner by throwing a football—if the ball is thrown too far ahead, the runner will miss it; and if the ball is thrown too far behind, no yardage is made. You may have to lead a bit but only in the direction that the other person is already going. Difficult but necessary confrontations, of course, are exceptions to this general guideline of passing the ball to people.

You can offer your own hunches about what you think is the real problem and see if the other person can use your view of it—but only if you are not so busy doing this that you interrupt the other person's self-examination process with your "wise ideas." People receiving help—especially premature advice (before the problem is specified and owned)—often find it more difficult to use others' ideas when they are busy seeking to define and understand their own thoughts and feelings. If you follow this advice (!), you will avoid the second most prevalent of the major problems beginning problem managers have: failing to define the problem and giving premature advice.

Perhaps the ideal time to share your definition of a problem with others is when they are stuck, or when you want to add some alternative ways for them to consider a problem. Do this tentatively and watch (use observing skills), and then check with the other person to determine the usefulness of your ideas or responses. Don't assume your perspectives will be internalized and used by the other person. We usually don't take others' advice carte blanche and then act on it! Give focused input at the right time.

The facilitative process of helping others see and take ownership of problems is much like the quarterback leading the runner by throwing a football— if the ball is thrown too far ahead, the runner will miss it; and if the ball is thrown too far behind, no yardage is made.

The more thoroughly a problem is explored and the more specifically it is defined, the greater probability there is for a high impact solution to be reached. The exploration of an internal or external problem with another person—or with self— begins by using all of the skills outlined above in the section on communication. As you understand meanings, feelings, and define the situation that has occurred, you will begin to get a sense of a pattern emerging.

As you lay a base of understanding using the communication skills— especially the skills of listening and responding—you are in a better position to formulate a specific problem statement using a format such as: **"Now you realize that you can't/haven't (specify what person cannot or has not done) because (specify reason), and that makes you feel (specify predominant feeling, using one word)."**

Or, you may choose to use a somewhat different format that gets at the same issue: **"You seem (identify main feeling) because you can't (specify what cannot be performed) due to (identify internal lacks or causes of problem, which could be overcome if identified)."**

Example of a Problem Exploration Dialog in a Coaching Relationship

Presented below is an example of a problem-specification dialog. An executive (Helen) was engaged in a dialog with a manager (Merle) who was having a difficult time sticking to timelines. He had turned in most assignments two weeks late. A high-performing employee in his previous job where he moved around and talked to people, Merle now was in a job role where much of what he did was an audit function at his desk. He had more critical managerial responsibility in his new role but less opportunity for innovation and human contact. He was also having medical problems in his family, his parents were aging rapidly and were 1,500 miles away, and he didn't really like the stress of living in a big city with a lot of traffic and smog.

Helen: Merle, I've noticed that you have been turning in several projects late during the past few weeks. Could we talk about this now, or do you want to set up a time to meet tomorrow?

Merle: Yes, we can talk now. I know I have been late on three important projects, but I'm in a slump and can't seem to keep myself on track. I don't really know what is wrong.

Helen: I noticed that you looked stressed just now, Merle (a response to immediate, observable feeling, to facilitate a supportive climate). I'm not trying to make you feel guilty, but I'd really like to work through this with you if I may be of any help. Your previous contributions have been on time and high quality and I want to do what I can to support you to continue the super job you normally do (recognizing previous strengths and achievements in the context of confronting weakness is respectful and supportive leadership behavior).

Merle: I've even been avoiding trying to face why I am repeatedly late with the projects. It's been bothering me a lot since the first one was late two weeks ago. I just feel depressed and I don't know why.

Helen: Yes, when I have glanced at you during the past few weeks, I have noticed your energy level is down and you seem to be in a slump—even sometimes your posture is actually slumping over, and it is even now. You seem to be sort of in pain, somehow. Does that fit for you? (A response to the predominant feeling nonverbally exhibited is often facilitative of deeper self-disclosure.)

Merle: Yes! I feel pain in my neck and back when I sit down to do these projects. I thought I would be motivated in this new area, but now that I am into it, I don't find it challenging—it's too repetitive, and I don't see any promotions sideways or up for quite sometime. I feel trapped, like I'm just doing time here all day long, not using my talents as I was in my other role. (At this point, because she went of her way to help Merle get this promotion, Helen could have become hooked and said, ...but I thought you wanted this job, you jerk, but she did well and suspended her frame of reference.)

Helen: OK, Merle, I think I am getting a clearer picture. Right now you seem down on yourself because you haven't taken responsibility for processing this off-key feeling for over two weeks and you have allowed your performance to drop because you can't see any way out of your dilemma.

Merle: Yeah. I know I'm stuck because I said I would take on this job for two years. And I can't go back on my word.

Helen: So you feel trapped because you believe you can't have integrity if you change your mind, due to your high standards about giving your word?

Merle: Yes. If I say I'm going to do something, I do it. No whining!

Helen: So, it's like you're sapped of enthusiasm because you can't see another way to maintain your integrity other than making yourself march through this job for a few years—even though you now realize it doesn't fit your goals and talents?

Merle: Is that what I'm doing?! I'm not that rigid, am I? I guess I am. I think I want to do something about that! I don't think I will be doing myself or the company the best I can by being so rigid. What other options do I have? (Merle now recognizes and takes ownership of his part of the problem.)

Helen: I'm not sure because I haven't thought about it. Maybe we could both jot down some ideas between now and Monday and see what we come up with. Can we meet at 10 in the morning?

Merle: Yes, definitely. Thanks for supporting me on this one, Helen. It's not everyone who is willing to look at more than one way things can work out for the better.

Helen: I need to be in the right spot, too, if I am going to use my talents and enthusiasm to produce good results. I'm thinking about making a move in about a year. I'll be ready for a change by then. Thanks for your trust in going through this personal area with me. Do you think you can get the report in on time tomorrow afternoon now that we have a better idea of what is happening?

Merle: Count on it.

Helen: Thanks.

It Doesn't Have to Take a Long Time

This sequence of problem-identification responses gives you a clear idea of some interventions that could be appropriate in a three- to five- minute conversation. It doesn't have to take a long time to facilitate a person through the process. In the long run, it will save many lost person-hours if Merle's performance goes up or if he gets into a more fitting job role—or even if you help him find another company so you can replace him with a person with a nature that fits the job.

TL Skill #27 Problem Specification: *The Most Complex Skill*

This specification skill is the main skill nearly everyone who attempts to develop these skills has difficulty implementing effectively. This is the case because problem exploration requires a complex set of qualities and abilities—patience; temporarily suspending personal hunches, judgments, emotions, and premature advice; careful empathic listening; a creative mind; and a perceptual receptivity to the other person's nonverbal cues. It also requires the ability to craft language that clearly defines the problem, and a belief that the root causes of a problem should eventually be explored when the person being helped can handle more depth. Although difficult to master, the skill of problem specification is very powerful in assisting others to move ahead in their understanding of their problems and to solve them—which can improve their morale and their work performance.

Example Problem Statement—An example of language that could be appropriate for a problem statement a leading manager might make to a coworker in trouble is as follows: **"You seem to be saying you're depressed because you realize that you can't stop drinking so much, because it's so difficult right now for you to face the painful reality of your wife's cancer."**

As you can see, this is a complex sentence, capturing the problem behavior, the difficult inner self-control problem, and the harsh external reality. The statement also contains no words that could be accusatory—just the facts as presented, for the most part. You can see why these statements are so difficult to formulate, and, therefore, why many people tend to oversimplify problems and give trite advice or pat answers they honestly hope will be helpful.

The More Solvable Problems are Best Addressed First

It is also important that problems with a high probability of being solved or managed effectively be focused on first so that motivation will be higher to take action. Searching for supports in the environment, strengths within the person, and problem-solving potentials inherent within the problem itself are important. Success will then more likely be the result. We all need the encourgement of early small-wins.

TL Skill #28 Problem Ownership: *Helping Ourselves and Others Own Up*

This is a difficult skill because many people often assume that if people were really motivated, they would get the lead out of their pants and solve the problem. When people are facing difficult and stressful problems, they are often stunned. They can be temporarily mentally or emotionally frozen, unable to think or function well. Helping others to take ownership of their part of an overall problem they believe they can do something about is our primary task as problem-managing leaders. Without their being able to willingly and honorably take ownership of their part of the problem, there will not be change.

We believe that an inability to personalize problems is most often an issue of personal development rather than stubbornness.

What if people will not take ownership of their problems?
This is often because they feel humiliated, ashamed, embarrassed, or fearful of not getting a hoped-for promotion—or they dread the pain of facing the problem and would rather live with the pain of the problem itself. As we create a culture where facing the truth about problems (and our personal responsibility in them), we can provide a climate where mistakes or difficulties can be overcome and dealt with honorably. It is even possible to create a culture where celebration and recognition can be given to those courageous souls who, with honor, face the facts and engage themselves in dealing with it.

The fact remains that some people will not take ownership, no matter what we do. In these cases, it is our job to act in good faith and continue to do our part in facilitating problem-solving even though the other person is frozen, unable, or just plain unwilling to face things. So long as we have the leadership responsibility to work with a person—and we have decided not to fire them, or they cannot be fired—we must act as though the glass is half-full and we are going do what we can to fill it up and run it over.

Here is a language format for specifying a problem so it facilitates ownership: **"You seem to feel (one feeling word) because you can't stop (problem behavior) due to (internal cause of problem)."**

Once we help someone crystallize the language that captures the essence of their internal difficulties and obstacles, we are in a position to help that individual set goals to overcome the internal difficulties causing the external manifestation we call the problem. Most often, external problems are caused by these internal difficulties that must be dealt with before progress can be made. This is where we can see that helping someone through this impasse can be very powerful in creating a climate where learning can occur.

Some people are good at doing what we call personalizing problems (taking ownership) so they can get into personal action to solve them. Others are not so good at it. We believe that an inability to personalize problems is most often an issue of personal development rather than stubbornness. An inability to personalize can also be due to previous emotional abuse or learning disabilities. Therefore, it is much more economical and effective to hire good problem-solvers in the first place than it is to coach and develop them to maturity and competence. If we are, however, having to work with people who are not competent at present, and they need to grow or need to be facilitated through this process, you can see how the problem-management process can work.

Jack Welch, CEO, held morning meetings at General Electric where he had managers go through this kind of processing of problems in a large group. He led the process himself and all those present dealt with emerging problems on a daily basis; they went through the problem-management process on each problem. Sometimes people had to own up to personal responsibility in front of the group. Sometimes Jack did. They were honored and recognized for this courage and humility. I wonder if this has something to do with General Electric's being the largest and most profitable company in the world?

TL Skill #29 Goal Setting: *Identifying Realistic and Motivating Targets*

Goal setting is the "what to do" part of the problem-management process. Action planning, the skill we will examine after goal setting, is the "how to get there" part of the process. For now, let's turn to your self-assessment of your goal setting skills.

Attacking high yield problems, where there is opportunity for both personal development and improvement in external circumstances, is preferable to setting goals that will alleviate only a personal problem or improve external circumstances. This is the case because often personal difficulties cause problem situations, and problem situations can, in turn, cause additional personal difficulties. The skill of goal setting is important because it provides a focus for defining future accomplishments which, when reached, can ideally alleviate the problem inside a person and improve the external problem situation at the same time. Goal setting is a practical and powerful skill for becoming a more intentional and successful person yourself, and in your leadership interventions with others, to assist them to do the same.

Goals should be set that are specific enough to solve a defined problem and give direction to action. Goal statements that are the most effective have these attributes.
1. Measurable and verifiable
2. Realistic and achievable within a reasonable time
3. Genuinely owned by the person with the problem
4. In accord with the values and beliefs of the person
5. Clearly envisioned and attractive enough to be motivating
6. Desirable enough to give rise to genuine commitment
7. Evaluated on an ongoing basis to check for realism

Thus, specific and careful goal setting that challenges our own or others' unused potentials are often not easy to specify. Often, people offer one another premature advice or "pat answers." Goal setting, however, requires time and careful consideration for effective formulation. By providing yourself and others with a clear sense of direction for managing problems, stress can be alleviated and constructive action, increased energy, and improved performance can result.

An example of a clear goal statement might be the one that Merle made to Helen during a subsequent meeting, when he realized that, for a number of reasons, he had to change jobs and geographic locations. After Helen and Merle met the next Monday morning, Merle realized he was not only disillusioned with his new job role, he was facing the fact that he did not want to live in the city where he now lived, wanted to move closer to his aging parents, and wanted to live in a city where pollution would not be such a problem.

His problem was related to a complex set of factors pushing him away from not only the job he was in, but away from the company he was working with, too. After Helen helped Merle sort through a more clear understanding of these factors, she helped him respecify his problem as a career and life planning problem. Then Merle formulated his own goal statement based on the increased clarity he found in his dialog with Helen: "I want to take the initiative to explore other career options and other cities so I can relocate to start a new life by next summer—where there are ample career opportunities, good family emphasis, clean air, and affordable housing."

Note how clearly the goal is defined here, with a timeline and Merle's values considered in the statement. Helen did a good job of helping Merle to be quite specific and concrete in his goal setting.

Helen began searching for another employee who could better fill Merle's position, instead of keeping Merle in the same job or switching him to another job in the same company in the city where he did not want to live. Helen is likely to see an overall increase in corporate performance if she does more careful staff selection for that same position and other positions the next time she has the opportunity.

TL Skill #30 Goal Ownership: *Securing Ownership to Get Commitment to Action*

In the same way, it is important to facilitate others to take ownership of goals that will resolve their part of the overall problem being faced. My experience is that until someone comes up with the language to move ahead successfully, they do not change their approach or perform any differently. Yes, some people are visual, but it still seems that language locks goals in to the people's action systems. Our observations are that goals that are written down are more than 50 percent more likely to be achieved than goals thought or spoken about. Goals that are prioritized are more likely to be accomplished than those that are on a long list of goals to be achieved "someday." If we are always working primarily on our top three or four goals, we are more focused, less distracted, and more successful. Goals that are timelined are also more likely to be achieved. So, if I want to get commitment to action, then I can help people set goals that follow the specificity guidelines set out here.

Here is an example of how I assisted a CEO to take ownership of a goal. For years, he was preoccupied with business. He agreed with the opinion of his wife and friends who thought he was neglectful of his marriage. Even though he had admitted his problem and set a goal to change, he had never really taken personal ownership for the goal. I challenged him by asking him to open up his daily scheduler and see if he could find a place in it during the last month where he had written her name. He looked, and was stunned that he still had not even planned "a date" with her, even though he had committed to do so. This time, he agreed with me that he would meet with her that evening and plan a two-week vacation. He was also going to schedule time for them to spend special evenings together, doing things they could both enjoy. He agreed to phone me the next day to tell me he had followed through with his plan. He did and he had.

There is a resource well worth mentioning now. Bill Bean, Ron Ford, and Richard Edler have written a fascinating workbook called *Living On Purpose.* It outlines over 300 well-formulated goals from which you can select, then prioritize and create an action plan to build a more balanced and meaningful life. The same *Strategic Planning Technology* that has worked so well in business can now be applied to personal life, too. Those interested in accessing a copy of this workbook can do so at http://www.strategia.com. Although not yet in its published form, it is accessible at this time.

TL Skill #31 Action Planning: *Exploring and Evaluating Specific Pathways for Achievement*

Once the goal has been defined, it is time to examine alternative pathways to reach it; then it is time to develop a realistic plan to implement that goal in a step-by-step fashion.

Exploring Alternative Strategies to Reach the Goal

Quite often, people fail to achieve goals for a number of reasons. Some of the main reasons are their strategies are not clear, the steps involved are too large for the timeline that has been set, or they lack the required material or emotional supports. It is important, therefore, to ensure that all possible alternative strategies are explored and evaluated before one is decided upon prematurely. Often, there is a better way to "get there," but people tend to do what is familiar and not explore other options thoroughly enough to evaluate better action alternatives. Being exhaustive in searching out alternative courses of action nearly always reveals attractive, motivating, and encouraging steps to take that were not previously clear.

Evaluating and Selecting Alternative Strategies to Reach the Goal

Once alternative strategies have been explored, it is important to evaluate which ones best fit your own or others' values and motivational structures. The action plan has to "turn us on" for some reason or we do not want to "go for it." Therefore, to evaluate the potential of an alternative action plan, we need to specify what is important to the person with the problem, and assess how much each alternative course of action fits what is felt to be important.

For example, Merle wanted to choose a new location to live, and after exploring what was important to him, his family, and others in his social setting, he made a comparison chart similar to the one below. He rated each city on a scale of 1 to 5 in terms of how much it might fulfill the values he deemed important.

| | **Alternatives** | | |
Values	Chicago	Denver	Dallas
Clear Air	2	5	3
Family City	2	4	3
Good Economy	3	4	4
Affordable Housing	2	4	2
Proximity to Aging Parents	2	5	3
TOTALS	11	22	15

It may not be necessary to actually make a chart on paper unless the problem is quite complex, but the steps you would go through in considering various alternatives—or helping someone else to consider them—would be the same.
1. Identify alternatives
2. Identify values in order of importance
3. Weigh alternatives against criteria
4. Get a more clear sense of which alternative course of action seems most desirable after careful assessment

TL Skill #32 Implementing Action Plans: *Increasing the Success Rate*

Helping self and others to reach goals and succeed in taking planned action steps is important to the problem-management process, perhaps ultimately the most important step. If we do not succeed in counseling ourselves and others to accomplish worthwhile goals, then how effective is our helping or problem management? Action plans may not get off the ground because people tend to cling to old, less functional patterns of behavior. It can be scary to give up familiar

> **Action plans may not get off the ground because people tend to cling to old, less functional patterns of behavior.**

patterns of action in favor of more effective but foreign ones. If action plans do get implemented, they tend to fall apart over time, or fade in intensity, and quite often, they are replaced by old patterns of behavior.

Leaders may get discouraged with how often people "fail" at living up to their expectations for improved performance. We find we can get discouraged with ourselves in certain areas of our lives because we want change, and it doesn't come easy. It would be good for us to accept that deeper changes often come about with great struggle, much encouragement, and quite a bit of time in the process. We have all seen that just because people set goals and plan to take new actions, that doesn't mean that the leader's task ends there, and the "follower" is now fully capable and responsible.

An implementation plan includes a clear—often written—statement of what will be accomplished, when, and by whom. When implementation breaks down, ongoing coaching or counseling may be required. With people who are more stuck or resistant, confrontation may be required.

TL Skill #33 Confrontation: *Facing Self-Defeating Behaviors*

You can challenge the discrepancies, distortions, smoke screens, and games that others seem to use to keep themselves and others from seeing their problem situations and unused potentials—or you can use confrontation to challenge people to move beyond discussion to action.

This skill is the most risky of all the other skills because it involves getting the other person to confront self directly. A great deal of trust is required for people to feel comfortable allowing you to challenge what you think may be self-deception, self-defeating behavior patterns, or destructive interpersonal "games." It would seem we have to earn the right to confront by developing the relationship over time, prior to engaging in a confrontation.

Strength Confrontation: You challenge others to focus on strengths you observe are present, but ones they tend to ignore or deny. Berenson and Mitchell (1974) found that more-facilitative helpers used strength confrontations significantly more often than less-facilitative helpers. They also found that people used this type of confrontation least often! An example of a strength confrontation could be: "You have lots of ability to perform and enjoy sports that you aren't using right now—and yet you say you want to get fit. Maybe you could find a sport you really like and use that to help you reach your goal?"

Weakness Confrontation: You can challenge others to face their weak spots because they are tending not to see them. This is the more risky type of confrontation because it requires that the other people have enough self-worth to face their deficits without feeling like losers. Many people cannot face weaknesses or faults directly without feeling shaky in the self-worth department. They can also feel threatened and fearful that others will judge them negatively and discriminate against them when it comes time for a promotion. In some environments, this is probably a realistic fear.

Recently I confronted a CEO I was coaching. I told him I believed he was underutilizing his superior visionary leadership abilities (a strength confrontation) and then confronted him with the fact that his implementation of action plans isn't nearly as strong when we look at his track record of execution. He agreed and realized that if his organization is to function at its optimum level, he will have to hire someone with an excellent track record in operations and execution to complement his visionary abilities. He also agreed that such a person should be able to more than generate his or her salary because we would hire someone with proven experience in that area.

> It is important that your sharing of your experiences does not turn into domination of the dialog, that it be well timed, and, most important, useful to facilitating further understanding or insight of the other person.

Didactic Confrontation: In this type of confrontation, you are sure that the other person simply has wrong information and it would be irresponsible or uncaring for you not to confront him or her about it. You could say, "I have different information that might help you solve this problem you are facing—are you willing to hear it?" Asking people if they are willing to hear a confrontation and getting their permission to confront is an important step in insuring that they will even hear you. Using confrontation to build the relationship and build others' successes makes you a more appreciated and credible leader.

TL Skill #34 Self-Sharing: *Giving Others Additional Perspective with Your Own Story*

You can share your own experience with others as a way of modeling nondefensive self-disclosure, or as a way of helping them move beyond blind spots, and as a way of seeing possibilities for problem-managing action.

This is perhaps the most encouraging of all the types of challenging. When you are genuine enough to share an experience—which shows the other person that you have some true sympathy with their experience—there develops a sense of camaraderie or mutuality. This is trust-building and eliminates a tone of judgment so often feared by many.

It is important that sharing of your experiences does not turn into a domination of the dialog, that it be well timed, and most important, useful to facilitating further understanding or insight in the other person. It is an especially valuable skill to use when a person is stuck when attempting to specify his or her own part of a problem, or when attempting to come up with action alternatives.

I used this skill when I shared my own experience of having difficulty in specifying my own purpose statement with a CEO with whom I was doing executive coaching. He really wanted clarity about his own purpose, but was expecting his purpose statement to take shape out of thin air in one try. When I shared with him that my own purpose statement is continuing to evolve, and that it took a few weeks of revision after revision for me to feel comfortable with the first one, he relaxed and made more realistic progress.

TL Skill #35 Immediacy: *Helping People get Unstuck in Their Immediate Context*

This is a very versatile and widely applicable skill that enables you to deal with issues that must be dealt with before other problems can be tackled. It could be considered a "process" skill that enables you to help get yourself or others "unstuck" when things aren't moving forward. This skill can assist you to improve your working alliance with others in two ways.
1. By using relationship immediacy—which focuses on your ability to discuss with another person your relationship with him or her, with a view to managing whatever problems have existed, and maintaining strengths in the relationship.
2. By using here-and-now immediacy—which focuses on your ability to discuss with others whatever is standing in the way of working together right now.

Immediacy is a powerful skill in establishing your genuineness as a person and as a helpful leader. It expresses your concern that the relationship go well and expresses your commitment that problems get solved. Using immediacy is an excellent way to "cut through" tension and a stuck feeling in the relationship if the other person is the type who can handle direct, face-to-face honesty. If the other person is too intimidated to deal directly with such intensity and openness, then this could be a risky skill to use, especially in the beginning of a relationship.

This type of immediacy is illustrated by the example above when I challenged the wife-neglecting executive to open up his daily scheduler and see if he could find a place in it where he had written her name.

TL Skill #36 Making an Effective Referral to a Professional Helper

When you realize the person with whom you are working is facing a personal problem that is over your head, it is appropriate to make a smooth referral to a professional helper. In making an effective referral, it would be best to refer the person to someone already known and respected by your friend, associate, or employee. When this is not possible, it is ideal if you personally know some good helpers you can recommend to others when they are in need. The following steps could be followed when making a referral.

> **When you realize that the person with whom you are working is facing a personal problem which is over your head, it is appropriate to make a smooth referral to a professional helper.**

1. Gather as much information about the counselor or therapist to whom you might make a referral.
2. Make sure the counselor is formally qualified (through university training and certification, as is appropriate in certain states and provinces) and whenever possible, verify that he or she has a track record of reputable practice.
3. Meet this professional helper face-to-face so that you get a sense of who the person is and what approaches this individual prefers.
4. When you are satisfied you have located a good counselor, suggest to the person needing assistance that you would like to make a personal introduction to a new helper who can help more effectively than you can in this instance, for very specific reasons.
5. Personally introduce the two who may work together and leave them alone to have their first session.
6. Follow up with both parties to see how things went (you may have to make another referral if the first one doesn't click).
7. Make sure that confidentiality agreements are specified and agreed upon by you, the person, and the therapist or you will lose trust and integrity in the eyes of others.
8. Continue supporting the person receiving help but do not enter into

confidential conversations that could counter the work being done by the therapist; if you do, there may be a frustrated therapist or counselor on the phone asking you to stay in your own territory.

Section Two: Understanding the Processes of Counseling and Problem Management

What is the Problem-Management Process?

The problem-management process is a step-by-step manner of approaching and solving all kinds of problems. It emerged from theory, research, and models of problem-solving and decision-making. This process is becoming more popularly integrated into counseling, leadership, and management practice because of its logical and systematic approach to defining problems, setting goals, exploring and implementing action alternatives, and evaluating the results.

Effective counseling or helper training programs have effectively used a problem-management approach (Egan, 1990). In his book, Egan offers a theoretical backdrop for the model he has developed. He reviews and integrates applied behavioral psychology, applied cognitive psychology, applied personality theory, and social influence and decision-making approaches, and weaves them into a comprehensive counseling model. This model has a three-stage process that assists practitioners to assess what they are doing and what they need to do next in the problem-management process.

Expertise in the use of a step-by-step process model such as this is developed as you apply it to real problems. The problem-management process gives structure to the application of appropriate skills at various stages. We will examine the stages, steps, and skills in this process later in this chapter.

Who Needs You to be a Skilled People-Problem Manager, Anyway?

Nearly anyone may need you to assist them in some way. The knowledge and techniques for facilitating problem-solving within and between individuals is perhaps more subtle and advanced than any other problem-solving body of knowledge. It can be applied to personal and interpersonal matters that affect overall human performance and morale in families and in work settings. If there is truth in the above statement, then everyone we contact (including ourselves) could potentially benefit from others who possess these skills.

During a consulting contract where my job was to assist twenty-eight managers to better understand and deal with high stress levels on the job, I heard one manager say: "Managers don't have time to deal with 'whiners' or people with problems. We are too busy dealing with more important operational issues and decisions and shouldn't be slowed down by ineffective people. If people can't hack it, get rid of them and get people in there who can do the job. If you have a disgruntled customer, tell him or her to leave—we don't have to put up with 'guff' from customers."

This general attitude of impatience, seeming unkindness, and intolerance is a signal that this person lacked what the research of Kouzes and Posner (1988) report that employees like very much in their leaders: a heart for people. The insensitive "bottomline" response to people with "problems" is what I call the "computer chip approach" to management: "If it is defective, just unplug it, and push in another one that works." Sometimes, because of collective agreements or labor legislation, managers are forced to make the best of employees with problems. Parents are leaders who definitely are "stuck" with their children who seem to nearly always have some kind of problem prior to leaving home. Business owners are stuck with finicky customers who will leave and bad mouth them and their business.

Someone Close to You May Need Your Help: It May Be You

It is realistic to say that some of the personal relationships that managers or leaders have may require a deeper level of helpful understanding and skills. Certainly for one's self, family, and friends, they are enviable skills to possess. Problems don't really happen between people in relationships, they happen inside of each person interacting within the context of a relationship. That is where problems must be solved— on the inside. This is the great contribution counseling skills can

A total of 150 well-established companies were evaluated as to their human resource effectiveness practices and attitudes. The ones that came out on top were also the ones assessed as having the highest morale and greatest revenues.

make toward strengthening our personal and even our business relationships. Another encouraging point is that you can learn the skills of solving (and helping others to solve) internal personal problems that interfere with personal relationships and work performance.

Often, it is someone in our immediate family, or the person working beside us who is going through a separation that could end in divorce, a battle with alcoholism, drug abuse, grief, depression or mid-life crisis. Leaders are in strategic positions to support, problem-solve, and intervene in the lives of many people. The results of counseling others can be increased morale, increased productivity, and a more positive organizational culture. Sometimes each of us is in the advantageous position of having established trust with someone—and that can enable us to assist that person in more powerful and deeper ways than anyone else could.

One of the most impressive studies I have seen on the efficacy of good communication, problem management, and effective culture-building—these three areas build upon one another—to produce bottomline results and positive worker-morale are those done by Kravetz (1988). A total of 150 well-established companies were evaluated as to their human resource effectiveness, practices, and attitudes. The ones that came out on top were also the ones assessed as having the highest morale and greatest revenues (compared to the other companies surveyed).

There is also some evidence that the best counseling occurs right in a person's own environment; and that most people facing a personal problem will not or do not seek the help of a professional (Carkhuff, 1971).

Furthermore, it is also true that even if everyone who needed help was to go to a professional helper (and no one else) to gain assistance in solving problems, there would likely be more than 200 people crowded into each psychologist's waiting room at any given time. This is another reason why it would be, ideally, everyone's responsibility to learn to help everyone else for the benefit of all.

Last, you may need to help yourself solve a problem. Perhaps you have some problems too personal to share with some others. Watson and Tharpe (1981) have devoted a whole book to self-management and problem solving that outlines how to apply the problem-management process to yourself.

Managers Do Not Have Time to Counsel

Because managers often do not have time to become involved in long-term or in-depth counseling relationships, it is important that they continually seek a balance between task and relationship factors in the environment. If supportive and helpful relationship factors are neglected for too long a time, this can affect performance. if the task aspects of the environment are not attended to properly, then they simply won't get done. This type of balance is much like surfing: If you step too far ahead trying to catch the wave, it will come crashing down on you; if you step back too far, you miss the wave entirely.

It is true that leaders cannot deal with all people with personal problems just because they happen to cross paths, but it is very desirable and advantageous for good leaders to selectively understand and be able to show genuine and skilled caring for some of the people. This can increase trust, commitment, morale, and productivity.

It is also a fact that people who are ordinarily effective go through periods of time when they face developmental crises; times of grief when performance is lower; times of personal, family, or marital stress when concentration is distracted; or times of physical health difficulties when performance is temporarily on the decline. An attitude of support, encouragement, tolerance, and compassion is what most of us would deeply appreciate from others around us—and is perhaps what we especially need from those "above" us in leadership positions.

When time or pressure does not allow a leader to take on counseling responsibilities, a Transforming Leader will develop other helpers within the organization or effectively refer the burdened person to a professional helper.

> **When time or pressure does not allow a leader to take on counseling responsibilities, then a Transforming Leader will develop other helpers within the organization or effectively refer the burdened person to a professional helper.**

Does Counseling Really Help?

A review of research literature on counseling outcomes reveals basic themes that might be best summarized by saying that some approaches do help some people, with some problems, in some situations, some of the time. We are not able to say with confidence that all helpers are helpful, but we can say with some confidence that some helpers have been and can be destructive!

Following is a summary of three statements from the literature on counseling effectiveness we reviewed to provide you with a clearer picture of some relevant findings that have been established through research.

#1 Counseling can be effective and can encourage personal development and can also enhance job performance (Bergin, 1971; Emrick, 1975; Landman and Dawes, 1982; Smith and Glass, 1977; Smith, Glass, and Miller 1980).

In view of the evidence in the studies referenced above, that counseling can be valid and helpful is not really in question. The studies referenced below indicate that the reliability of counseling may in question.

#2 Counseling can also be questionable because there is some evidence that it can be ineffective and/or destructive (Levitt, 1963; Bergin, 1980; Mays and Franks, 1980; Orwin and Cordray, 1984).

This statement may summarize why so many managers, leaders, and others are fearful of trying to help people solve problems that interfere with morale or performance at home or on the job. It is clear that if you don't know what you are doing when you enter others' personal worlds, you might inadvertently damage self-worth, morale, and performance—and perhaps even increase turnover and absenteeism at the same time. Therefore, it is important to be able to recognize the major mistakes of counseling, and to develop the key skills to be a facilitative helper.

Three Major Mistakes Untrained Leaders Make when Attempting to Do Counseling

In video-taping sessions that I have conducted of untrained (in counseling skills) leaders and managers at the beginning of a counseling skills-training session, I see several frequently made mistakes.

Mistake One: The first one is simply that most leaders are so task-focused, they fail to actually hear the content and check for the intended meaning of the messages being sent to them.

Mistake Two: The leaders presume that they accurately understand—without checking with the other person.

Mistake Three: The leaders give premature advice without jointly arriving at a specific definition of the problem. This advice is usually not followed by the other person because the solution offered does not fit the real nature of the problem.

Other problems showed up less frequently, such as failing to temporarily suspend personal judgmental reactions, emotions—and the giving of inappropriate or even destructive advice.

> It is clear that if you don't know what you are doing when you enter others' personal worlds, you might inadvertently damage self-worth, morale and performance; and perhaps even increase turnover and absenteeism at the same time.

The Good News about Transferable Skills Training

We know from many other studies on the efficacy of training people in interpersonal and counseling skills that it is possible to train them in a relatively short period of time to be effective in counseling others to solve problems not long term and pervasive in nature. We know it is possible to help most trainees quite rapidly give up ineffective patterns.

#3 Helper Training Programs that bring forward core facilitative conditions through systematic skills training have been demonstrated to be most effective. (Carkhuff (1971); Carkhuff and Berenson (1967); Ivey and Authier (1978); Larson (1984)).

Based on the positive statement of skills-training outcomes like the ones above, counseling skills have powerful potential to assist transforming leaders to produce positive changes in self, in others, and, therefore, in organizations.

Gain Self-Confidence and Self-Esteem

After managers had developed a minimum level of competency in counseling skills in my college and university courses, they reported on the evaluations that they felt a greater sense of calm, confidence, and self-esteem because they knew they could now really be of help to others in need without feeling they were "fumbling around in an area I don't know anything about." They also reported being glad to learn how to make effective referrals to professional helpers when appropriate to do so. We will review this skill at the end of the chapter. You will also have the opportunity to assess your knowledge of it.

> **This approach of defining the situation as a problem to be better faced through learning and development avoids having people feel like they are losers, "basket cases," or "unpromotables."**

Dispel Fears of Judgment and Earn Trust

By developing a culture in your group, organization, or family—where people agree in advance to face problems openly and see one another as resources rather than judges—there can be a resultant increase in morale and performance. There are decreases in productivity and increases in absenteeism, staff turnover, and stress-related illnesses in situations where people are supervised in negative-culture environments by overly task-oriented managers who miss out on the people side of enterprise. When they fail to attend to the relationship dimensions of their supervisory or managerial roles, these managers contribute to a higher level of corporate stress. The same is true when children are put down and undervalued: they often rebel or even run away from home.

Problem-Solving, Not People-Blaming

Many, if not most, problems are a result of a person's not having a more effective response to a given situation. In most cases, people can learn new ways of perceiving, thinking, and acting that will enable them to solve problems. This approach of defining the situation as a problem to be better faced through learning and development avoids having people feel like they are losers, "basket cases," or "unpromotables."

When is Counseling Appropriate?

It is inappropriate to counsel people when trust has not been established, when there is no cause to counsel, and when there is no permission to counsel. Peters (1985) suggests counseling is most needed when an individual follower shows some or several of these indicators.
1. Has a solid track record but isn't performing.
2. Has been educated and coached but without results.
3. Asks for help in solving a personal problem.
4. Is "stuck," unsure about how to proceed.
5. Is having difficulty coping with organizational change.
6. Cannot bounce back after a failure or loss experience.

More specifically, counseling can be used constructively in several ways.

For Improving Performance: It is appropriately used for leadership impact when coworkers, colleagues, subordinates, or learners are having personal difficulties that are interfering with their performance on a task or in relationships with others. Assisting them to specify and take ownership for their own problems in a problem situation is germane. Supporting or guiding them to set realistic goals and take effective action can also be a great help in keeping people, groups, and organizations "unblocked."

For Supporting Others: The problem-management process and counseling skills are also appropriately used with those seeking or needing brief personal assistance in your own family, with friends, or in work situations. These skills do not replace professional counseling or long-term psychotherapy when it is needed. By understanding and practicing the skills of counseling, you can better specify, manage, and solve problems yourself.

When You Get Permission to Counsel: Most people have to be willing to enter into a helpful type of communication with you and often will do so only because they trust you. They will more likely trust you if you have integrity and if you are genuine, respectful, empathic, and skilled. You must have people's permission to enter into a deeper level of communication with them, which can involve your seeing their personal difficulties that are interfering with their relationships at home or their performance at work.

Getting and Giving Mutual Commitment through Formalized Mentoring Relationships

As reported by Gray (1987), it was clear that a key set of skills identified as effective in the process of formalized mentoring are the skills of supporting and helping protégés through the stages of the problem-management process. The mentor/protégé relationship is a further development and extension of the leader-helping-follower relationship as there is an agreement in advance to engage in problem management, personal growth, and professional development. This agreement avoids the often uncomfortable crossing of the "line" into what is traditionally considered to be the personal territory of the follower. The importance and impact of developing a mentoring or consultative type relationship with subordinates will be discussed more fully in Chapter 7.

Example of a Major Problem and an Appropriate Counseling Intervention

The Assessment

A CEO in a large government department became aware of a serious stress problem among most of the managers in his region. They were ill more often than usual, and did not deal well with problems he thought should have been dealt with swiftly and effectively; he was suspicious that there was a "hidden" problem.

The senior executive talked with some of the managers in an attempt to identify the causes of the problem, but not one of the managers wanted to come right out and say what the real problem was. The senior executive sought assistance from a consultant who interviewed him and the five top managers in the region. Aside from the fact there was a "trimming" of management positions due to budget cuts, it became clear from the interviews that all five managers felt afraid that their job security was threatened. This was because they had received virtually no feedback from the senior executive in over a year, had observed him firing two other managers for "confidential" reasons, and had experienced his leadership style as being very authoritarian— he did a great deal of telling. He was distant—he held only one weekly meeting where he informed them of new developments and changes—and threatening—he yelled frequently and listened very little.

The Intervention

The consultant confidentially presented his findings in summary written form to the senior executive, and asked him for his assessment of the validity of the findings. Surprisingly, he responded very openly, and said he had been very domineering all of his life, had felt close to hardly anyone, and had alienated his wife and three children with his intimidating stance to the point that she threatened to leave him. He asked for direct counseling assistance in overcoming this problem.

Then, with the CEO's permission, the consultant shifted into a supportive counseling mode—because he had the skills and ability to do so—and had several productive two-hour sessions with him. After these sessions, the consultant shifted back into the consultant "mode" so he and the CEO could plan and arrange a team development session. He and all twelve managers clarified the purpose and concrete goals of the team for the first time, assisted them to clarify each of their roles and the goals they were attempting to reach, and negotiated an appropriate and agreeable leadership style for the senior executive to use with this group of managers.

Transforming leaders can be "outside consultants," as in this case, or they can act as a flexible counselor-consultant within their own organizations if they have the knowledge and skills to do so. It would have been most preferable if the CEO himself had had the personal and interpersonal development and counseling skills to deal with these problems himself.

The Results

The absenteeism levels dropped, two-way communication was established among nearly all members, problems were managed more effectively, goals were reached more swiftly, and the CEO sought continuing marriage and family counseling outside of the work setting. This is an unusually ideal series of events where most everything worked out well, but without the *Transforming Leadership* intervention, the outcome could otherwise have been far worse.

The main point in the above example is that the consultant was able to shift into a helpful, supportive, developmental mode to assist the Senior Executive to develop in a problem area causing distress among twelve managers—and their employees, and their families, etc. If the senior executive had had these skills from the beginning, the stress and morale problems would likely not have developed to nearly the degree they had. The advantage is clear when communication and counseling skills are present within individual leaders, regardless of their role.

Counseling Skills Training is Becoming More Recognized

On the basis of extensive research on the impact of counseling in various environments, Carkhuff (1969) has stated two propositions that suggest counseling can be a potent tool for leaders. The first one states, "All interpersonal processes may have constructive or deteriorative consequences." This implies that management, leadership, psychotherapy, counseling, parenting, teaching, training, and all other significant relationships are not neutral, and may effect people (and performance) for "better or for worse."

The second proposition is, "All effective interpersonal processes share a common core of conditions conducive to facilitative human experiences." Those leaders, managers, counselors, psychotherapists, teachers, parents, trainers, and significant others who are supportive, facilitative, and action-motivating will be more effective than those leaders/helpers who are not.

These propositions—and the research on which they were based—roughly cut the edge of a new movement within counseling, one toward the education and training of a wide range of people in the skills that only counselors and therapists had previously learned. The new focus on skills training for members external to the "expert" psychologist community marked the beginning of a new awareness of the need for facilitative interpersonal and counseling skills in many fields.

It used to be that managers appreciated the value of communication skills, and that "communication" was the training buzzword for management training—and often still is. Now many managers want further training in how to deal with followers' deeper issues and with the problems in their own personal and professional lives. When there is a rich body of transferable knowledge and skills available to managers to help them develop personal effectiveness and leadership potency, then why not avail ourselves of it?

Since the late 1960s, this movement has taken these face-to-face human resource development skills into a wide range of environments, from elementary school classrooms to corporate boardrooms. Most colleges and universities now offer competency-based courses in interpersonal and problem-management skills. But these skills-oriented courses are often limited to social work, counseling, corrections, and education departments. In more progressive business, law, and medical schools, systematic competency-based courses have begun to appear during the past ten to fifteen years.

In response to demands from the professional community, Ivey (1987) has developed a well-researched and effective helper training program that has been taken by a wide range of people—from executives, managers, doctors, social workers, nurses, social services workers, correctional workers, to parents and volunteers in community service agencies.

The need for all people to become good people-problem managers is on the increase as problems in our world increase in intensity and frequency.

Transformative leaders can pass on some of these important skills to others they help and lead as we move toward the new millenium—perhaps when problem management will likely be most needed.

The Conditions that Facilitate Effective Problem-Management

These are the "core conditions" found to be facilitative when present in the behaviors of leaders who are helpful.

1. **Genuineness:** The willingness and ability to be role-free, honest in a kind way, and open about one's self to others makes leaders more free to open up and explore themselves without fear of judgment.
2. **Empathy:** The willingness and ability to perceive others' world views, to see through others' eyes, and to communicate back to them an accurate understanding of their feelings and ideas encourages others to trust you and explore problems more deeply and specifically with you.
3. **Respect:** The willingness and ability to actively show that you highly value the people with whom you work—regardless of their present performance—is an important quality to communicate to others when you need their respect and participation toward reaching goals.
4. **Specificity:** The willingness and ability to be highly specific when using language to describe others' views and experiences can help others increase the clarity of their understanding and solve problems more effectively.

Transforming Leadership and Counseling are Integrally Linked

When leaders learn to apply counseling skills and the problem-management process in themselves and in their work with others, they internalize a powerful set of knowledge and skills at a deep and personal level.

Good leaders understand the problem-management processes both cognitively, when analyzing an organizational problem—and affectively, when understanding the inner workings of self or another person. They understand the stages and steps in the process, and are able to deal with their own personal and interpersonal problems. It is important that a leader's personal life be in good shape so that he or she is not distracted by internal unresolved emotional or interpersonal problems at home or at work. Good leaders are personal, interpersonal, and organizational problem-solvers and managers, directly in their own lives.

Transforming leaders also help other people solve problems. If an employee is facing a personal problem but not seeking outside help for it—which often is the case—a transforming leader is able to respond with genuine caring and effective counseling skills. This leader may be a principal of a school counseling a student, a teacher or counselor on staff, or a parent. The leader may also be an executive who intimately and quietly assists an executive team mate having marriage, family, drug, alcohol, or stress problems— problems typical to some executives.

Counseling skills are an integral part of *Transforming Leadership*'s problem management skill repertoire because some problems are simply inside individuals. Whether a leader is managing a problem within self or others or between self and others; mediating a conflict between others; doing a performance appraisal counseling interview; a career planning interview; or assisting a person or employee to overcome a personal difficulty, basic counseling/problem-management skills are invaluable.

Style-Shift Counseling: a Developmental Approach

Anderson (1987) has developed a theoretically integrated and developmentally based helper-style assessment and training instrument and leader's manual. While Style-Shift Counseling integrates familiar concepts from a number of theoretical approaches, it is novel in its usage of them because assessment and intervention are presented from a developmental perspective. In this chapter, we will briefly discuss the *Developmental Level Assessment Grid*, which integrates developmental theories into a counseling tool for assessment, intervention planning, and tracking progress.

Style-Shift Counseling is a systematic counseling plan that organizes psychotherapeutic methods into a working model that provides guidelines for the appropriate use of helping and developmental approaches and interventions. For the purposes of this book, a review of the basic assumptions of the approach is summarized below.

1. No one approach works with all people.
2. No one approach always works with the same person.
3. It can be difficult to decide which approach will work best.
4. It is difficult for most helpers to use more than one approach at one time, or shift from one approach to another.
5. It can be easy to get discouraged and give up when working with failure-oriented or undeveloped people.
6. A more practical and flexible approach to counseling that would allow for client individuality and facilitate development and performance was needed.
7. A method for assessing a person's developmental readiness to receive help is needed, which would also allow for helper flexibility in shifting to fit people's helping style preferences and ability levels.
8. Helper training often acquaints students with a wide range of counseling theories, but seldom gives them a framework for the appropriate application of those theories and methods in a systematic and integrative manner.

Style-Shift Counseling offers such a framework for the effective application of theory. The developmental theories and counseling approaches that form the basis of *Style-Shift Counseling* can be examined in Anderson's, *Leader's Manual* (1987), referenced below.

Understanding Developmental Levels for Situational Effectiveness

The following developmental levels are presented for you to gain additional understanding that different levels of functioning exist due to varying levels of development. This is a very important reality to observe in people because it will help us learn to adapt our methods and approach to the level of the person with whom we are dealing.

Level One—Resistant or Undeveloped Individuals: People who function at Level One are distinguished by low levels of individual readiness and willingness, which often result in their becoming detractors in the helping and problem-solving process. They are predominantly preoccupied with self, are underdeveloped, reactionary, unaware of problems, and/or deny ownership of and responsibility for personal problems. People who function at this level sometimes attempt to escape reality by trying to live in fantasy.

Some examples of Level One client populations might include: preschool children, drug addicts, alcoholics, severely mentally retarded or mentally ill people, autistic children, "hard-core" juvenile delinquents who are highly resistant, and potentially violent prisoners.

Level Two—Rational Individuals: People functioning at Level Two demonstrate some readiness and willingness to be helped but usually at a cognitive level only. They are willing to think and talk about behavior change but need help defining problems in concrete terms, and often need follow-up support and reinforcement programs. These people can be good observers who notice many things but seldom take corrective action without support and follow-up from others.

Some examples of Level Two client populations might include: underdeveloped teenagers, "soft-core" juvenile delinquents, immature high school, college, and university students, underdeveloped adults in general, and mildly mentally retarded or mentally ill people.

Level Three—Reflective Individuals: People who function at this level tend to seek self-understanding, are willing and able to explore internal personal problems that may interfere with performance, are often more willing to take ownership for personal problems and behaviors, have the ability to learn independently with occasional support, are often concerned about interpersonal development and problem-solving, care about others as well as self, and are more able to make lasting commitments to change.

Some examples of Level Three clients might include: mature teenagers, responsible adults, some college and university students, and personal development seekers in general. These are the employees who make ideal employees and followers because they are ready and willing to learn, and take responsibility for their own performance.

Level Four—Resourceful Individuals: People functioning at this level tend to be independent learners, good decision-makers, and creative problem-solvers. They are often able to teach others, have developed a self-responsible lifestyles, and often are only in need of additional information, resources, or additional perspectives. They seek and use expert consultative advice.

Some examples of Level Four clients might include: successful professionals, creative homemakers, educators, plumbers, electricians, managers, artists, etc.

The Style-Shift Counseling model provides a clear way to assess levels of development and functioning. Each level has corresponding helping styles, behaviors, and interventions that best match levels of readiness, ability, willingness, and preference. A foundational concept of the model is that it is the helper's responsibility to shift his or her counseling style to fit the client's willingness and ability to receive that approach. For a review of the literature that forms the base for this approach, see the *Leader's Manual for the Therapeutic Style Indicator.*

The Developmental Level Assessment Grid

The Assessment Grid presented on page 158 can be a useful tool to do a quick assessment of a person's general level of functioning in relation to a specific task he or she is attempting to do or that you may be asking the individual to complete. The developmental level of a person is task-specific. It includes the following dimensions: general functioning level, cognitive, affective, interpersonal, ego development, and needs hierarchy level. An example of a person with different levels of functioning in two areas of life is a prisoner doing a life sentence for molesting and murdering children and who is also an accomplished concert pianist. At controlling his abnormal sexual impulses, he is functioning at Level One, but he functions at Level Four on the piano.

As you can see from the *Developmental Assessment Grid* on the following pages, it is possible to estimate what levels of functioning or development a person moves in and out of depending on the situational context. Assessing a person's functioning level will assist you to plan the approach you should generally take with him or her in relation to a specific problem that that individual is facing.

Four Intervention Styles

Four styles of intervention correspond to the four functioning levels. What we do to help people move ahead in their development must be more appropriate to their readiness and ability levels for our interventions to be more catalytic to their development. In Helping Tasks Appropriate to the Four Development Levels (below), you will see four levels with appropriate strategies of intervention.

These guidelines are meant to be a useful beginning—a starting place for you to learn to use developmental considerations when approaching people facing problems. If you wish further study in this area of using developmental considerations to plan your interventions, you could take courses in developmental psychology or counseling theory and practice, or read Ivey's book (1986).

Facilitative Leaders are Not Psychotherapists

The field of psychotherapy—not counseling or helping, as the terms are used in this chapter—includes those therapists who use predominantly one or two orientations of therapy and generally work with emotionally disturbed or mentally ill people over longer periods of time (months or years). Psychotherapists, at least in the beginning, tended to work with institutionalized patients—including both inpatients and outpatients. Helpers are people who have developed counseling skills and who work with members of the general public concerning issues of social adjustment and/or minor emotional and behavioral problem-solving. It is usually short-term in comparison to psychotherapy and often is educationally related. Leaders can have a transforming impact without pretending to be psychotherapists.

The differences between counseling and psychotherapy can be summarized in the following statement by Pietrofesa, Hoffman, and Splete (1984). Counseling focuses more on developmental-educational-preventative concerns, whereas psychotherapy focuses more on remediative-adjustive-therapeutic concerns. *Transforming Leadership* focuses mainly on the developmental, educational, and preventive concerns.

Performance Appraisal and Discipline Interviews Require Facilitative Counseling Skills

The one situation where you do not need "permission" to shift into a counseling mode is when you are doing performance appraisal or reprimand interviews. Then, it is your role and job to assist employees to specify problems that block performance and even job security. Your position gives you the right to specify problems, goals, and action plans with employees. Under these more

The Developmental Level Assessment Grid

D-Levels	D-Level 1	D-Level 2	D-Level 3	D-Level 4
Assessment Dimensions	*Resistant/ Undeveloped*	*Reasonable*	*Reflective*	*Resourceful*
General Capability	Unable, unwilling, and/or insecure	Unable as yet, but willing	Able, but somewhat insecure	A degree of competence with creativity
Cognitive Functioning (Neo-Piagetian)	"Magical," unrealistic, or illogical thinking	Concrete, rational thinking— linear, simpler	Formal operational, self-reflective thinking—more complex	Dialectic, abstract, creative thinking
Ego/ Affective Functioning	Lacks inner controls or denies emotions— lacks self-worth and self-confidence	Begins responsible integration and controlled expression of emotion	Integrates own emotion with appropriate control and responds to others' emotions	Has integrated emotion and can understand and care for others' feelings
Inter-Personal Functioning	Self-oriented detractor	Self-oriented observer, interacts for self interest	Minimally capable of intimacy and two-way communication	Seeks to develop relationships and to develop others
Consciousness Level	Blind belief or imagining	Unvalidated rigid belief based on understanding of a system of belief	Validated belief based on examination of alternatives	Direct sense of "knowing" self and "life"

Helping Tasks Appropriate to the Four Developmental Levels

Structure	Coach	Counsel	Consult
With Resistant People	**With Relational People**	**With Reflective People**	**With Resourceful People**
Design safe environments	Gain credibility	Establish rapport in relationship	Do problem management
Structure therapeutic environments	Clarify problem behavior	Explore problem situation with the person	Consult and give expert info
Control violent people with restraints	Clarify problem behavior	Assist person to own personal responsibility	Provide life planning consultation
Provide constructive releases	Coach problem thinking	Specify internal problems of person	Personal development (advanced)
Provide positive reinforcement	Plan for improved behavior	Focus on problem which has good potential	Focus on new perspectives
Administer humane discipline	Confront irrational assumptions	Confront person's internal discrepancies	Challenge in a mutual way
Temporary isolation programs	Set action goals and programs	Mutually set action goals and programs	Explore goal options
Evaluate and communicate progress	Mutually evaluate progress	Mutually evaluate progress	Explore possible scenarios

difficult circumstances, it is even more important that you be positive, skilled, and wise in your approach.

Conclusion

You may be feeling somewhat intimidated by the complexity and difficulty of these skills, or you may be saying to yourself that you have been doing these things all along but didn't have specific names for them. In either case, having gone through this material gives you the advantage of greater intentionality in the use of the skills—a perspective from which to evaluate your own counseling behavior and a model to use in planning your own professional development.

In the next chapter—Chapter 7—we will be examining how to build upon the interpersonal, counseling, and problem-management skills to intervene in a consultative role in groups or organizations to make a transforming impact. This is the most cognitively complex mode in which to function because you constantly and directly interface with dynamic human systems and organizations. Then in Chapter 8, we will examine the concepts of style, skill, and role-shifting for greater appropriateness and effectiveness. This will complete Section 2 of the book, and we will then move into learning to use the tools of *Transforming Leadership*.

Research has established that basic counseling skills and core facilitative conditions are foundational to most successful relationships. Counseling roles and skills, as parts of a leader's transforming tools, are not ones to be taken lightly. Neither are they to be neglected, avoided, or overused.

References

I. **Janis**, *Short-Term Counseling*. (New Haven: Yale, 1983).

R. **Marx**, "Improving Management Development Through Relapse Prevention Strategies," *Journal of Management Development*, vol. 5, 2, 1986, 27-40.

B. **Berenson** and K. **Mitchell**, *Confrontation for Better or Worse!* (Amherst, Mass.: Human Resource Development Press, 1974).

G. **Egan**, *The Skilled Helper*. 5th ed. (Monterey, California: Brooks/Cole Publishing Company, 1994).

J. M. **Kouzes** and J. **Posner**, *The Leadership Challenge*. (San Francisco: Jossey-Bass Publishing Company, 1988).

D. **Kravetz**, *The Human Resources Revolution*. (San Francisco:

Jossey-Bass Publishing Company, 1988).

R. R. **Carkhuff**, *The Development of Human Resources.* (New York: Holt, Rinehart & Winston, 1971), 167-168.

D. **Watson** and R. **Tharpe**, *Self-directed Behavior.*, 3rd. ed. (Monterey, California: Brooks/Cole, 1981).

A. E. **Bergin**, "The Evaluating of Therapeutic Outcomes." In A. E. Bergin and S. L. Garfield (eds.), *Handbook of Psychotherapy and Behavior Change* (New York: Wiley, 1971).

C. D. **Emrick**, "A Review of Psychologically Oriented Treatment in Alcoholism," *Journal of Studies of Alcohol,* 1975, 36, 88-108.

J. T. **Landman** and R. M. **Dawes**, "Psychotherapy Outcome: Smith and Glass' Conclusions Stand Up Under Scrutiny," *American Psychologist,* 1982, 37, 504-516.

M.C. **Smith** and G.V. **Glass**, "Meta-analysis of Psychotherapy Outcome Studies," *American Psychologist,* 1977, 32, 752-761.

M. C. **Smith**, G.V. **Glass**, and T.J. **Miller**, *The Benefits of Psychotherapy.* (Baltimore: Johns Hopkins University Press, 1980).

E. E. **Levitt**, "Psychotherapy With Children: A Further Evaluation," *Behavior Research and Therapy,* 1963, 1, 45-51.

A. E. **Bergin**, "Negative Effects Revisited: A Reply," *Professional Psychology,* 1980, 11, 93-100.

D. T. **Mays** and C. M. **Franks**, "Getting Worse: Psychotherapy or No Treatment—The Jury Should Still Be Out," *Professional Psychology,* 1980, 11, 78-92.

R. G. **Orwin** and D.S. **Cordray**, "Smith and Glass's Psychotherapy Conclusions Need Further Probing: On Landman and Dawes' Re-analysis," *American Psychologist,* 1984, 39, 71-72.

R. R. **Carkhuff**, *The Development of Human Resources.* (New York: Holt, Rinehart & Winston, 1971).

R. **Carkhuff** and B. **Berenson**, *Beyond Counseling and Therapy.* (New York: Holt, Rinehart & Winston, 1967).

A. **Ivey** and J. **Authier**, *Microcounseling: Innovations in Interviewing, Counseling, Psychotherapy, and Psychoeducation.* (2nd. ed.) (Springfield, Ill., Charles C Thomas, 1978).

D. **Larson**, *Teaching Psychological Skills: Models for Giving Psychology Away.* (Monterey, California: Brooks/Cole, 1984).

T. **Peters**, *A Passion for Excellence: The Leadership Difference.* (New York: Random House, 1985), 367-368.

W. **Gray**, International Journal of Mentoring (Vancouver, B.C.), vol. 1, no. 1, 1987.

R. **Carkhuff**, *Helping and Human Relations, vols. I and II,* (New York: Holt, Rinehart, & Winston, 1969).

A. **Ivey**, *Intentional Interviewing and Counseling,* 2nd ed., (Monterey, California: Brooks/Cole, 1987).

T. **Anderson**, *The Therapeutic Style Indicator (Amherst, Mass.:* Microtraining Associates, 1987).

A. **Ivey**, *Developmental Therapy.* (San Francisco: Jossey-Bass, 1986).

J. J. **Pietrofesa**, A. **Hoffman,** and H.H. **Splete**, *Counseling, an Introduction,* 2nd ed. (Boston: Houghton Mifflin Company, 1984).

G. **Egan**, *The Skilled Helper,* 4th ed. (Monterey, California: Brooks/Cole Publishing Company: 1990).

R. **Carkhuff**, *Helping and Human Relations, vols. I and II* (New York: Holt, Rinehart, & Winston, 1969).

Chapter 7

THE SKILLS OF TEAM AND ORGANIZATIONAL DEVELOPMENT

There are three types of executives in the world. There are those who can get short-term results and haven't a clue where they're going to take the company in the future. Conversely, there are those who have a great ten-year plan but are going to be out of business in ten months. And then there are those who can get short-term results in conjunction with a vision for the future. These are the good ones. But they are in unbelievably short supply.

Al Dunlap,
former Chairman of the
Scott Paper Company

It [leadership] happens in the symphony, in the ballet, in the theater, in sports, and equally in business. It is easy to recognize and impossible to define. It is a mystique. It cannot be achieved without immense effort, training, and cooperation, but effort, training, and cooperation alone rarely create it. Some groups reach it consistently. Few can sustain it.

(Schlesinger, Eccles, and Gabarro, 1983.)

Introduction

Faced with an unprecedented climate of fast, unsettling change, both organizations and individual leaders tend to react in predictably self-defeating ways. They feel victimized, overwhelmed, and work compulsively harder, doing the same things, or they try to pretend that everything is fine. According to David Noer, author of, *Breaking Free: A Prescription for Personal and Organization Change*: "The only response that works is the positive willingness to learn and meet change head-on. Learning to learn is the best tool for growing beyond the victim mentality."

In this chapter, you will be exposed to knowledge and a set of skills that address this need to face change head-on and learn to learn instead of being overwhelmed, entrenched, or retreating into denial. Although these skills are increasingly abstract and more difficult to learn and integrate into your work and life, they are also the most powerful in their potential to get larger-scale results. They build on the knowledge and skills that you understand from previous chapters. By putting all these skills together into one process, the effect is that you will have the capacity to become a more effective transformational change agent as you lead.

A transformational change agent is another descriptive phrase for a transforming leader: a leader who has developed the awareness, knowledge, skills, and care to exercise a significant impact on the development of individuals, teams, and organizations to accomplish a premeditated purpose. Leaders who can act as change agents are needed now and will be needed in the years ahead—as the world becomes increasingly competitive, and as great performances for customers become a requirement—not an option. The pay-off for all the hard work required to bring a team or organization to the point of high performance is described by Robert Quinn (1984): "The interface of big dreams, hard work, and successful outcomes is potent. The sensation that accompanies the phenomenon is a feeling of exhilaration." It is important, therefore, that leaders light the way toward strategically managed change and innovation. When they are acting in the consultative role, they not only ardently practice experimentation and problem-solving, they also develop the tendency in others to be more explorative and prudently adventuresome. Your organization will not become a learning organization until the leaders in it build a leadership organization of competent leaders who learn to lead change and protect and value people in the process.

The Transforming Leadership skills that will be discussed in this chapter include the following.

This chapter is divided into two Sections.

Section One: We will look at the nature of the consulting process. You may want to skip this first part and go straight to Section Two, which deals specifically with the skills you feel are your weakest, but be sure not to miss reading Section One at some future time. The overview and principles described in it are essential for helping you be most effective in developing and mastering the complex skills in this skill set.

Section Two: You will explore the various skills appropriate to the consultative role.

In summary, although more difficult and abstract in nature, the knowledge and skills presented and assessed in this chapter are more powerful and far-reaching in their implications. As a communicator (Chapter 5), you saw you have significant impact on the quality of relationships with others in an organization. In the role of counselor and problem manager (Chapter 6), you recognized you can have specific preventative and remedial capabilities. In this chapter, by acting in the role of consultant, you will gain awareness and ability as a change agent to increase your impact with individuals, teams, and organizations. Then in Chapter 8, we will explore applications of the various skills to a wide range of settings and review the advantages of learning to shift style, skill, and role to maximize leadership effectiveness. Now we will examine the importance of intentionality when effecting the development of teams and organizations.

Section One: An Overview of the Consulting Role

Intentionality: A Cornerstone of Transformation

Although exploration and experimentation are both important characteristics of transforming leaders and excellent organizations, competency and technical know-how are also important factors to include in the recipe for success in managing and innovating change. The main difference between a professional and an amateur is that an amateur is often using the trial-and-error method, and the professional has a backlog of knowledge and experience as an inner guidance system—the professional "knows" what he or she is doing. Consider the example of the brain surgeon who has specifically analyzed the exact part of the brain that must receive a keenly refined surgical intervention. He or she does not touch a surgical instrument to the person's brain unless established procedures are being followed. Only

> **It is possible that the impact of these interventions can be even more far-reaching than that of the brain surgeon.**

a person with a skilled and experienced hand, with the highest level of training, would dare intervene in such an invasive way. And finally, such an operation would occur only with the constant monitoring of the physical system of the patient during the surgery. In many cases today, the patient remains awake to report to the surgeon.

I trust this analogy has meaning for leaders who intervene in the lives of teams and organizations, because it is possible that the impact of these interventions can be even more far-reaching than that of the brain surgeon. Acting intentionally and purposefully is critical to success. For a further exploration of intentionality, we refer you to the *Center for Constructive Change* (1984).

Building the Consultant Inside of the Leader

As a leader becomes increasingly capable of being objective by seeing an overarching view of situations, there is greater opportunity for the strategic kind of intervention we see in the example of the brain surgeon. The manager becomes a leader with an objective perspective, able to "touch" teams or organizations with more precise effects to achieve agreed-upon and justifiable ends. Oddly enough, like a successful brain surgery, a good consultative leadership intervention seems very impersonal, removed, objective, or even aloof. Yet, at the same time, it is intimately personal, getting at the very nerve roots of teams and organizations and producing healing effects with developmental impact; alternatively, it is possible for a leader to exert a destructive or neutral effect. But certainly, every intervention has a consequence for better or for worse; even actions that seem neutral in their impact rarely are without consequence.

The leader in the consultative role can have many functions and "hats" and each of these hats—which can be put on or taken off—has its own requisite set of skills. The consultative role may include such functions as: catalyst, developer, researcher, strategizer, trainer, analyst, motivator, group or team facilitator, problem-solver, organizational auditor, mentor, and coach. The range of consultative functions leaders can play in organizations is as varied as the organizations in which leader-consultants find themselves. In many instances, several roles are being played at the same time. The skills involved in fulfilling these functions are the skills of transforming leadership, outlined in Chapters Four through Eight. These skills are generic in that they are basic to, and flexible enough to fulfill the demands of, the various consultative roles and functions. For a more in-depth analysis of the various roles and skills consultants can use see Menzel (1975).

> **Every intervention has a consequence for better or for worse; even actions that seem neutral in their impact rarely are without consequence.**

The Importance of Consultative Roles and Skills in Transforming Leadership

The following example will illustrate the diversity of roles and stages that naturally occur in the course of a consultative intervention. Either a leader from outside an organization or team or someone on the inside could perform the behaviors outlined below.

During the initial assessment phase of a consulting contract, a vice-president and general manager of a manufacturing firm confided in me that he had "tried everything" to increase employee productivity. He had put pressure on managers and supervisors to up the production quotas, had threatened firings if production did not go up, and tried to "pump" all the managers with "excellence" audio and video tape programs. He even instituted a "Quality is Free" program. In my interviews with his managers, supervisors, and frontline workers, however, it became clear that the company was experiencing what I call "excellence burn-out." The workers were pushed to the limit of what they believed was reasonable for what they were receiving in return—and they weren't willing to give any more unless they could see where there would be "something in it for me." As a team, they were, according to industry standards, functioning at only about 60 percent of the real potential of the equipment they had to work with—and the vice-president made sure they heard this on a daily basis. The more he pushed, the more they complained about being overworked and underpaid. As in some union situations, the people who did the work decided how much work was going to get done and anyone who stepped out of line to perform above this norm would be disciplined by the work-group members in very quiet and effective ways.

Upon further investigation through interviews with frontline staff—the ones who directly control productivity—it became clear they were angry. This anger came across in nearly every interview. I listened carefully for many hours without turning my interviews with them into sessions that could be seen as "encouraging whiners to whine," as the vice-president put it. During my thirty interviews with them—which included a random cross-section of frontline staff—I made a list of complaints and a list of what they appreciated about working for this company. Here, in order of priority of importance is the list of their complaints.

1. Nobody cares about us around here—why should we put out for them? They won't even fix up the restrooms and lunchroom. They treat us like migrant workers. (This one complaint about the restrooms and lunchroom was the most frequently mentioned of all complaints!)

2. They (management) say they care about us "people" and that "people are important to the company" but really, they just talk the talk, but don't walk the walk. When Bill got seriously injured on the job, they just called the ambulance. Not one supervisor, manager, or executive in this place even visited him in the hospital for two weeks. That's sick. (The fact was that management did make a visit, then they had to go out of town for a week. Not all 197 staff members knew this.)

3. Some low performers connected to the president's family get to stick around and continue to "sluff off" their responsibilities on the job, and we have to pick up the slack. The boss plays favorites, and we aren't his favorites. (From the boss's view, this one person was an old-time friend of the family, and out of kindness and respect for this person's age, the boss decided not to fire him.)

4. Good performance is not even noticed or rewarded around here. Why should I put out my best when we don't get raises even when production does go up for a whole month? If I put out more on the job, then I get pressure from most other workers to fall back into line so they don't have to work harder.

5. People can get fired at any time around here, and without enough of a chance to better their job performance. They fired three receptionists in the head office without even giving them any training to do the job. Other

people have just disappeared around here and no one knows why. You wonder if you are next! (The boss didn't fire the receptionists; they just couldn't do the job so he released them at the end of their probationary period. They couldn't keep up with a position around which we later had to build two positions, due to the complexity of that job role.)

6. I've been here for four years and I still don't know if I will ever get a promotion. I don't know if I'm being seen as "just another worker" or not. I think I could do a good job as a supervisor, and I have taken the training, but no one will tell me if I should have any hope or not. I'm looking for another place to work where there is more opportunity. (This has been remedied by including the issue of career-path planning in the performance review process.)

7. Management continues to change their minds about how things should be done they don't involve any of us in making changes, and they don't even ask us how the changes are working! (This problem area has also been remedied through more effective team meetings.)

From these complaints, which I collated and summarized into a brief report, the vice-president and I arrived at the following understandings.

1. Managers who aren't listened to and shown respect by the VP often do not listen to and show basic human decency and respect for their workers.

2. Managers demonstrated role, skill, and style rigidity in the traditional "old school" fashion.

3. People won't work hard over the long haul for people they don't like.

4. The president of the company had set the "impersonal tone" of the corporate culture by treating previous executive and management staff with a "transistor" approach to management: "If it doesn't work, unplug it, throw it away, and get another one in there." There had been a 35 percent turnover in managers and supervisors during the past three years since the company had really gotten off the ground, and a corresponding 40 percent (per year!) turnover in frontline staff. No one calculated the cost of training or hiring people who didn't fit their jobs.

5. No one in management acted as an internal consultant to the organization. No one was reading the "nonrational" factors in the workplace to respond to things like fixing up the restrooms and lunchrooms (at least)—considered to be the major sign of disrespect by management toward the employees (who were 65 percent women)!

It is clear from this list of complaints that I had discovered—in my role as external consultant—a series of problems that could be remedied if I could get the understanding and cooperation of the vice-president and the president.

In a series of meetings and planning sessions, we came to the conclusion some changes were needed in the way people treated people in this organization. Changes were immediately made to address the specific complaints of the workers. The washrooms and lunchroom were upgraded. Human resource systems were put into place to find, hire, place, orient, and train the right people to fit the jobs available. A profit-sharing program was installed. The results have been that the company has increased its productivity significantly. The employees who have stayed on have accepted Crosby's, *Quality is Free* program with the resulting effects of decreased turnover, decreased absenteeism, increased performance, and higher morale.

Leaders are often expected by those "below" them to act in a traditionally independent and decisive manner, but as we can see in the above example, in day-to-day affairs, they are more likely to need to use the skills of consulting with others in a collaborative manner. It is ideal when all people involved can arrive at decisions for which there is team commitment and consensus. If the vice-president had been the internal consultant, this could have been ideal! "Team leadership"—once called participative management—is becoming even more popular because of the results achieved through team efforts in many business environments (Peters and Austin, 1985). Many Japanese companies have demonstrated the effectiveness of well-functioning teams, and some North American companies find themselves attempting to emulate their efforts.

> **It would be preferable to develop the leadership capacity within each manager to set up, monitor, and develop people, morale, and unique systems to facilitate the organization's success.**

In another important and innovative work, referred to above, Philip Crosby (Crosby, 1979) has developed a book and training program for managers called, *Quality is Free*. This program outlines many of the critical factors that appear to be required for organizational success. Although Crosby places importance on the role of managers as internal quality consultants to the organization (calling them "quality managers"), he does not provide a means for training those managers to become skilled transforming leaders. The success of his program rests on the existing competencies of those who implement it, however undeveloped they may be.

Crosby's focus on developing "management participation and attitude" is a good start, but if we want to go the full distance, we will provide a means to develop the manager into a skilled and competent internal consultant to the organization. This manager will be a leader who can do more than manage a good system for quality or productivity improvement. It would be preferable to develop the capacity within each manager to set up, monitor, and develop people, morale, and unique systems to facilitate an organization's success. But let's not sell Crosby short—he himself is an example of a transforming leader and does provide a tested system for improving quality and productivity.

Interpersonal communication, counseling and problem-management, and consultative skills are required to carry out successful team and organizational leadership. Even though it is important for those exerting leadership influence to shift at times from a mutually communicative to a helpful counseling role, it is perhaps even more important that they be able to shift from the communicative and counseling roles to the consultative role.

The Nature of the Consultative Role

The consultative manner of dealing with people and problems is an innovative and creative one—a more "global" one. It is characterized by careful assessment and strategically planned action and combined with empathy toward others. The consultative role also requires pronounced detachment and objectivity about the team and/or organizational context in which a team's problem is occurring. The skilled leader is capable of transforming people and organizations by moving from a mutual communication role to a counseling and problem-management approach, and then

> A consultative leader, while having the ultimate authority to make final decisions, can be more of a humble "servant," attempting to discover and meet needs to facilitate the accomplishment of agreed-upon goals while keeping the "big picture" in mind.

shifting to a consultative role when the situation requires this type of "skill and role-shifting" (discussed in depth in Chapter 8).

Many leaders demonstrate role, skill, and style rigidity and this lack of receptivity and responsiveness to change and to people limits their potential to function effectively. Developing consultative awareness—objective awareness of the process and the context of people and events—and skills will assist you to be more effective in the consulting process. The multifaceted and flexible leader functions in this "fluid" manner, not closing down options or opportunities. He or she uses both intuition and rational calculation—theorizing, strategizing, and then taking action—only to reevaluate the impact and shift again.

This type of circular *modus operandi* is similar to what has been called "MBWA," or Management By Wandering Around, by Tom Peters. There is a certain informal quality, a genuine and mutual—but expert—quality of leading in this manner. A consultative leader, while having the ultimate authority to make final decisions, can be more of a humble "servant," attempting to discover and meet needs to facilitate the accomplishment of agreed-upon goals while keeping the "big picture" in mind at the same time.

This image of leading while wandering around talking with people for a purpose captures the spirit of the "hi-touch" but objective and result-oriented leader who can function in the consultative role, and the other two roles—communicating and counseling—alternatively, or in a blended fashion.

Difficulties in Developing Consultative Skills

As mentioned above, the consultative role, and the skills that are appropriate to it, are more difficult to develop than the communication and counseling skills, because they are more complex. They require a more comprehensive awareness of self, others, teams, technical know-how, and the organizational and environmental contexts involved in each changing situation.

When functioning in the consultative role, it is as though a part of the your self is reserved and "perched upon the roof," looking down into the context of the team or organizational setting in which events are taking place. When you shift into the consultative role, you practice seeing patterns in the environment, much as the eagle soars above—constantly "casing the territory," looking for movement, irregularities, or patterns below. When we work with executive teams, we get them up on the "roof" of their organization so that they can begin to work "on" the organization, not just "in" it.

The consultative skills also require that you have a strong base of communication and problem-management skills to be most effective. Many people in positions of authority have few skills that they consciously and deliberately employ. Some people in positions of responsibility over others seem to have one or two sets of skills. Few managers seem to have developed all three sets of skills and integrated them into practice.

Even though the consultative level of awareness, and the skills that accompany it, are the most difficult to develop, they are perhaps the most influential. Therefore, they are potentially the most rewarding. It is the challenge for the transforming leader—functioning in the role of consultant—to stay open, to deal

> **When we work with executive teams, we get them up on the "roof" of their organization so they can begin to work "on" the organization, not just "in" it.**

with complexity, and to be at least as complex as the complexity of the situation at hand. The capacity to be complex and versatile is vital to both effective processing of information and creativity.

The consultative role includes such roles as listener, interviewer, observer, data collector, reporter, teacher, trainer, coach, educator, sponsor, support-giver, advisor, challenger, mediator, mentor, advisor, advocate, researcher, problem-solver, entrepreneur, and creator. All of these roles capture the complexity of leadership and require all three sets of skills in transforming leadership. With this complexity in mind, you now have an opportunity to familiarize yourself with the steps in the consulting process.

The Consulting Process

Egan (1988) outlines a practical systems-based model for changing and developing organizations that results in action that leads to valued outcomes.
1. **Current Scenario:** Find out what is not going right or what's going wrong in terms of problems, unmet needs, unused resources, unmet challenges, and so forth.
2. **Preferred Scenario:** Determine what the organization, organization unit, or project would look like if it were in better shape. A preferred scenario deals with what an organization needs and wants, not with how it is to be achieved.
3. **The Plan for Getting There:** Develop an action program or strategy for moving the current scenario to the preferred scenario. This stage deals with how results are to be accomplished. It projects action plans that lead to valued outcomes.

In Egan's model above, there is a systematic and objective attempt to gather and interpret relevant information for the purpose of gaining insight about the nature of a need, problem, or overlooked strength. This "diagnosis" provides the consultant with the information needed to design interventions that will more likely result in improvement of performance, morale, and/or climate of a particular person, team, or organization.

There are many models of strategic planning, implementation, change management, and evaluation that could be referred to here, but I have distilled these into steps that may be appropriate for you to use when you attempt to facilitate positive change in your organization. Outlined on the following page is the amplified summary of the consulting process so that you can gain better perspective on the steps involved.

Step 1: Assessment of Needs, Wants, and Problems
During this first step, some kind of organizational needs assessment or organizational audit can fruitfully be undertaken. This needs, strengths, or problems audit can take the form of administering standardized questionnaires for organizational assessment, interviews can be conducted with key people in the organization, or a systems effectiveness analysis can be conducted by an outside specialist (i.e., an accountant, engineer, etc.). Although the

identification of problems and unmet needs is essential, the pinpointing of strengths and unrealized potential is also critical to discover and communicate to all members of the organization. Assessing both the technical and relationship aspects of a problem are equally important. Currently, we are using an organizational survey we designed called the *Organizational Assessment Review (OAR)* to do a comprehensive assessment of all areas of the organization.

Steps In The Consulting Process

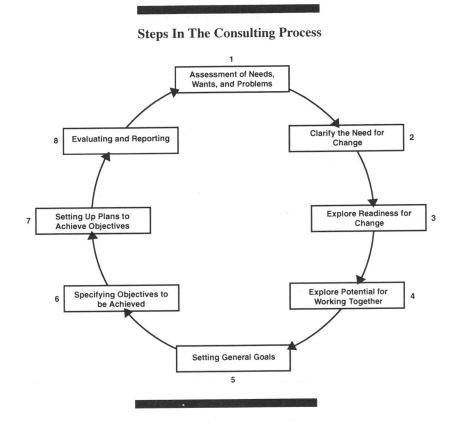

Step 2: Clarify the Need for Change in a Language Others Will Understand and Accept

The consulting process is very similar to the problem-management process in this respect: problem identification and specification is a most critical phase of the process. The more specific and careful the definition of the problem or need, the greater the likelihood of a successful intervention.

There are both informal and formal ways of defining problems and assessing needs. Some informal ways include small group interviews with representatives from various parts of an organization, small group simulations of problem situations perceived to be occurring frequently in the organization, or anonymous surveys with key workteams, supervisors, and managers. More formal methods of data collection will be specifically explored below. The problem must be communicated to the team in such a way that leaders and members will be able to usefully identify it as a valid problem or need.

Step 3: Exploring the Readiness for Change

As each team or organization endeavors to make a positive difference, the change agent and the individuals involved must assess one another's willingness and ability to make the change happen successfully. There are many obstacles to effective change and many forces that can promote change effectively. Personal insecurity, interpersonal or interteam conflict, financial pressures, political forces, and timing can all affect a change attempt adversely. When intervening in a consultative role, regardless of your role, it is good to do a "force field analysis," identify all the possible blocks, and test to see if there are ways to remove some of the blocks before they hamper the effectiveness of your efforts.

For example, a principal of a large elementary school called me to assist her in planning professional development activities for her teaching staff. During my mandatory interviews with some of the teachers, a few of them confided in me that nothing would likely be well received because the principal was not consulting with the teachers about what they felt was needed in the coming year. She was just planning to "lay on" some training. The resentment was so great that I confronted the principal with this perception. We thought through how we could overcome this block, and the principal decided to hold a meeting to specify the teachers' areas of need, using me as a planning facilitator.

The teachers appreciated that the principal had asked an outsider to facilitate staff consensus on training events because her communication and leadership styles were autocratic and authoritarian in nature. The principal did not want to change her management style because she feared losing some of the authority and control she thought she had established. But because she was participating in the planning process as a mutual leader/member of the team, instead of the "boss," the principal was also able to get many of the things she wanted into the program.

People on her team who perceived themselves as mature or as deserving more respect resented being "bossed around" by her in the past, so we had to overcome this block before a positive difference could be made. She had to develop some additional style versatility in dealing with these followers or delegate some leadership to one of them to get the results she wanted. She also had to learn basic interpersonal communication skills because she had never been trained in these skills. She grew up in a family that had taught her to be the way she was.

The principal subsequently used the same consultative role of operating she saw me use to solve two other problems that arose in her teaching team—with good results. Her performance was under review that year by her school district's director of instruction and she was greatly relieved at the increasingly positive evaluations she was receiving from her teachers. Her readiness for change, inspired by her observations of how the consultative process can solve problems without losing authority, increased as time went by. This resulted in the teachers changing their perceptions and approaches with her, much to the relief of everyone. She made small changes that resulted in big pay-offs.

Step 4: Exploring the Potential for Working Together in Concert
A good working relationship is imperative if we are to make the positive difference we would like to make. Establishing bonds of common values, beliefs, or approaches can help in developing trust with those with whom you work. Being open about differences can also be important when it can prevent future expectation gaps and clashes in values or styles, and that can allow you an opportunity to work through agreements about how you will deal with problems and resolve the conflicts that will inevitably emerge. We use the *Values Preference Indicator* and the *Personal Style Indicator* to help team members understand their strengths and accept their differences.

When expectations are not clear, anxiety levels often escalate and nonrational, even irrational, behavior can result. One of the ways of managing nonrationality is to be clear about what you will not do and what you can be expected to do. Then see how much support you can get from the people with whom you are working on key issues. Not only can you test to see how much potential compatibility or conflict there is among three or more people, you can communicate a certain degree of willingness to respect the values and approaches of others involved in the change effort. Establishing clear and agreed-upon values and procedures in any group can help create compatibility in your work relationships with others.

I was asked to accept an eight-month contract as an organization development consultant with a juvenile correctional facility. Prior to beginning this contract, I became aware that the administrator was perceived by most supervisors and workers as a "spineless jellyfish"; I told this man there was a lot of evidence from initial surveys and interviews that his behavior was being perceived as inconsistent. He was also seen as too easily pressured by various kids or staff to change his mind on key issues. I informed the administrator that this behavior was causing specific problems, including undermining the behavior-modification reward system, and also staff and "kid" morale problems due to his being seen to "play favorites"—and financial problems because he had approved spending by one department and left little money in the bank for some of the other programs.

I decided to work on getting the commitment from him that he would meet weekly with his senior staff and consult with them about the likely consequences of various actions before he made major decisions that would affect them. I told him that, otherwise, I doubted there could be a positive difference made by my presence as a consultant. He agreed to the consultative sessions—because he hated saying no? Actually, he was greatly relieved to get some assistance in making some of the more difficult management decisions. He had never had training in leadership or management before, and as a result of our having several meetings together, he decided to quit his position to become a counselor in an alcohol and drug treatment program. He realized that administrative roles really weren't for him. We developed a good working relationship over the eight months of the contract. Without developing these clear working agreements with him and his staff, my efforts at unblocking and developing this organization would likely have been entirely foiled.

Step 5: Setting General Goals
A parallel to this step in the "counseling" role outlined in the previous chapter would be the goal-setting step. In this phase of the process, agreements are made with others about what achievements or accomplishments are being attempted. These goals need to be stated concretely enough—and usually in writing, as much as most people resist doing this—so that their attainment can actually be observed and measured. General goals are stated as things we hope for: "We want to improve our hiring process" or "We want to use time more wisely in our meetings." It is important to come to consensus about general goals before moving on to seek consensus among members of a workgroup or team. Otherwise, you may be attempting to set more specific objectives to be achieved when there is no real commitment to do so. These goals can become an important part of a written contract—if this more formal type of agreement is appropriate.

Step 6: Specifying Objectives to be Achieved: A Practical View of a Preferred Future
For most people busy doing the "job"—whether that job is leadership in a home, a classroom, a school, a hospital ward, a company, or an army—there is some reluctance to take the time to do careful planning. It takes time and a stretching of the imagination. It is hard work to be specific with language! It is risky to announce to others that you have a plan, because then you will be asked by them whether or not your plan worked! So quite often, people just keep going along with the status quo; they don't rock the boat or set even slightly risky goals that could later prove to be embarrassing if they aren't achieved.

The director of a large church youth group called and asked me if I could assist him to develop the team of people involved in working with about 150 youth in the church. On this staff, there was one full-time director, three paid part-time staff, and twenty-five volunteer adult staff. The youth program had been going along steadily for seven years or so with the same director, but no long-range planning or annual goal setting had taken place at the team level. It was "top down" leadership where the director—to this point—had taken most of the responsibility for structuring activities and motivating the youth, with other volunteer leaders following along whether they liked the way things were going or not. They did not want to confront the leader's authority because they valued showing respect to their leaders by not "disagreeing" with them. As the church became larger, the need for more staff and more diverse programs became evident.

One primary problem became clear. No one had systematically determined what the needs and wants were from the points of view of the youth, and no one had assessed the needs, skills, and abilities of the staff or twenty-five volunteers. They were hired or accepted as volunteers based on their personal qualities and their willingness to serve. This scenario is typical of most volunteer groups and committees where one leader is taking most of the responsibility, and the followers are not specifically qualified for the roles they are assuming. I spent one day with the four leaders and their spouses—since they worked together as couples—to decide what they would like to do to strengthen their team effectiveness and the impact of their work with the youth in their church and in their community. With my assistance in wording their objective statements, they wrote out the following.

1. We will conduct an informal needs assessment (personal interviews) of the youth in our church and community, and also use a more formal questionnaire approach to see how much the two match.
2. We will create a comprehensive mission, goals, and programs statement based upon the above needs assessment of youth in our church and community.
3. We will write a proposal to the board that will include an outline of our departmental statements and a budget that will outline the financial requirements to achieve our goals; this proposal will be given to them on May 1 for their consideration.
4. We will involve youth in the decision-making process about programs we are planning for them in the future by getting their ideas and input at planning meetings we schedule each month.
5. We will engage in staff training for ourselves when we determine areas of need, assess the training needs of our twenty-five volunteer staff, and provide training for them, and we will begin both training programs in June.
6. We will discover and appreciate one another's strengths and create job descriptions for ourselves that reflect our individual abilities. We will communicate these job descriptions to one another and review their appropriateness every six months.
7. We will bring in people external to our church to assist in meeting needs we don't have the expertise to meet, i.e., career and life planning seminar for senior high and college age youth, self-esteem seminar for junior and senior high youth, premarital and marriage seminars for those who marry young. We will provide longer-term professional counseling for youth who have emotional and family problems.

This group needed assistance in specifying their objectives because they clearly would not have put them together in this complete and specific way without external assistance. It would have been best, however, if someone within the church organization had consultative knowledge and skills to accomplish this end without external consultation. The board was so impressed with the clarity of this department's plans, they funded all of their proposals without reservation and gave the youth pastor a promotion to assistant pastor.

Step 7: Setting Up Plans to Achieve Objectives

Strategic planning is 5 percent of the equation for success, and implementation is the other 95 percent. After objectives have been set with the agreement of those involved, you will be in a much better position to plan and implement the objectives in a step-by-step fashion, with timelines for implementation. It is also more likely that you will assign the most appropriate people to do various parts of the task if you have specified exactly what needs to be done. This must be stated in terms of action to be taken and accomplishments to be achieved so that your team can achieve its goals and purpose within specified timeframes.

Step 8: Evaluating and Reporting the Impact of Your Intervention

It is important to assess the impact of your interventions as you intervene at set time intervals during a project. Normally, you would do some type of assessment after the first session, another one-third of the way through, another two-thirds of the way, and one at the end. This regular evaluation will assist you to set a new course as your planned intervention will need some fine-tuning to perfectly hit the mark .

When you have determined there is a problem, you will need to communicate that challenge to the group and give them an opportunity to suggest alternative solutions. These suggestions can be integrated into an overall plan for improving their approach or strategies. You will win the respect of group members when you can "head problems off at the pass," rather than ignoring problems or avoiding any awareness of them altogether. It is far better to "correct course" than to stick to the "plan" and run the ship onto dry ground.

An example of how this type of evaluation can be effective is to use the same survey both before and after a time of planned change. We use the *OAR* to assess the current state of an organization and to measure change after a specified period of time. Also, the strategic planning and implementation document itself can act as a reference point to determine how well the plan has been implemented because you can determine the extent to which you have achieved what you intended.

Another way to illustrate this type of evaluation and reporting is for me to tell you about my own practice teaching at the university level. At the beginning of each session, I hand out a three-by-five-inch file card to all students and ask them to jot down on one side what "worked," and on the other side what didn't work in that class, with suggestions for improvements. When I read all thirty or forty cards, I know how to better approach the class next session. I tell the students what I have learned from their feedback and thereby model being open to suggestions and criticisms. By opening up this simple channel of evaluative communication between myself and the students in my classes, I have prevented many problems from developing and have received many exciting ideas from students. My teaching evaluations have gone up over the years as a result of this practice, and so has my teaching effectiveness.

Section Two: 12 Skills in the Consulting Role

The skills in this part of the chapter are summarized and explained in concrete terms so that you can gain insight into what is required to perform each skill. Reading about these skills is often not enough, however. As with the communication and counseling problem-management skills, to develop these skills to their fullest, you will need a coach or a mentor or at least take some training specific to your areas of need.

TL Skill #37 Informal Assessment Skills: *Walking Around Talking with People*

This area of skill involves your using all the communication skills outlined in Chapter 5. This requires you to informally engage in assessing and reporting needs, wants, fears, problems, opportunities, or threats in several different ways. This can be done in a casual way by walking around talking to people. Or it can be done by scheduling one-on-one interviews over coffee with key people, to gain insight into their concerns or to learn their perceptions about issues you have determined are important. Good leaders stay in touch with the people implementing the team's strategies and help them in the trenches, on a daily or weekly basis, to prevent and manage problems. This kind of leadership cannot be done without informal interviewing on an ongoing basis. Some of the very best information I have received has been from this type of "grapevine" communication. After you gather information, you can introduce it in a team or executive leadership meeting for further consideration and discussion.

I am reminded of my own psychology professor who told me about his experience trying to research to determine morale issues when he was in the army. His team designed questionnaires, did surveys, collected data, crunched the numbers, and yet the team members felt they were not in touch with what was going on with the over 2,000 officers in their charge. Finally, after months of investigation, the four researchers decided to go out and talk with the people face-to-face. The information they collected made the "data" come alive with meaning. This has been so true in my own experience: it is important to talk with a cross-section of the people who do the work and who have the concerns. These individuals can design and implement solutions to many of their own problems, when they come up with solutions themselves. People implement ideas they help create.

TL Skill #38 Formal Assessment: *Research, Interviewing, and Reporting*

This skill area is critical to the success of the change process because, without careful and accurate assessment of needs, wants, and problems in a team or organization, there can be little or no effective intervention. To make a positive difference, goals must to be accurately and specifically stated and programs implemented so that targeted problems are solved and felt-needs are met. Here are examples of such information gathering.

1. A leader does a survey of what a workgroup or team members would most like to do during a given session.
2. A teacher assesses the reading levels of students to plan individually tailored reading programs.
3. A manager or supervisor does a job satisfaction survey each week to determine problem areas, and takes appropriate action based upon feedback.
4. A salesman reviews monthly data by geographic sales areas to better target the achievement of next month's sales objectives.
5. A consultant assesses the factors related to absenteeism in a large company in an attempt to alleviate the absenteeism problem and increase overall productivity.
6. A university president conducts an institutional self-study to determine areas of effectiveness and potential problems, or to identify unmet needs.

> **Good leaders stay in touch with the people implementing the team's strategies and helping them in the trenches, on a daily or weekly basis, to prevent and manage problems. This kind of leadership cannot be done without informal dialog on an ongoing basis.**

7. A parent has a family meeting to determine needs, problems, and wants and creates some strategies for meeting these.
8. A consulting accountant provides cash flow or sales projections to plan effectively for future capital expenditures or project sales or for the results needed to achieve the desired business goals.

The information-gathering and interpreting process follows a number of steps adapted from Kilburg (1978) and are outlined below.

1. Clarify the purpose of gathering information so that the information will assist people to make better decisions in specific areas.
2. Formulate expected results so you can compare the real results with the expected results.
3. Use proper assessment tools, surveys, interviews, questionnaires, or tests so the information you collect will be focused and useful.
4. Sample all or a representative selection of the members of a team or organization so you can have confidence that your results reflect the needs or problems of the whole team.
5. Analyze and interpret the information so the results can be used to make better decisions about solving problems or meeting needs.

Before designing or administering various measures, first discover if the people responding to the questionnaire or survey will perceive it worthy of their response.

6. Summarize and present the results of the information-gathering in a way others can understand and use it.
7. Make decisions based on careful assessments instead of "hunches," intuitions, "gut feeling," team member opinion, or "revelation" alone.

The data-gathering process can be assisted by using already validated instruments or questionnaires appropriate to your environment. Specific ones that meet your exact needs may not be easy to come by, and you may have to create your own. Quite often, it is more effective to design the key questions for an interview or on a questionnaire as you can then be somewhat more assured that the questions you ask are appropriately focused and that they address real concerns.

A cautionary note is warranted about administering questionnaires or doing surveys in an organization. Before designing or administering various measures, first discover if the people responding to the questionnaire or survey will perceive it worthy of their response. Sometimes, people are "surveyed out," or they have no confidence that spending their time responding to a survey will result in any change they view as positive.

General Guidelines to Use for Considering the Various Approaches to Gathering Information

In Small Groups (in the range of four to fifteen): Where the members are relatively mature, simply ask them what you want to know—using direct and pointed questions that require a yes or a no—or ask open-ended questions to gather information by using general questions that can be answered in any way the respondents choose. With a group of shy teenagers or slightly paranoid adults, you might ask them to write down their concerns anonymously and place their notes in a "hat" for later reading and response.

In Larger Groups (sixteen to sixty): You may consider using a simple questionnaire that can be developed with the assistance of a few key members in touch with the general concerns of the group. Keep the size of the questionnaire to one or two pages each time you administer it, and make the response time no more than just a few minutes, to increase the response rate. Ask both closed and open questions, as is appropriate. Alternatively, have the key people in the group each approach five members with the same questions. Ask the key people to record the answers and report back to the group leader when the interviews are complete.

In Large Groups (sixty to 200): Groups of this size can be approached in a similar manner but can often be more effectively assessed by using a more involved and carefully designed questionnaire that—ideally—can be computer-scored. As soon as the group gets to be this large, the time involved in getting the data and collating it into meaningful interpretation can be unruly. It can be easier if you have access to a computerized organizational assessment program—such as Campbell's Organizational Survey—or if you know how to use a software program such as "Statistical Program for the SS" (SPSS), a statistical package. (See Gale Research's directory of computer programs, 1-800-877-GALE.)

Groups Larger Than 200: These groups will require high-tech research methods lest the time and expense of distribution, collection, collation, interpretation, and presentation of the data become unwieldy. As a part of the

> **When he looked over the results of the survey, he decided to change his role to that of a more visionary president, and to bring in outside professionals to oversee the operations.**

assessment skill area, in more advanced assessment projects, you may need to develop these research and statistical skills yourself. There are questionnaire-development and scoring software programs that make many of these more difficult tasks quite "user friendly." A working knowledge of the research process and statistical analysis would be an asset in providing you with a greater sense of confidence that the information you have collected is representative of your total population, and not a biased sample. You can take courses in research tests and measurements, and in statistics. Or you can call on those more experienced in this area if you need assistance in developing these skills. You could also delegate this task to qualified researchers if you are in a position to do so; this could be especially important if the research you are doing requires high levels of confidentiality or impartiality by the investigating parties. In politically sensitive situations, you wouldn't want to be accused of being a biased data collector or reporter.

TL Skill #39 Problem-Management Facilitation: *Leading Teams Through Resistance to Change*

This skill is required to prepare the ground for change. People do not want to change simply because there is a need for change. People must understand the need for change, the benefits and downsides of change, what is required of them, and they want to know how their future will look after the change has taken place. Without support, many people become anxious, negative, and unproductive—until they can embrace a clear vision of how change can result in a preferred future. Your job is to use your problem-management skills to uncover the "shadow side" of the resistance to change, help people understand why changes must be made, get them to see what's in it for them if they help you, and get them to enlist in making necessary change happen. Some theorists have called this the "unfreezing" stage of change management, where people get help to become unstuck from old ways of thinking and acting. Most people need help and encouragement to get "out of the box" of what is familiar, and then step out into new territory.

Recently, for example, I worked with a CEO to administer an *OAR* to evaluate how his fifty-million dollar company was doing in twelve areas of performance. I also assessed his own strengths, talents, gifts, personal vision, and life goals in light of what the company needed from a CEO during its current time of rapid growth.

When he looked over the results of the survey, he decided to change his role to being a more visionary president, and to bring in outside professionals to oversee the operations. Previous to this date, he was overseeing the operational aspects of the company with a team of managers who had grown up in the company. A few had been there for thirty-five years. None of the managers wanted any "new blood" to come in from the outside because they each felt deserving of the title of VP of Operations and they were threatened by the unknown person who could hold them accountable to new standards. To facilitate the organization's leaders through this impasse toward change, I suggested to the president—and he agreed—that I could help him implement the following solutions to deal with the resistance to change.

1. Meet with the existing managers to share the results of the *OAR* (available through Strategia at http://www.strategia.com, or from CRG at http://www.crgleader.com) and the CEO's newly clarified role and goals.
2. Assess what they feel is needed for the organization to move ahead.
3. Ask them to catalogue their own strengths, talents, and motivations in

helping move the organization from an entrepreneurially run company to a professionally run business.

4. Tell them the decision has been made to hire an experienced and previously successful VP of Operations. The plan is to advertise and find a person in whom most managers have confidence and with whom they can work agreeably.

5. Involve them in the final interviews to select the person who will, in a practical sense, become their new day-to-day leader.

6. Allow any of them to apply and compete for the job if they feel their expertise and qualifications surpass those of the final short list of applicants.

After this meeting, the managers agreed to the desirability of at least looking for someone who might be the best person to lead the organization into its next stage of development. Of course, it was difficult for them to disagree with the CEO, but they all had the opportunity to process how they felt about the proposed change. They were relieved to know they would have a part in the decision of selecting a new leader of operations, and had a sense of excitement about the CEO's commitment to learn and move ahead into a preferred future for the organization.

> **Before people are really willing to embrace change, they have to be convinced it is truly necessary.**

TL Skill #40   Need Clarification: *Clarifying the Need for Change*

Before people are really willing to embrace change, they have to be convinced it is truly necessary. None of us wants to change just for the "heck of it." It takes work, understanding, patience, and persistence to get key team leaders to the point where their heads and hearts are committed to change. Sometimes people's heads will be convinced, but their hearts will be reserved.

The managers in the above example still weren't fully buying into the need for the impending changes to the organization or their job roles. In particular, two of them were very negative and began bad-mouthing the whole venture—blaming me and the CEO for "messing up what has worked for so long." The CEO and I discussed this lack of enlistment to moving ahead into a preferred future—as they saw it. The following happened as a result of our discussion.

1. We had another team meeting with the managers.

2. We reviewed the results of the *OAR*. This helped the managers pinpoint some changes they wanted to improve things from their points of view, and the CEO agreed to help them move ahead with those changes.

3. They reported liking these new meetings where their concerns and views were heard and where response was immediate with decisions and action.

4. The CEO further explained his own personal need to move out of the role of operational overseer into the role of ambassador for foreign projects, vision-caster, political figurehead in negotiation sessions, etc.

5. He also told them he couldn't make the best use of his time and talents if he continued on in his current role—they agreed with him that he wasn't the very best operational manager that they could have.

6. I explained the differences between an entrepreneur-style organization and a professionally run one, and the "lights began to go on" regarding the benefits of this difference. They agreed they wanted to see the organization move ahead from fifty million to 100 million in the next few years.

7. They agreed that they, too, needed to have some changes in their roles and that if there could be a VP of Human Resources hired as well as a VP of Operations, they could get on in a less distracted way with doing what they each did best. They also agreed that the overall profitability of the company would most likely increase (beyond the cost of the salary for the position) as a result of hiring a VP with a proven track record.

They finally got the message that making planned change happen could benefit them and that they could trust it and the CEO—and even me, an external consultant. They started to "gel" as a team in a new way. But their full enlistment and wholehearted commitment was not yet secured. More is required, as you will see when we explore the next skill in this leadership skill set.

TL Skill #41 Readiness Checking: *Overcoming the Real Blocks to Change*

Helping people get ready for major change is difficult, complex, and fraught with the unexpected. It is hard to manage the "shadow side" of the events that inevitably emerge. There are "skeletons in the closet," old resentments among team members that go "way back," and fears about the uncertainty of an ill-defined kaleidoscopic future. Sometimes the real obstacles to change have to be ferreted out and confronted head-on.

The CEO and myself met again after the final session with his managers. The man was both troubled and encouraged. He was encouraged we'd gotten this far; he had frankly expected far more resistance or even a refusal to move ahead from a few of the managers. He was troubled because there was one person on his team that he couldn't trust.

He felt that more than half of the twelve managers were "on board" and ready for the launch of a new and better organization. He also felt empathy for the other half still passively looking on, or the two who were still somewhat negative in their attitudes. He was determined to give them a reason to either get "on the bus" or not continue to work with the organization.

He didn't want the poison he had tolerated in the past. He realized he was no longer willing to tolerate the draining negativity and pessimistic attitude of two of his team leaders. He realized he wanted to communicate to people in the organization that mediocrity, acceptance of negativity, or minimal performance were no longer acceptable. After a long conversation and some soul searching, he asked me to assist him to do the following tasks while I coached him in the further development of his interpersonal, problem management, and consultative skills.

1. We asked all managers to rewrite their job descriptions based on what they really did. Their current job descriptions were so far outdated that many of them started with a clean piece of paper. We asked them each to prioritize the tasks on their new job description in the order of what they did best and what would best achieve their departmental goals and the organization's strategic plan. The managers consulted the supervisory level below them and went through the same process, delegating some things to various supervisors who wanted some of the tasks the managers off-loaded.

> **Helping people get ready for major change is difficult, complex, and fraught with the unexpected. It is hard to manage the "shadow side" of the events that inevitably emerge. There are "skeletons in the closet," old resentments among team members that go "way back," and fears about the uncertainty of an ill-defined kaleidoscopic future.**

2. Then, we met with each manager and revised his or her job description to reflect what we could all see were the best uses of the manager's time and talents. We helped them see how they could delegate the rest of the tasks that were distracting them from performing from their strengths. We also reengineered their work roles so that they were relieved from doing tasks that were not as strategically important to accomplishing what was most critical for their department or for the organization's success.

3. The CEO shared and revised his job description based on feedback from each manager. He off-loaded some of the things that had been "on his plate" for years onto the new VP of Operation's job description, or onto other managers' job descriptions—to managers who had the talents to perform the tasks well.

4. From the implementation plan of the organization's strategic plan, we added a prioritized list of projects and accountabilities—with timelines

for accomplishment—to the last page of the job description, and the CEO and manager each signed off on them. In this way, what they had together was an agreement for the work they were committing themselves to doing in the coming year.

5. We agreed that this job description document would be open-ended because a new, upcoming strategic review session was planned to further clarify roles and responsibilities for the coming year.

6. We dealt with the one person the CEO couldn't trust because that person had engaged in some manipulative behaviors: lying to protect himself, "lording" his authority over key supervisors, and refusing to own up to these things. All the managers felt intimidated by this one fellow because of his history of threats, destructive put-downs, and spreading false rumors that hurt people's reputations. Because the man refused to take ownership of his destructive behaviors, he was given the choice of losing his authority and function as an advisor to another manager—or leaving the organization. Interestingly, he chose the former option. Because of a medical problem that was giving him warnings, he had to back off on his stress levels before his retirement in a few years. He also abandoned most of his negative approaches to people.

The results of going through this process were that each of the managers now felt that the major obstacle to team harmony and progress was removed! The one manager who had been demoralizing the rest of the team had been repositioned. The other fellow who was mainly negative in his attitude turned around because he was no longer in the clutches of the leader who represented the "old guard" values of the organization.

The values of the organization throughout the decades of its existence had remained predominantly authoritarian and "good ol' boy networkish." In other words, if you got promoted, it was likely because that the boss of your division liked you or that you were a relative of someone in "higher places." Many people had received raises based on their connections rather than their performance. This practice is found too often—masked in sneaky or "quick-and-dirty" personnel selection procedures. Some low performers got raises and their slack performance was tolerated because of whose sons or daughters they were. People of lesser "status" in the kingdom were given the more difficult and stressful jobs. It was just the way things were done from the beginning. Was this culture hard to change? Yes! It was similar to some military, police, or correctional cultures in some ways. The need for a new charter, new culture, new values, new vision, new strategy was at hand.

After getting people ready to accept change, the next step is that the operating values of the organization need to be clarified. Some consultants would argue that we should have done this in step one. Based on my experience, if we had done that, our major obstacles would not have been removed and the probability of achieving some measure of real consensus around operating values would have been decreased.

Values Must Make a Difference

Many people are sick of the whole values-clarification and consensus-seeking process because they have been through the exercise of specifying organizational and team values before, and it didn't make any significant difference—the values became mouthed, notional values, rather than action-based, guiding values in reality. Once articulated and agreed upon, the values must carry some weight!

For example, Norm Stamper, Chief of the Seattle Police Department, made a public statement on local TV that if any employee of the police department were observed discriminating against anyone because of race, belief, or sex, that person would be dismissed immediately. This put the commitment to values in plain sight for everyone to see. Chief Stamper did this based upon consensus developed about the preferred values of those who worked in the organization. He also made this announcement because he is upholding the worth of all people, and the value of the Constitution.

Agreed-upon values must become operational values that carry genuine consequences when they are not followed. Even more important, behavior in alignment with the desired values of the organization must be recognized, appreciated, and rewarded or those values will have a tendency to fade.

Bill Bean and Ron Ford have written and produced a workbook entitled *Turbocharging Your Business* (available from Strategia at http://www.strategia.com), which includes a team-based exercise to identify and prioritize organizational values. This technology also provides a fine model and process to accomplish strategic planning and implementation planning that involves key stakeholders. The steps in the model are very similar to the skills outlined in the last part of this chapter.

Clarifying Values at the Organizational and then Team Levels

Both team and organizational values may need to be specified. Organizational values are more global, and are often agreed upon at the executive or management level. Acceptance and adoption of these values is sought by people in all areas of the organization. Once the organizational values are specified, then teams can identify their own team values that are based on the organizational values. Teams must have some cohesion to exist over time. Cohesion is made up of good reasons to get together—to meet one another's needs, to solve problems, and to reach goals.

When team members are at odds with one another about how people should be treated, about how rules and regulations should be interpreted or followed, about how to conduct the meetings, about who has leadership and final decision-making authority, then the team will be divided and dysfunctional and may merely exist in mediocrity for years. Therefore, it is of critical importance that the issues of team norms (rules, regulations, manners of treating people, and solving problems), values (priorities, importances), and beliefs (assumptions about what is good, true, worthwhile, etc.) be addressed in the first stage of a team's development.

In the same manner as outlined above for specifying a purpose, a team can be facilitated to seek and arrive at consensus about the issues of norms, values, and beliefs. Where conflict is not resolvable, team members must compromise, follow the authority of a leader given the ultimate decision-making authority by the team or by a higher authority—or leave the team.

Problems Incurred from a Failure to Secure Values Alignment

When value alignment is not handled in the development of a team or organization, there is bound to be undue and ongoing conflict, strife, and unresolved problems. I am not suggesting that people should all believe the same things and have the same priorities or values, but I am asserting that when people don't agree that it is OK to disagree; then there is often an intolerable clash of expectations and hard feelings, coupled with people blaming one another for the demise of the organization or team.

A college faculty had a departmental meeting and sought consensus about—and then agreed upon—their written purpose, goals, norms, values, and beliefs statements. One person only pretended to "buy into" the statements because to resist the team's momentum would have meant she was clearly out of line with the very basic human values prized by all the other team members. She neither wanted to give up her values in favor of the team's nor be openly at odds with the other team members, so she just quietly operated from her own opposing values without the team's immediate knowledge.

Over time, several of the team's members began to notice that students were being treated in an arbitrary fashion, without due respect or according to principles that the other members of the department did not value. This kind of internal sabotaging of a team's key values happens in organizations when people are hired who claim they have a certain type of character and then turn out to be the exact opposite. These problems are the more difficult ones to solve. These problems represent the "shadow side" of the organization and are more difficult to manage.

A comprehensive program titled *TeamLead*, written by Everett Robinson, is available from Consulting Resource Group (CRG) at http://www.crgleader.com. In this process, a team values assessment and prioritization activity is outlined. More than twenty other assessments and activities designed to build high-performance teams are also available from CRG.

TL Skill #43 Vision and Purpose Consensus-Building

Many visionaries or strategic planners use an analytic approach to planning that doesn't unify people into a force for change. This approach has the following characteristics.
1. It begins with an assessment of the current state, issues, and problems.
2. It breaks the issues or problems into their smallest components.
3. It solves each component separately, i.e., maximizes the solution.
4. It has no far-reaching vision or goal—it merely seeks the absence of the problem.

Transforming Leadership takes a systems approach to envisioning and problem-solving. The systems approach has the following distinctive characteristics.
1. It begins with a vision of a preferred state of affairs in the future.
2. It articulates ways to know when we arrive at the preferred state.
3. It assesses where we are now.
4. It then articulates strategy to get there, to close the gap between where we are and where we want to be.

The following graphic and description of the systemic approach to strategic planning was developed by Ron Ford.

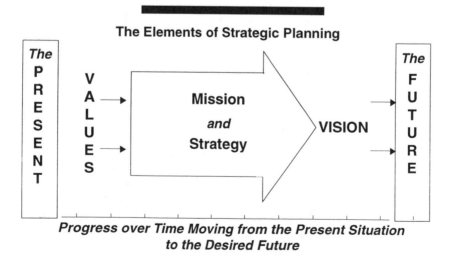

The Elements of Strategic Planning

The PRESENT — VALUES → Mission and Strategy → VISION → The FUTURE

Progress over Time Moving from the Present Situation to the Desired Future

Description of Key Elements in Systems Approach

Element One: VISION
The role of *vision* is infinitely more powerful than the average leader realizes. Vision pulls us toward the future with an image of what that future could look like. It gives us a compelling reason for the sacrifice and effort needed to accomplish something significant.

Element Two: VALUES
The *values* held individually and corporately are primary sources of motivation in the enterprise. Priorities and activities that do not reflect our values are easily procrastinated, compromised, and even abandoned. Values drive us and empower us for accomplishment.

Element Three: THE PRESENT
Every determined step toward the future—no matter how bright and promising it appears—must always begin upon the ground of the present. Present realities must be understood and considered as future planning takes shape in your thinking.

Element Four: MISSION
The *mission* of the enterprise is the tactical and operational focus for the company's resources and efforts. While vision concerns what you are ultimately seeking to build in the company, mission is more concerned with the actual business activities in which you will be engaging in the immediate and short-range future.

Element Five: STRATEGY
With all of the above in view and in proper perspective, a careful, comprehensive plan can be developed. This will consist of priority actions, which will leverage corporate resources and opportunities, and accountable assignments, which will ensure that the plan gets done.

An experienced leader knows that you cannot get people enlisted in moving toward a preferred future unless they are willing to do so. If people are involved in creating or defining the vision—instead of having one "laid on them from on high"—they will be much more likely to accept it and work hard to achieve it. This is one of the most difficult skills for leaders to develop and practice.

Most of the leaders I have worked with have had difficulty projecting beyond the next few months in their corporate lives or their personal lives. This is a major challenge, especially for organizations experiencing or desiring rapid growth. Planned change is obviously preferred to spastic change. I am often told, "I can't plan anything because everything is changing so fast, I can't count on things staying the same for very long." Although this is true to an extent, it is still a fact that some people lead market changes and other types of major change. In Switzerland in 1954, they laughed at Mr. Seiko when he proposed a quartz watch at an international watch makers conference. No one is laughing now.

Bill Bean, in his book *Strategic Planning that Makes Things Happen* (1993), differentiates between Vision and Mission/Purpose. The following clarifications (even formulas) are offered.

1. A vision statement answers the question, "Where are we going?"
   a. What will be our primary products or services be in five years?
   b. What will our primary markets be in five years?
   c. Who will our primary customers be in five years?
   d. What will our exclusive differentiating benefit be in five years?
   e. What will the geographic coverage of our enterprise be in five years?
   f. How big will our enterprise be in five years in terms of total sales, total number of employees, locations, types of locations, etc.?
2. A mission/purpose statement answers the question, "Who are we and what do we do?" Look at the examples below for clarification.
   a. XYZ company delivers performance technologies and profitability systems (what we intend to accomplish/provide),
   b. resulting in enhanced performance for our clients and proper returns for our stockholders (results to customer and owners),
   c. based upon a foundation of integrity and respect for the individual (values and beliefs).

Examples of Vision and Mission Statements

Here are the conceptual statements developed by Consulting Resource Group to articulate their understanding of their long-range vision and their shorter-range mission.

Vision Statement

Consulting Resource Group (CRG) is a global resource that strengthens and develops growth and Leadership in individuals, families, and organizations.

Mission Statement

CRG creates, produces, and teaches innovative learning and Leadership systems for key Leaders around the world, so they can teach these systems to others.

Once there is some reasonable level of consensus regarding the vision and mission/purpose statements, it is then time to move on to developing strategy that will close the gap between the current state and the future state. Most companies find vision-casting and arriving at true consensus to be very difficult. It is, however, the foundation of all else that will occur in the enterprise—and it must be dealt with in a genuine and honest way. Kotter (1996), in his new book, *Leading Change*, is emphatic when he states, according to his research at Harvard University, that there are eight major reasons why organizations fail. Several of them relate to the issue of vision.

Error 1: Allowing too much complacency
Error 2: Failing to create a sufficiently powerful guiding coalition
Error 3: Underestimating the power of vision
Error 4: Undercommunicating the power of vision by a power of 100
Error 5: Permitting obstacles to block the new vision
Error 6: Failing to create short-term wins
Error 7: Declaring victory too soon
Error 8: Neglecting to anchor changes firmly in the corporate culture

Finally, by way of example, let's return to the company we discussed earlier in this chapter. When it came time for them to articulate their vision and mission, they found it incredibly difficult. No one could seem to articulate how the future might look, three to five years down the road. They were a very established, mature organization, accustomed to success (like GM and IBM before the competition gained on them).

They are currently vulnerable because they are building strategy for only the next year, to carry on doing what they now do, but hopefully better. Change seems to be especially difficult for more mature businesses or for government organizations. The future trends forming must be discerned and responded to in a proactive way to catch the next "wave" with a creative new "surfboard" that people will want to buy. That's why we turn now to the issue of strategy. We need two strategies—one to strengthen and improve on current business, and one to anticipate and prepare for a preferred future that keeps moving around on us.

TL Skill #44 Strategy Consensus-Building

We combine the words strategy and consensus here because strategy doesn't get implemented without consensus. Ken Blanchard, in his new book, *Mission Possible*, says it well when he says, "Getting people to break out of their current world view while continuing to operate within it is difficult even for the best of us. Yet in today's hyper competitive markets, it must be done. We have no choice. We must work on the present and the future at the same time."

The *Strategic Planning Technology* process designed by Bill Bean and Ron Ford does exactly this, and is available at www.strategia.com. We highly recommend this process for planning because it is extremely practical, comprehensive, systems-based, as simple as possible—"Everything should be done as simply as possible, but not simpler," as Einstein said—and is based on a review and further development of other approaches to strategic planning.

Another comprehensive model and process for strategic change management that is more detailed and that has even more supportive materials is to be found at the Centre for Strategic Management in San Diego, California (we have found this model more appropriate for sophisticated audiences). Steve Haines' comprehensive strategic planning workbook is titled, *Reinventing Strategic Planning for the 21st Century: A Systems Solution*. The workbook is based upon Haines' book, *Sustaining High Performance* (1995).

Bill Bean's and Steve Haines' approaches cover many of the skills outlined so far in this chapter and are recommended reading for understanding in more depth and with more precision what this strategic change and planning process is about. Most people have never seen a strategic planning document with an implementation plan attached to it. It would be very helpful for you to get a copy of one of the above references so that you can learn more about it than space permits here.

Plan a Two- or Three-Day Strategic Planning Retreat

Unless you already know how to carry out strategic planning, find a consultant with a track record of doing it very well and hire him or her. A good plan and a leadership team that can function with consensus will produce far more benefits than the cost of the consultant. A leadership team, consisting of senior management and representative leaders throughout the organization, needs to be present for such a planning session. Otherwise, it will be difficult to attain any measure of consensus, acceptance, and enlistment in the plan.

Strategic planning can be done in regularly scheduled meetings, but if you are like most leaders, planning just doesn't get done well unless you can get away for a few days each year for focused reflection and planning. Many leaders do their own review of progress and long-range planning at regularly scheduled times, both corporately and personally. This can become an annual tradition that is both refreshing and challenging.

In describing this skill of strategy consensus-building, we will be as brief as possible to specify what a leader must learn in order to have the transforming impact we are seeking and expecting. This skill involves leading—or having a facilitator or consultant lead—your leadership team through reviewing past performance, and setting goals and objectives to close the gap between the present and the preferred future you have articulated. If the facilitator or consultant is brought in from the outside and won't be staying on to help, you or someone in the organization must be prepared and available to lead the implementation process. Fail to give sustained, determined leadership to the implementation process and it will likely falter.

The steps involved in this skill are as follows.

1. **Review all data.** This could be the data you collected when you did the informal and formal assessments by using skills #37 and #38. There needs to be some type of organizational assessment for you to pinpoint successes, failures, strengths, weaknesses, opportunities, and threats.

2. **Conduct an S.F.S.W.O.T.** This is an expanded version of what used to be called the S.W.O.T. (strengths, weaknesses, opportunities, and threats analysis). For obvious reasons, it is important to include facing failures and celebrating successes in the assessment formula. This involves an honest appraisal of the organization and using this data to identify and prioritize all of the above issues so they can be addressed. We use the *OAR* available from www.strategia.com. There are other such tools you can use. Many times, they should be used in conjunction with interviews to gain a better sense of what is currently occurring in the organization and its surrounding environment. This can also be done interactively in a meeting or at a retreat setting. It is best to have objectively collected data—through questionnaires—and subjective data from face-to-fact interviews. The findings from both sources should support each other or you would begin to suspect the validity of one approach or the other. One thing you don't want is information that is false or wrong!

> **Strategic planning can be done in regularly scheduled meetings, but if you are like most leaders, planning just doesn't get done well unless you can get away for a few days each year for focused reflection and planning.**

3. **Prioritize Five to Seven Major Goals that Will Move Everyone Toward the Vision.** Steve Haines calls these major goals Key Success Factors because when accomplished, they will result in successfully realizing at least a part of the preferred future scenario. It is fine to have more than five to seven goals, but most teams find it difficult to focus on five to seven main goals at a time. It is based on the "eighty/twenty rule" that suggests you want to spend 80 percent of your time doing the right 20 percent of the things that achieve 80 percent of the results you want to achieve. The other goals are important as well, but not nearly as important as the success factors that will transform the organization and its people from where they are now to where they want to be. State the goals in concrete, believable, achievable, and challenging language. See the following example of what we think are clear goals.

Ideally, the following will result from your being skilled enough to facilitate the strategic consensus-building process, and you will be smart enough to have an experienced planner do it if you aren't ready or are not the right person to do it.

1. You will leave your planning meetings with a living document—a strategic plan that does not become like the familiar S.P.O.T.S. (Strategic Plan On the Top Shelves).

2. You will have a plan on which the attending leaders agree, and that they will take back to their teams for review and editing—only to bring it back to the next meeting for additional refinements.

If you ask them, the people who do the work will tell you if they have agreed to "buy into" the plan. And ask them! If they don't buy into it, the plan won't get implemented very well. In a government organization with whom I worked, six leaders attended the planning retreat. They then returned to the workplace to meet with twenty-four supervisors to explain the plan and get their input and revisions. The final draft was discussed with each supervisor's workteam members—by the supervisors in face-to-face, one-to-one interviews—and further revisions and refinements were made.

> **Through this process, people found out they could be heard, that there was a pipeline to senior management, and that their comments were taken seriously. No one said he or she was not consulted or heard when objections or suggestions were made.**

Through this process, people found that they could be heard, that there was a pipeline to senior management, and that their comments were taken seriously. No one said he or she was not consulted or heard when the individual made objections or suggestions! Some employees recommended fundamental changes in the workplace and processes that enabled better customer service, better working conditions, lower stress, and higher morale as a result. "Frontline" workers had a transforming effect on the organization. And they were transformed into team members who were important and were, in fact, significant to the overall organizational health and performance. They also implemented the plan to about 85 percent—a good score compared to most teams!

Once the plan has been accepted by a critical mass of people in an organization—at least 60 percent of all staff and 90 percent of all leaders, it has a chance of succeeding. This is especially true if you deal proactively with the negative leaders, who can put a damper on the progress of change. Negative team members can do the same thing but on a smaller scale. Jack Welch

XYZ Company Strategic Goals List

Goal #	Goal Description

1. Develop comprehensive, leadership-supported marketing plan.

2. Refocus Total Quality Management plans to align with overall XYZ Company strategic plan.

3. Develop formal cost control program.

4. Develop comprehensive new hire recruiting and training plan.

5. Develop continuous workload plan, with backlog and smooth flow.

6. Review health insurance coverage and make recommendations.

dismissed many of the managers when he took over as CEO at GE because he wasn't willing to work with people who were either not high performers or people he believed would not support his vision. Chief Stamper of the Seattle Police Department challenged every leader in the organization to get on board with the vision, values, and plan—or get off! Most got on board; some got off or were asked to get off. Most people would agree it is a better place to work now. There are still a few grumblers, as always. In a small organization, it is possible for the implementation planning to take place in one leadership team and then be delegated to team leaders.

In larger organizations, it is likely that each leader will do implementation planning in each department and meet with the senior leadership team to insure cross-functional team communication and effectiveness. Once goals are set, implementation planning can take place. Let's look at the skill that is involved, and the process of planning itself.

TL Skill #45 Implementation Planning: *Specifying and Implementing Steps, Dates, and People to Expedite the Achievement of Goals*

This skill involves formulating a set of steps that translates the general goals into action-oriented language to make them more achievable and exciting.

Being as specific as possible about these steps, timelines, and responsibilities for action can bring team members together and cause a synergistic, energy-releasing effect that gets results.

The increased energy released by careful implementation planning is well worth the trouble and time it takes to formulate such plans. A thorough plan makes it possible for you to clarify—in the minds of team members—who will do what, why they will do it, and how they will do it. A brainstorming approach is often most effective in stimulating a discussion of a wide range of options for possible implementation.

An example of an effective goals and planning sheet is presented below for you to consider. This sample of what Bill Bean calls a Chronological Action Plan List, is a key step to turning carefully crafted goals into action and results. Without translating goals into clear, time-bounded, person-responsible actions, it is unlikely that disciplined implementation will ever occur. If we carefully plan our interventions, we will create more effective scenarios and implementation will be enhanced. Some planners even use project planning software to track the implementation of their strategic plan. Here is an example of what a plan might look like.

The list of action plans demonstrated on the following page, once developed, can then be sorted according to due dates. This then becomes a vital tool for use by the leadership of the organization for tracking and managing the ongoing strategic initiatives of the company or group. It provides a simple method to stay focused on a monthly basis in a way that maximizes clarity, specificity, and accountability for action.

TL Skill #46 Strategic Plan and Team Performance

For some reason, the moon shows up every month as some kind of reminder that a cycle has occurred. We have monthly financial statements, invoices, bills, etc. How about a monthly meeting to discuss what we all said we were going to do to move the strategic plan ahead and to review and improve our team performance? Even among committed partners, this is extremely difficult to do. Those who discipline themselves to do this, however, will enjoy the following results.

1. You will celebrate together the various accomplishments you have achieved.
2. You will track how realistic your plan is and make course corrections early.
3. You will keep minutes up to date so that all team members have a brief record of plans and results.
4. You and other leaders will report about what you said you would do to hold one another accountable.
5. You will balance the long-term plan with the demands of daily operations.
6. You will keep the "big picture" view of your organization and discuss how to improve current operations and prepare for the shifting future.

XYZ Company Chronological Action Plan List (unsorted)

Goal #	Action #	Action Plan	By Who	By When
1.		**Create Comprehensive Marketing Plan**		
	1A.	Analyze XYZ product performance and profitablity matrix and develop recommendations	Carl	June
	1B.	Develop international strategy with selected joint venture partners and selected country priorites and next actions	Jim	July
	1C.	Develop hiring plan and timetable for new Marketing Director	Mary	July
2.		**Refocus Total Quality Management Plans**		
	2A.	Assess current state of XYZ TQM process with Business Unit leaders and identify key areas for remedial action	Jack	Sept.
	2B.	Make simple company-wide announcement of refocused TQM direction	Jack	Oct.
3.		**Develop Formal Cost-Control Program**		
	3A	Analyze current XYZ budgets and develop recommendations	Helen	May
	3B.	Design plan for transforming Business Units into Cost Centers	Larry	July
4.		**Develop Hiring and Recruiting Plan**		
	4A	Identify new hire volume requirements for next 18 months	Jane	Feb.
	4.B	Design new recruitment and employee-interviewing system	Jane	Mar.

The globally competitive marketplace has driven the excellence movement. Now, we must do excellent strategic planning and operational implementation of the plan or, as Tom Peters said, "we may die in the marketplace." I believe that Bill Bean's Monthly Executive Review meeting (Bean, 1993, p. 235) is more important than anything we can do to insure that implementation is achieved in the most effective way possible. I have had more success in building executive teams in the context of this type of meeting than anywhere else because we develop the team, learn the skills of teaming, and get the job done at the same time. I have seen this in operation with my own clients and a number of Bill's clients.

I have also seen many, if not most, strategic planners and well-meaning, busy executives fail to teach and install a review system that really functions on a monthly basis. This is a matter of critical importance. If we have designed a beautiful and versatile plan but do not implement it, what use is it? Above you will see a sample agenda from Bill Bean illustrates how the relationship between planning and implementation can be strengthened to achieve maximum potential.

To build the monthly executive review into your executive team's agenda, it is necessary to understand the benefits and the process. Outlined below are a list of the benefits.

1. It stimulates getting the job done.
2. It's extremely time-efficient— one to two hours per month.
3. It insures that the strategic plan becomes a living plan, continuously updated with new action plans as necessary.
4. The right people are kept up to date with the right information at the right time, with the right level of executive focus and individual accountability.

> **The globally competitive marketplace has driven the excellence movement. Now, we must do excellent strategic planning and operational implementation of the plan or, as Tom Peters said, "we may die in the marketplace."**

5. You have the benefits of a monthly check of the two critical components of performance: monthly operational performance and strategic action plan implementation success. The process involves having those leaders responsible for the implementation of the strategic plan meet together in person or via teleconference or televideo conference to review the following agenda items.

XYZ Company Monthly Executive Review

Agenda

I. **Review of Key indicators**
   A. **Financial iIndicators**
   B. **Business indicators**
   C. **Other indicators**

II. **"Two-Minute" Drills**
   A. **Each person, key highlights from his/her area**
   B. **New issues to be addressed in plan (see IV.A)**

III. **Review of Strategic Action Plans**
   A. **Past-due (done yet?)**
   B. **Current (on time?)**
   C. **Upcoming (on track?)**

IV. **Address New Items/Adjust Strategic Plan**
   A. **Discuss new items, reach closure**
   B. **Assign new action plans as needed**

Adapted from Bill Bean and Ron Ford, *Turbocharging Your Business*. Used by permission.

TL Skill #47   TQM Leadership: *Leading Teams Toward Continuous Learning for Continuous Improvement*

As we have said in various parts of this book, we must build a leadership organization that can have its act together enough to implement such complex change as Total Quality Management (TQM) to become what Senge has called a learning organization. Senge describes the new leader as a "designer, steward, and teacher responsible for building organizations where people continually expand their capabilities to understand complexity, clarify vision, and improve shared mental models." He says that they are responsible for making sure that learning happens.

Whether or not you choose to implement a full-blown TQM program as it is done by this theorist or other theorists is not as important as whether or not you make the commitment to learning. We need to commit to learning what customers want, what our staff wants, and how we can continuously do better to meet and exceed customers' expectations so we create what Blanchard calls "raving fans."

TQM theory states that quality is defined by the customer. TQM is a systems approach to being accountable for checking to make sure we are in communication and we are being responsive to both internal and external "customers." We want to create return customers who are "wowed" by the way we treat them. We push the golden rule—of treating others the way we would like to be treated—to the maximum. TQM is characterized by this customer focus, total organizational involvement, continuous improvement of processes, and fact-based decision-making.

A transforming leader leads a quality movement within his or her own organization—with his executive teammates and with his partners—to do most of the work These people used to be called employees. We do not have the space to go into the detail needed to do justice to introduce you to TQM. It would be important for you to learn more about it. We recommend you consider reading *Juran On Quality by Design* (New York: Free Press, 1992) or read the most recent and innovative addition to the literature on TQM Leadership by Michael Cowley and Ellen Domb (1997). These will give you a more in-depth understanding of the nature and applicability of the quality improvement processes that have revolutionized—not evolutionized—modern business in the past 30 years.

TL Skill #48 Building Accountability

It is possible to install accountability at all levels within the organization so that everyone experiences what I call "no-doubt contracting." This means that all interchanges, both verbal and written, are characterized by agreements between people.

For example, all job descriptions can become working agreements if they are perceived as living documents that describe what we promise to do for one another, what we hope to accomplish, what roles we will play, etc. Having fair, equitable, nondiscriminatory personnel policies is another way to be accountable. It is also possible that all partnership agreements, contracts with clients, and customers—both internal and external—are a reflection of agreements that took place in conversations characterized by two-way communication and mutual commitment. To be accountable, you can use executive monthly review meetings and initiate TQM initiatives. In other words, no-doubt, no-surprise contracts and commitments can become the dominant way of life in your organization. And everyone wants this.

The International Standards Organization (ISO) wanted accountability and no-doubt contracting among countries when it started the ISO 9000 series in 1945 as a preferred way of doing international business. As a result of this commitment over fifty years ago, you may have to certify and register your company with ISO in the future to engage in certain types of international business because some of your customers won't do business with you unless you are registered.

Accountability is a Part of Honest Leadership that Leads to Credibility

Jim Kouzes and Barry Posner, in *Credibility* (1993), share strong research evidence that this may be the most important factor that determines success as a leader. They quote a study by the Columbia University Graduate School of Business that surveyed over 1,500 top executives in twenty countries. The study reports that "ethics are rated most highly among the personal characteristics needed by the ideal CEO in the year 2000. Respondents expect their CEO to be above reproach." In addition to honesty, being forward-looking, inspiring, and competent were among the top characteristics Kouzes and Posner found to be preferred by those who may be willing to follow someone's lead.

Based on the above, it seems clear it is best for you to be seen as honest, caring, competent, inspired, informed, knowledgeable, capable, likeable, in a position of authority, and trustworthy by team members—if you are to be given the trust you need to unify and move a team in a particular direction. This can first be accomplished by making sure that you, in fact, are leading a team that you have some real ability and knowledge to lead. Tell about yourself openly, but not boastfully. The team members need to know something about your background and how you deserve to be in this leadership position because of your confidence, experience, knowledge, or power.

Kotter (1979) studied many of the ways leaders gain credibility and power in teams and organizations. He illustrates how many of the "success" behaviors of influential leaders can be learned. Your personal credibility will be better established if you can follow Kotter's general guidelines.

1. State your own purpose (based on your own inner clarity) for being in your role as leader. Let team members know you are in harmony with and attempting to achieve your organization's purposes in ways that uphold the organization's values.
2. Communicate and check for the validity of the needs and wants you hope to meet. In this way, you will gain awareness of the degree of real or imagined consensus about these critical issues. This can save you the embarrassment of attempting to meet needs or solve problems only perceived as relevant by a few.
3. Communicate how you intend to work in a respectful and helpful manner. This is critical if you want people to feel comfortable and have a sense of trust in you. If they perceive you as a potential threat or a noncaring person, you won't get their support to accomplish goals.
4. Value the worth and potential contributions of the other members of the team. Look for opportunities where team members can gain various kinds of recognition or rewards for being involved in the workgroup's endeavors.
5. Model good team-member and leader behaviors, which include all of the communication and problem-management skills outlined in the previous two chapters. In this way, you will gain acceptance and trust more readily.

In the next chapter, we will discuss how the knowledge and skills presented in previous chapters can be applied in a creative, flexible, and responsive manner through "style, role, and skill-shifting." It will assist you to develop the versatility skills so important for transforming leadership success.

References

B. M. **Bass**, *Leadership Beyond Performance Expectations.* (New York: Free Press, 1985).

B. **Bean** and R. **Ford**, *Turbocharging Your Business.* (Cardiff, CA: Strategia, 1996).

J. M. **Burns**, *Leadership.* (New York: Harper & Row, 1978).

P. B. **Crosby**, *Quality Is Free: The Art of Making Quality Certain.* (New York: McGraw Hill, 1979).

M. **Cowley** and E. **Domb,** *Beyond Strategic Vision: Effective Corporate Action with Hoshin Planning.* (Newton, MA: Butterworth-Heinemann, 1997).

G. **Egan**, *Change Agent Skills(B): Managing Innovation & Change.* (San Diego, California: University Associates, Inc., 1988).

G. R. **Kilmer**, "Consumer Survey as Needs Assessment Method: A Case Study." *Evaluation and Program Planning,* 1978, I, 286-292.

J. **Kotter**, *Power in Management.* (New York: AMACOM, 1979).

R. **Menzel**, "A Taxonomy of Change Agent Skills." *The Journal of European Training,* 1975, 4(5), 289-291.

Robert K. **Menzel**, "A Taxonomy of Change Agent Skills," *Journal of European Training,* 1975, 4(5), 289-291.

G. **Morgan**, *Riding The Waves of Change: Developing Managerial Competencies for a Turbulent World.* (San Francisco: Jossey-Bass Publishers, 1988).

T. **Peters** and N. **Austin**, *A Passion for Excellence.* (New York: Random House, 1985).

R. **Quinn**, *Beyond Rational Management: Mastering the Paradoxes and Competing Demands of High Performance.* (San Francisco: Jossey-Bass, 1988).

L. **Schlesinger**, R. **Eccles**, and J. **Gabarro**, *Managerial Behavior in Organizations: Texts, Cases, and Readings.* (New York: McGraw-Hill, 1983), 486.

Chapter 8

THE SKILLS OF VERSATILITY IN STYLE, SKILL, AND ROLE

Think about the productivity of employees who bring motivation, imagination, and energy to their work—who have spirit. If you wish all your employees were that way, you know that work spirit is a serious, not soft, subject.

Sharon L. Connelly

Introduction

It is one thing to compose or begin to play a piece of music; it is quite another to practice and develop one's potential enough to play well. Quality, productivity, motivation, imagination, the willingness to sweat and persist in the face of stress and occasional exhaustion—all these factors, when blended together, can produce unforgettable performances. People who are willing to "go all out" are doing so for good reasons. Someone has mobilized them with hopes, ideals, and expectations of rewards and has instilled in them some enthusiasm. Star athletes are an example of those who train until their maximum potential is unleashed.

In a similar way, *Transforming Leadership* has the potential to empower leaders and followers to achieve higher levels of impact to motivate and move people to take new action, reach for new levels of achievement and reward, and simultaneously facilitate the development of all those involved together in an endeavor. To achieve these heights, leaders do not necessarily have to be charismatic. But they do have to be effective in shifting to meet the needs of people and the changing demands of fast-moving surroundings.

The *Transforming Leadership* skills that will be discussed in this chapter include the following.

What we want to accomplish in this chapter can be summarized in the following specific objective statements.

1. Learn about *Transforming Leadership*'s facilitative, "style, role, and skill-shifting" approach, which leaders can use to facilitate individual, group, or organization development.
2. Learn about the developmental stages of a group or organization so you can assess what interventions are appropriate in each stage and thereby intervene more effectively.
3. Learn the steps and processes to design and set up a group or organization.
4. Explore the future of *Transforming Leadership* as a new practice of designing and managing change.

Max DePree (1989) in his fascinating book titled, *Leadership Is An Art*, states:

."...it is fundamental that leaders endorse a concept of the value of persons. This begins with an understanding of the diversity of people's gifts and talents and skills. Understanding and accepting diversity enables us to see that each of us is needed. It also enables us to begin to think about being abandoned to the strengths of others, of admitting that we cannot know or do everything. The simple act of recognizing diversity in corporate life helps us to connect the great variety of gifts that people bring to the work and service of the organization. Diversity allows each of us to contribute in a special way, to make our special talents a part of the corporate effort."

Essential to the *Transforming Leadership* approach are concepts that relate to the acceptance and integration of diversity in others: the concepts of "style-shifting," "role-shifting," and "skill-shifting." Learning to recognize different personal styles in others' behaviors can lead to more appropriate leadership responses, and can bring forth the best in others. Moreover, trying to shift roles appropriately—which also involves shifting sets of skills—to respond accurately to individual differences and preferences can improve communication, problem management, learning, and leadership effectiveness. Thus, style, role, and skill-shifting are presented together to provide a more

> **Essential to the *Transforming Leadership* approach are concepts that relate to the acceptance and integration of diversity in others: the concepts of "style-shifting," "role-shifting," and "skill-shifting."**

comprehensive and versatile model to subtly capture many of the important aspects of leadership complexity. The model is defined, however, so that it will be practical and applicable in a wide range of settings.

With the new understanding you gain in this chapter, you will find yourself responding more flexibly—and therefore more appropriately—to others and to situations. This chapter builds upon the knowledge and skills in previous chapters so you can develop expertise and even finesse in expressing your own individual approach to leadership—especially when your goal is to facilitate group and organization development. The final thrust of this chapter will be to examine how to do more than just develop a group or organization. It presents some direction on how to transform a well-functioning group or organization into a dynamic one.

> **Organizations do not have a life of their own separate from the individuals in them. Wittingly or unwittingly, it is especially the leaders who shape the climate that influences performance and morale.**

The Impact of Leadership in Teams and Organizations

Organizations do not have a life of their own separate from the individuals in them. Wittingly or unwittingly, it is especially the leaders who shape the climate that influences performance and morale. They can and do have a tremendous influence on how people think, feel, and behave. If you look back into the history of your own life in the context of the social systems that have surrounded you, you will become more aware of how many social factors and certain leaders have had profound effects on your own development. When we consider the staggering impact that all social systems—and especially the leaders in these systems—can potentially have on the development or destruction of the morale and fabric of people, the need to develop innovative approaches to design and develop positive organizational spirit becomes evident. As Bass (1985) has concluded from his research: "...transformational leadership will contribute in an incremental way to extra effort, effectiveness, and satisfaction with the leader as well as to appraise subordinate performance beyond expectations..."

Transforming Leadership moves the development of a leader one step further toward effectiveness and competency. It goes beyond communicating the important quality of charisma, the kindness of empathy, the insight of intellectual stimulation, and the benefits of providing rewards. *Transforming Leadership* proposes to develop the core of a leader into a more versatile and creative master of positive change. This leader will then design and manage the quality, health, and performance of an organization or group.

Style, Role, and Skill-Shifting: Versatile Wisdom for Inducing Positive Change

It is of prime importance in the development of such mastery, as is suggested above, that leaders develop not only skills, but versatility, as well. The fluid concept of "shifting" styles, roles, and skills was adopted to capture the essence of the artistry and intelligence-in-action that *Transforming Leadership* asserts is so vital. As we move into examining the complexity of effective leadership, you will learn to see your own behavior more keenly within the context of the overall environment. Further definition of terms for each of the three aspects of style-shifting will assist you to understand some of the basic ideas that underlie the notion of "shifting."

Style-shifting is the ability to assess the personal style of another person and adjust your responses to better fit what is most effective in achieving your purposes, and to do this genuinely, without manipulation, while meeting the needs of the other person.

Role-shifting is the ability to recognize which of three major roles is most appropriate in any given moment to thereby alternate among communication, counseling, and consulting interventions as the situation or person requires.

Skill-shifting is the ability to move gracefully between three different sets of skills to accomplish various tasks, depending upon the circumstance or the developmental level of a person, group, or organization. As you skill-shift more appropriately, you will subtly increase your effectiveness in each of the three major roles.

It is important to develop the ability to act consciously and intentionally but also to spontaneously "oscillate" among and within each of the three roles and sets of skills. This could seem to make the process of leadership complex and difficult. Of course, it is complex, but the style-shift approach breaks down some of the complex reality of leadership behaviors into small enough "chunks" so we can learn each part before integrating it into a more fluid practice.

Effective leadership requires the ability to deal with complexity, break it into manageable pieces, intervene with a continuous alertness to the impact we are making to correct course, and respond afresh to a changing environment. Continuous vigilance to the impact of your interventions will better enable you to shift styles, roles, or skills again and again as it becomes appropriate to do so.

Transforming Leadership's Style, Role, and Skill-Shifting Model

Transforming Leadership is built upon a metamodel for lifelong personal and professional development that consists of several skills training modules, the skills for which were outlined in the previous chapters. A new and practical synthesis of the various areas of skill is what the style-shift model attempts to present.

The remainder of this chapter is divided into four sections:

1. Introduction to Personal Style Theory and its application to *Transforming Leadership* in the form of style-shifting.
2. Role-shifting to increase your effectiveness in recognizing and shifting into appropriate role behaviors.
3. Skill-shifting to increase your effectiveness by recognizing and shifting into the appropriate skills to be used in different situations.
4. Application of these various skills to develop and even transform a group or organization into one that functions and performs more dynamically and successfully.

The shifting model, in its most basic form, can be expressed visually in the following way.

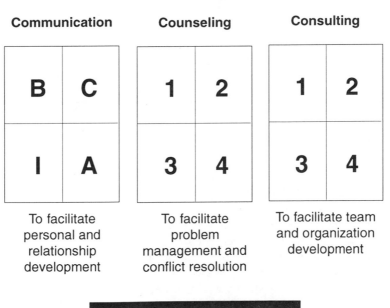

The Basic "Shifting" Model

Communication	Counseling	Consulting
B C	1 2	1 2
I A	3 4	3 4
To facilitate personal and relationship development	To facilitate problem management and conflict resolution	To facilitate team and organization development

Further Explanation

In the **communication** part of the model above, the B, C, I, and A letters represent different quadrants of personal style (to be explained further below). If we are aware of them, they will tend to influence how we approach an individual person or even how we approach a group or organization.

In the **counseling** part of the model, the numbers 1, 2, 3, and 4 represent levels of task-specific functioning or development of the individual, which provide indications of how you might best approach that particular person for optimum appropriateness and effectiveness (as indicated in the chapter on counseling skills).

In the **consulting** part of the model, the numbers 1, 2, 3, and 4 represent stages of group or organization development that require different approaches and skills in optimize the results you desire.

Therefore, when utilizing the model above to plan for more effective interventions, we can take into consideration the following:
1. The factor of individual style.
2. The appropriate role we should be playing in the situation we are in.
3. An individual, group, or organization's stage of development and functioning.

Style-Shifting for More Effective Leadership Impact

Skills #49 and #50: Assessment of Personal Styles and Style Shifting

Now we will examine the issue of personal style assessment and style-shifting into various types of behavioral responses to match the needs and preferences of others—which will increase your effectiveness when relating or solving problems with them. It should be pointed out that style-shifting can also be used with groups and organizations as well as with individuals.

What Personal Style Means

People tend to approach and interact with their surroundings (i.e., people, things, situations, and time) based upon their perceptions of them. This part of the personality superstructure is believed, by both Anderson and Robinson (1988), to be largely predisposed from birth, further conditioned throughout life, and tends to strongly influence individual perception of and response to the environment throughout a person's life. If this kind of natural "filter" through which each individual perceives the environment does exist, then it is important to identify and specify what it is. Personal Style Theory asserts that such a filter does indeed exist, and attempts to provide theoretical constructs

Behavioral — ACTION

This style dimension is characterized by a strong tendency toward altering the environment in a way that will achieve well-thought-out goals. Therefore, people who naturally operate mainly from this quadrant of style are likely to seem self-assured and driven, many times oblivious to other people's feelings and on a track of their own. When their vision is shared by a group, they are often seen as heroes and leaders because they tend to forge ahead to meet challenges with unusual fearlessness. This style position by itself is extroverted and can withstand greater stress. It does not favor artistic, aesthetic, or emotional modes of operating, but prefers a planned method by which previously defined goals and results are achieved. In this style, there is a clear sense of acting upon the environment to achieve these results.

Cognitive — ANALYSIS

This style dimension is characterized by a strong tendency to avoid being influenced negatively by people or environmental influences. This type moves toward goals often perceived as requirements of others in positions of authority. Attention to details and being on the alert for potential dangers or inconsistencies enable people with this style to maintain a better position of security and control. People with this style tend to avoid emotional intensity and unpredictability; they may especially need intimacy because they find that trust in others is not easily attained. This style position by itself is introverted, being more sensitive to stimulation. It does not prefer the sensory, emotional modes of operating, but tends toward logical analysis and correct performance of tasks, with an additional interest in the fine arts.

Affective — EXPRESSION

This style dimension is characterized by a strong tendency to intuitively explore the environment and interact with it to assess the outcome. Spontaneous exploration and expression of ideas and feelings mark the natural tendencies of this style. People with a natural tendency toward this dimension of style are often attempting to influence others through the creative media of speaking, writing, dance, art, or music. They would like to sell others on themselves, and ideas or products that they believe will be helpful. They will go out of their way to help others, even if it inconveniences them because often they believe in the value of people. By itself, this style is extroverted, not being easily overstimulated by the environment. It does not favor the analytical modes of operating, but is more intuitive and creative in its way of functioning.

Interpersonal — HARMONY

This style dimension is characterized by a strong tendency to adapt to people and surroundings to promote harmony and comfort for self and others. The approach to life and people in a practical, friendly, and naturally warm manner is typical of this style dimension. Adaptation to all other styles is a way of life, providing the desired security and balance needed and preferred by those who score higher in this style dimension. A desire to support others to gain a sense of validation and approval is a natural tendency. This style position by itself is introverted, being more sensitive to stimulation. It favors a practical balance of both the logical and intuitive modes of functioning, thereby avoiding extremes. In this style, there can also be a tendency toward stubbornness, especially if others are being overbearing.

that delineate and explain such a phenomenon. Without "pigeonholing" people, the term "personal style" reflects each individual's predisposed and usually preferred way of behaving.

I have defined personal style in the above-referenced manual (1988) as, "a person's habitual way of behaving, or predisposition to act, in everyday situations with most people." Robinson further defined it as, "a person's natural predisposition to perceive, approach, and interact with the environment." Thus, personal style includes characteristics of personality and behavior.

> **People who are versatile in their approaches to others will consider the individual style preferences of others and tend, therefore, to be more versatile and effective than those who do not.**

1. Preferred manner of accomplishing a task
2. Preferred manner of reacting to individuals
3. Strengths and difficulties characteristic of his or her unique style
4. Natural reaction to stressful events
5. Preferred manner of functioning in group
6. Propensity to lead or follow
7. Predisposition to be extroverted or introverted
8. Predisposition to be task vs. relationship-oriented
9. Predisposition to be right or left-brain-oriented
10. Predisposition to be verbal or nonverbal

When we can understand others in such a detailed and specific manner, we are in a better position to respond to them in ways that lead them in directions they are more naturally inclined to go, and to assign them to tasks at which they are more likely to succeed.

The Process of Style-Shifting

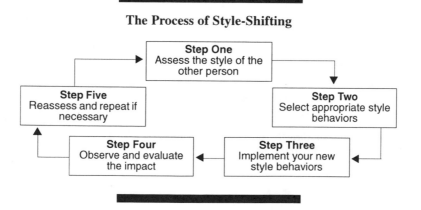

Step One
Assess the style of the other person

Step Two
Select appropriate style behaviors

Step Three
Implement your new style behaviors

Step Four
Observe and evaluate the impact

Step Five
Reassess and repeat if necessary

Personal Style Assessment

People who are versatile in their approaches to others will consider the individual style preferences of others and tend, therefore, to be more versatile and effective than those who do not.

To accurately assess another person's style, you need to be able to observe and predict how a person—or a group—will tend to act. If you have a model for style assessment, you can observe and listen to a person and thereby determine which two or three quadrants of personal style are preferred by that individual.

Since it is a critical factor in the practice of *Transforming Leadership* to appreciate the unique tendencies, needs, and preferences of other people, groups, or organizations, it is important that we become more proficient in assessing others' style tendencies so our responses will be much more appropriate and well received.

For you to gain a general assessment of your own style, you will see descriptions of four general quadrants of personal style extracted from a more extensive instrument that I have developed with Everett Robinson (1988). When you have read these descriptions of the four style tendencies, you will be able to gain a general picture of your own style tendencies, which have an impact on how you tend to approach others. You can also do a complete *Personal Style Indicator* on-line interactively at http://www.crgleader.com, and get an *In-depth Interpretation*, as well. The paper-based learning tool is also available to those who prefer that medium for training groups. Also available for further reading is Robinson's (1997) book on personal style titled, *Why Aren't You More Like Me?*

Now that you have read through the four personal style dimension descriptions, you will do a general assessment of your personal style. After reading the instructions, read through the following page, "Understanding Your General Style Tendencies." This information will assist you to become more familiar with your own and others' general style tendencies.

Instructions for General Style Assessment:

1. Place the number "1" in the quadrant (where you see the word "score") that you believe best describes you.
2. Place the number "2" in the quadrant that describes the style behaviors you would likely shift into next.
3. Place the number "3" in the quadrant that describes behaviors less typical of you.
4. Place the number "4" in the quadrant that least describes how you would act.

Understanding Your General Style Tendencies

Behavioral—*Action*   ☐
Score:

General Orientation:

To tasks:	wants results now
To people:	seeks authority
To problems:	is tactical, strategic
To stress:	doubles efforts
To time:	sees future and present

Typical Strengths:

Acts rapidly to get results
Is inventive and productive
Shows endurance under stress
Is driven to achieve goals
Can take authority boldly

Common Difficulties:

Can be too forceful or impatient
Can often think his/her way is best
Can be insensitive to others
Can be manipulative or coercive
Can be lonely or fatigued

Cognitive—*Analysis*   ☐
Score:

General Orientation:

To tasks:	wants quality
To people:	seeks security
To problems:	analyzes data
To stress:	withdraws
To time:	sees past and future

Typical Strengths:

Acts cautiously to avoid errors
Engages in critical analysis
Seeks to create a low-stress climate
Wants to insure quality-control
Can follow directives and standards

Common Difficulties:

Can bog down in details and lose time
Can be too critical or finicky
Can be overly sensitive to feedback
Can seem to be lacking in courage
Can be too self-sufficient, alone

Affective—*Expression*   ☐
Score:

General Orientation:

To tasks:	people come first
To people:	seeks to influence
To problems:	intuitive and creative
To stress:	escapes from it
To time:	present and future

Typical Strengths:

Acts creatively on intuition
Is sensitive to others' feelings
Is resilient in times of stress
Develops a network of contacts
Is often willing to help others

Common Difficulties:

Can lose track of time
Can "overburn" and overindulge
Can be too talkative
Can lose objectivity, be emotional
Can be self-orientated, self-assured

Interpersonal—*Harmony*   ☐
Score:

General Orientation:

To tasks:	perfoms reliably
To people:	seeks to help others
To problems:	gives practical solutions
To stress:	adjusts to it
To time:	sees present

Typical Strengths:

Promotes harmony and balance
Is reliable and consistent
Tries to adapt to stress
Sees the obvious things others miss
Is often easygoing and warm

Common Difficulties:

Can be too easygoing and accepting
Can allow others to take advantage of him/her
Can become bitter if unappreciated
Can be low in self-worth
Can be too dependent on others

Now that you have reviewed your general style tendencies and have become more familiar with the four quadrants of style, you can begin to explore the value of assessing the styles of others and shifting into the various style behaviors they would likely prefer. Keep in mind you have done only a general estimate of your personal style

Assessing Others' Styles and Style-Shifting

According to my field research with Robinson (1988) and the experimental investigations of Merrill and Reid (1981), we believe that learning to assess the personal styles of others, and to shift into an interpersonal style that best allows others to receive and understand your messages, is an often overlooked and effective skill that can be learned in a relatively short period of time.

To learn some basics of how to assess others' styles and practice this style-shifting skill, please see the four-quadrant grid, titled "Style-Shifting Guidelines" on the next page that offers general direction and hints for style-shifting effectively with the four style types.

Instructions: Place a person's name (whom you know well) in the quadrant or two near the guidelines that you believe could assist you to approach that person more effectively.

General Style-Shifting Considerations

If we examine the various needs and preferences of each style type, we can see why it is so easy to make mistakes out of ignorance with such individual differences among people. Below are some general considerations that can act as guidelines for planning a response to the four types of people.

Behavioral Action-Oriented: If you assess that a person is mainly action-oriented in style, then you would give this person "bottomline" facts in summary fashion and challenging assignments and opportunities. Don't distract the person with too many details or personal issues; get on with the "task" or job at hand; don't challenge him or her personally but provide brief evidence to support your challenge, and respect this person's high need for cooperation from others—these interpersonal behaviors appear especially important to this type of person.

Cognitive, Analytical: If you assess that a person has mainly an analytical, introverted style, then you would provide detailed and comprehensive factual information, give ample time for decision-making, announce changes in advance, respect any areas of special competency, and show appreciation for efforts and accomplishments—these things appear to be especially important to people with this style.

Interpersonal, Harmonious: If you assess that a person has mainly a need for a harmonious approach to people and the environment, you would

Behavioral Styles *Action*

Wants others to:
Provide summarized facts
Respect his/her judgements
Support him/her to reach goals
Cope with unwanted details
Cooperate with him/her

Gets most upset when others:
Are too slow
Get in his/her way
Talk too much
Try to be in control
Waste time

Responds best to:
Direct, honest confrontations
Logical, rational arguments
Fair, open competition
An impersonal approach
Getting results quickly

Cognitive Styles *Analysis*

Wants others to:
Give detailed information
Ask for his/her opinions
Not interrupt his/her work
Treat him/her with respect
Do quality work the first time

Gets most upset when others:
Move ahead too quickly
Don't give him/her enough time
Are vague in their communications
Don't appreciate his/her efforts
Are too personal or emotional

Responds best to:
Diplomatic, factual, challenges
Arguments based on known facts
Freedom from competitive strain
Friendliness, not personal contact
Doing tasks well and completely

Affective Styles *Expression*

Wants others to:
Give him/her opportunity to speak
Admire his/her achievements
Be influenced in some ways
Take care of details
Value his/her opinions

Gets most upset when others:
Are too task-orientated
Confine them to one place
Are not interested in them
Compete for and win attention
Seem judgemental of them

Responds best to:
Being challenged in a kind way
An influencing, sales approach
Enjoyable competitions
Affection and personal contact
Having a good time

Interpersonal Styles *Harmony*

Wants others to:
Make him/her feel like he/she belongs
Appreciate him/her for efforts
Be kind, considerate, thoughtful
Trust him/her with important tasks
Value him/her as a person

Gets most upset when others:
Get angry, blow up, or are mean
Demand that he/she be too mobile
Take advantage of his/her goodness
Are manipulative or unfair
Are judgemental of others

Responds best to:
A gradual approach to challenging
A factual, practical approach
Comfortable, friendly times
Respecting of his/her boundaries
Conventional, established ways

shift into providing social behaviors that show recognition and appreciation of services and efforts provided, offer a safe relationship climate relatively free of judgments and high pressures to perform, and provide opportunities for success by service to others instead of achievement of results—people with this style seem to appreciate and respond well to this approach.

Affective, Expressive: If you assess that a person has mainly this type of outgoing style orientation, then you could best relate by giving recognition for achievements and self-presentations (performances, clothes, successes); listen more than you speak; provide opportunity for promotions and for earning money, traveling, and mobility; and do not supervise too closely or you can kill creativity in this type of person.

Developing Style Versatility: a Case Study

The Case of Sandy: General Manager for a west coast paper distribution company that sells and delivers paper to printing companies.

Sandy's Profile:
High Behavioral (Action) and Cognitive (Analysis). Low Interpersonal (Harmony) and Affective (Expressive).

Sandy's Personal Style Graph

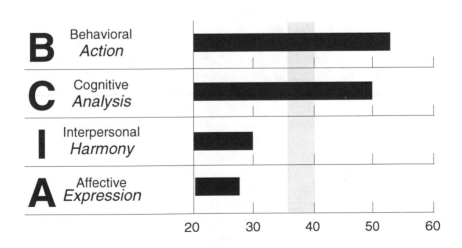

Sandy's Strengths:
1. Often gets quality results the first time
2. Can process large volumes of information
3. Can make objective decisions using a large data base of information from many sources
4. Challenges others toward excellence
5. Acts as a model for others
6. Is inventive and original
7. Is careful to avoid pitfalls
8. Provides guidelines others can use
9. Insures quality control
10. Endures and persists when under stress

Sandy's Difficult Areas:
1. Is impatient with lower performers
2. Can appear smug and "know-it-all-ish"
3. Can be insensitive to others' feelings
4. Can be lonely and fatigued
5. Can be too critical
6. Can be "touchy" with critical feedback
7. Can be too self-sufficient
8. Can lack in courage to face emotions
9. Can get lost in details before deciding
10. Can seem to be manipulative or coercive

Upon reading his In-depth Interpretation, Sandy laughed. He said that the description of him was better than 90 percent accurate and that he became more aware of some things about himself that he figured were often "blind spots."

The Problem: Sandy is in charge of a salesforce of nine people who tend to be predominantly high in the Affective/Expressive and Interpersonal/ Harmony dimensions of style. They resent Sandy's air of superiority and demands of high performance without any promises of rewards. They need recognition and appreciation from Sandy, but he rarely has time to give such "soft" rewards. He has only rewarded people for sales results that affect the "bottom line." He has, over the years, demonstrated inflexibility in his approach to others and gets really irritable at people who don't accept his domineering approach, putting them down in front of others. The increases in company profitability were 3 percent and 5 percent during the past two years, respectively, not enough to keep up with inflation. The turnover rate in the sales division and in the secretary and receptionist positions has been over 34 percent per year, primarily because these employees have had frequent contact with Sandy—and as a result, reported that their primary reason for seeking work elsewhere was to avoid working for him. Sandy's wife left him three months ago.

The Intervention: Sandy took a one-day *Personal Style Indicator* workshop and learned that his relationships with the people in his life have been characterized by a rather self-oriented and caustic approach, because he often got short-term results by intimidating people in subtle ways. As a result of the workshop, and the feedback Sandy got from his wife and the other managers just below him, he decided to change the way he treated the high A and I sales and support staff (and his A-I marriage partner); to eliminate "put-down" statements and behaviors from his management style; add more interpersonal behaviors such as expressing appreciation for a job well done, host an awards ceremony every six months for those in the company who achieved agreed-upon reasonable levels of performance; institute an employee-of-the month recognition program for exceptional performance beyond what is expected; and institute interpersonal skills training and team-building sessions for him and his management staff.

The Results: After one year, the turnover rate had decreased to 7 percent from the previous 34 percent. Two-way communication improved between Sandy and his employees at all levels. Problems were solved that had been previously "swept under the carpet" because most people avoided Sandy altogether. Overall profitability of the company increased 14 percent. Sandy's wife decided to go back and try to reestablish their marriage relationship.

This is a dramatic example of how Sandy's having developed some interpersonal skills and developing versatility in his approach to people with styles opposite to his had a dramatic effect on the performance of his subordinates.

It is important to realize that style shows up in organizational orientations and government leaders' approaches to politics and international relations, and that certain style tendencies can pervade whole societies. For example, President Clinton is often perceived as demonstrating an Affective Expressive and Behavioral Action orientation, acting upon the environment in an assertive and highly verbal manner. The United States and Great Britain, as cultures, are often perceived quite differently from one another. The English, however, have described the U.S. as appearing to be more "bizarre" (expressive) than the U.K.; and the U.K. is described by Americans to tend toward an analytical approach, being more reserved and "stuffy." The English can be heard saying that the Americans are too impulsive and run headlong into situations without thinking through the consequences first.

Of course, England and France have been experiencing "clashes" of style for centuries, in the same way that English-speaking and French-speaking Canada have (although, in general, Canada could be seen, like Switzerland, as having an Interpersonal Harmony orientation). The English find the free expressiveness of the French to be overwhelming and even revolting (in the extreme). The stuffiness and formality of the English make the French feel restricted, giving them the impression that the English are "phony." Modern Japan could be seen as having a more complex combination of Action, Analytical, and Interpersonal orientations (with an emphasis on the

Interpersonal). German culture would likely be seen as action and analysis in its orientation.

Style assessment is complex and difficult, but that style differences can cause difficulties between people cannot be denied. Learning to shift approaches to people can increase our effectiveness with them, reduce conflict, enhance leadership credibility, and facilitate relationship development.

In the next section of this chapter, we will examine the nature of the three major roles—and the tasks appropriate to accomplish in each role the transforming leader fulfills. It is important to keep in mind that a continuing awareness of "style" has a catalytic effect when a person is functioning in all three of the major roles of communicator, counselor, and consultant.

Role-Shifting For Greater Effectiveness and Appropriateness

Skills #51 and #52: Assessment of Roles and Role-Shifting

Appropriate role-shifting makes the leader's responses more effective and, in turn, a follower's response is often more favorable. Proper role-shifting as a foundation of appropriateness is needed in order to build the base of influence and trust that leaders need to help develop both people and organizations in a positive manner. It is quite ineffective for a leader to attempt to function in a mutual-communicative or advisory-consultative manner with a resistant employee who clearly needs the problem-management approach of the counseling role. It is likewise counterproductive to "counsel" with people who first need to develop a mutual, open-communicative relationship or to see that they can work as effective team members with the leader as consultant and group facilitator.

What Is Role-Shifting?

Role-shifting is the ability to shift moment-to-moment among three different sets of skills—depending upon the situations or people encountered. It is important that you become able to shift among these three sets of skills when interacting with colleagues or followers so your interventions will have a greater likelihood of meeting expectations, needs, and preferences. This could seem to make the process of leadership very complex and difficult. It is complex, but a style-shift model breaks reality down into small enough "chunks" so that we can learn each part of it before integrating the chunk into a larger picture. Effective leadership requires the ability to deal with complexity, break it into manageable pieces, and intervene with a continuous alertness to the impact we are making.

In keeping with the evidence that effectiveness is related to complexity and versatility of leader behavior, it would assist leaders to be more effective if they could discern which of the three roles are appropriate with each individual, group, or organization in each moment. Here is a further delineation of the three roles involved in role-shifting.

1. **In the Communication Role**—Positive interpersonal communication is the appropriate mode in which to be functioning when you want to develop a mutual relationship with a person. It is appropriate with coworkers, family, friends, and even acquaintances on a day-to-day basis. It forms the foundation of all relationships, and is usually appropriate at the beginning of a relationship and for maintaining and building relationships. It is the informal "glue" that bonds any relationship, and without it, there can be a kind of robotic formality that can interfere with the fostering of easygoing and effective relating with others. This mode can also include the more difficult aspects of interpersonal communication such as giving and receiving feedback, assertiveness, and confrontation.

2. **In the Counseling Role**—Effective counseling and coaching, which involves personal and interpersonal problem management and personal problem solving, is most appropriate when coworkers, colleagues, or subordinates are having personal difficulties that are interfering with their performance or relationships with others. Your acting as a facilitator of their personal and interpersonal development by assisting them to specify their own problems in relation to a problem situation (and then take effective action) can be a great impetus in keeping people, groups, and organizations "unblocked." Coaching is related to counseling in that it is a process by which a manager guides the development of a subordinate by continuous observation and assessment, discussion, guidance, and encouragement so the subordinate learns more from completing the task and the manager's own expertise is passed on.

3. **In the Consultative Role**—It is appropriate to shift into the consultative mode or role when the person, group, or organization with which you are interacting requires and expects you to do some kind of assessment, intervention, evaluation, and ongoing monitoring. Sometimes you may find yourself under pressure to respond authoritatively or even sternly, perhaps because your position as leader causes others to expect you to be decisive and resolute—especially when time is limited for key decisions. When you have to make decisions that require an overall awareness of organizational factors of which others may not be aware, then it is especially important to act cautiously using this consultative mode. Even if you are not in a leadership position, it can be appropriate at times to act in this role, especially if your action can be seen as effective and appreciated by those in positions "above" and "below" you.

Blending Roles to Increase Effectiveness

Sometimes, situations occur where it is important to accomplish the goals of two or three of these roles. These interchanges are more complex. For example, suppose you have an employee named Manuel who has recently lost his brother in an automobile accident.

In some situations like this, which require greater complexity on your part, you may find it is more effective to begin your conversation with role-free communication, with a response such as: "Is it possible you might join us for that round of golf on Saturday that we have been meaning to have?"

Then, as the conversation progresses to more personal material, you could appropriately intervene with a counseling response: "I can understand how you are finding it difficult to get into traveling on your sales route this next week because of the recent loss you have experienced in your family."

> **Sometimes, situations occur where it is important to accomplish the goals of two or three of these roles. These interchanges are more complex.**

Then, intervene with a consultative response as you get into exploring options with Manuel about how to deal with the grief: "I think I can arrange for Bill and Sue to take your sales route next week if you would like that. The company would cover your time off."

Manuel needs time off work to spend with his family and your caring about his pain by giving him time off will likely be of great value to him. He is an employee who will likely never steal from you, will likely defend you when others may be unfairly critical, and is likely to find working for you and with you a refreshing change from what he would receive from many other employers.

The creative combining of the three leadership roles can provide you with greater freedom of choice in how you will respond to another person. By changing roles, role-shifting allows you to communicate the value you place on people.

How Role-Shifting Communicates Your Valuing Others, and Builds Positive Culture

The critical difference in *Transforming Leadership* is that it attempts to meet organizational objectives and, at the same time, communicates the value of the individuals in each interchange. In fact, one of the organizational objectives in an organization led by a Transforming Leader is to communicate the value of people to coworkers and followers, and encourage them to understand and communicate that same value to others. In this way, you can better create a value-driven organization that lives and breathes what it believes. This positive culture encourages and nurtures the development of people, which, in turn, can promote well-being, creativity, and productivity of workgroups and organizations.

Compare this vision with the one of the rigid, role-bound bureaucratic manager who responds mainly by the "book," who does not "flex" self or procedures for the sake of people. Demoralization occurs when people are treated in this depersonalizing manner. Leading others the way we would like to be led—by considering them and even asking them how we can respond to meet their needs—is leading by the "golden rule." Using the communication role to make friends and develop relationships, the counseling role to resolve personal and interpersonal problems, and the consultative role to implement group or organizational interventions will increase the complexity and, therefore, the effectiveness of your responses.

The Importance of Being Genuine and Respectful when Acting in Various Roles

Most people prefer a leader who is a genuine person at all times, and who treats them as individuals. Sincerity and respect are key qualities to communicate in all three roles. If I am myself when I attempt to communicate, counsel, or consult with someone, my credibility will increase nearly automatically. Making statements that clearly identify your personal opinions and feelings can encourage others to see that you aren't "role-bound," that you are approachable, and that you, too, are a person who can also make mistakes, learn, and develop.

> **The creative combining of the three leadership roles can provide you with greater freedom of choice in how you will respond to another person.**

This genuine and respectful attitude and approach communicates the qualities of honesty and humility. Even when you have to exercise difficult leadership authority in stressful situations, you can still communicate this kind of humility, a willingness to serve, and a willingness to be wrong. By communicating these qualities in your language, your tone of voice, and your actions, others will feel more respected and will have a greater sense of trust in, and respect for, you.

There are specific tasks appropriate in each role. These tasks are typical of the kinds of things that you would normally discover need to be handled in each role. The achievement of these three sets of tasks requires the three sets of skills for their accomplishment. We will summarize these tasks in the next section to further elucidate the complexity and potential in style, role, and skill-shifting.

Role-Shifting: Tasks Inherent in the Three Roles

The relationship among the three roles (or modes of functioning) and the tasks in each of the three roles are illustrated in the chart below.

Appropriate Shifting of Roles and Typical Tasks

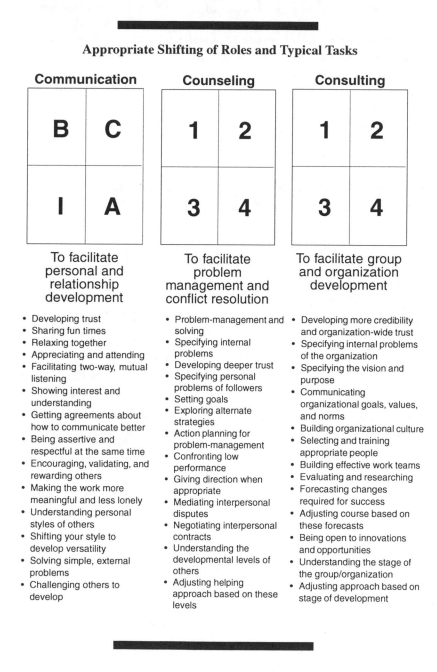

Communication	Counseling	Consulting
B **C** **I** **A**	**1** **2** **3** **4**	**1** **2** **3** **4**
To facilitate personal and relationship development	To facilitate problem management and conflict resolution	To facilitate group and organization development

Communication — To facilitate personal and relationship development

- Developing trust
- Sharing fun times
- Relaxing together
- Appreciating and attending
- Facilitating two-way, mutual listening
- Showing interest and understanding
- Getting agreements about how to communicate better
- Being assertive and respectful at the same time
- Encouraging, validating, and rewarding others
- Making the work more meaningful and less lonely
- Understanding personal styles of others
- Shifting your style to develop versatility
- Solving simple, external problems
- Challenging others to develop

Counseling — To facilitate problem management and conflict resolution

- Problem-management and solving
- Specifying internal problems
- Developing deeper trust
- Specifying personal problems of followers
- Setting goals
- Exploring alternate strategies
- Action planning for problem-management
- Confronting low performance
- Giving direction when appropriate
- Mediating interpersonal disputes
- Negotiating interpersonal contracts
- Understanding the developmental levels of others
- Adjusting helping approach based on these levels

Consulting — To facilitate group and organization development

- Developing more credibility and organization-wide trust
- Specifying internal problems of the organization
- Specifying the vision and purpose
- Communicating organizational goals, values, and norms
- Building organizational culture
- Selecting and training appropriate people
- Building effective work teams
- Evaluating and researching
- Forecasting changes required for success
- Adjusting course based on these forecasts
- Being open to innovations and opportunities
- Understanding the stage of the group/organization
- Adjusting approach based on stage of development

The tasks outlined above are typical of each role, the achievement of which requires the practice of the three sets of skills appropriate to each of the three roles. Understanding that these tasks are often needed to facilitate development of people and organizations is another step toward exerting a transforming effect wherever you go.

Role Rigidity Obstructs Leadership Effectiveness

A parent who cannot become a friend to his or her child is an all too common situation. An overly friendly boss can lose credibility and clout when it comes time for confrontation. Trying to act in the consultative role when others are not asking for it or expecting it can cause others to see you as overly officious or "high-minded." With practice, however, your increased ability to shift roles gracefully and appropriately will assist you to meet the challenge of constant change and complexity in your organization, with groups, and with individuals—at work or at home.

In addition, more appropriate interventions with individuals, groups, and organizations can be better understood by using Personal Style Theory. Once you internalize a clear understanding of the theory, you can learn to better "read" the style tendencies of groups and organizations.

Skill-Shifting for Greater Versatility in Leadership Roles

Skills #53 and #54: Intentionally Assessing and Shifting Skills

Assessing the skills appropriate to a particular situation is relatively easy if you know what role is appropriate in the given situation or with a particular person or group. The examples below will help clarify how this skill-shifting approach works.

Example of shifting into the communication role: A few months back, I was coaching a CEO to build his executive team. He rarely played the consultative role because he didn't have the skills to do so. That wasn't his fault. He had an MBA that taught him analytical skills he could apply to managing his company well. But they did not teach him the skills he needed to build a team, to work on designing and developing a better organization, and to do strategic planning and implementation.

As I coached him, I modeled all three sets of skills. Over lunch, we discussed, in a very mutual way, how difficult was for me to develop the skills and apply them consistently in my own life and business. I shared with him some ways I have failed to use what I know. He was relieved and saw me as being more humble and approachable, and not so much the "expert" he had imagined me to be. I intentionally shared my mistakes and shortcomings with him to move our relationship into greater intimacy and mutuality. We were in the very mutual communication role together over lunch and I became more "real" to him. This was appropriate and was a natural development of the personal side of our relationship.

Example of shifting into the counseling role: Then, in the afternoon session with the CEO and his Senior VP who was not functioning up to the CEO's standards, I had to shift into the counseling role. I asked both parties for their permission to act as the problem manager/mediator in their scheduled conflict-resolution encounter with one another. As they each voiced their disappointments and concerns with one another, I acted as a mediator to ensure that two-way communication occurred. I also functioned in the closely related counselor role to ensure that each party understood and took ownership of some behaviors in which they each engaged that were not effective. We resolved some unresolved issues that had been troubling their work and personal relationship for years. After about an hour, when we finished talking, they each said something very strange. They confessed they had never really talked with each other before! This is all too typical of many business and marriage relationships! People just don't have the skills to make it work, and don't always apply the skills even when they do have them!

Example of shifting into the consulting role: In the late afternoon session, we spent two hours with the executive team in order to conduct their monthly Executive Review. The CEO chaired the meeting and I was there to coach his group leadership and meeting facilitation skills. Before the meeting started, I enlisted their agreement that I would be functioning, for the most part, in the consultative mode for this afternoon's meeting. They all wanted to learn these skills because they all had to go back to their functional teams and lead their own meetings. So we worked with three agendas all at once: 1) we had a meeting; 2) we were doing a training session on how to run better meetings and lead better; 3) we wanted to get real work done. Training, learning, and getting the job done needed to occur simultaneously.

You will notice in the chart above on page 230 that the tasks under each of the three roles require the use of the skills in order to do the tasks well. These tasks are the work of *Transforming Leadership*. The skills required to perform these tasks are the three sets of skills on which we were focusing in the previous three chapters. All the skills build upon one another—sometimes overlap—and at other times are used separately, intentionally.

Recognizing and Facilitating the Stages of Organization Development

TL Skill #55: The Recognition of Organizational Developmental Stages

In the next section of this chapter, we will examine the developmental stages of a group or organization and the skills appropriate to each stage.

Stages of Development in a Group or Organization

Understanding stages of development is beneficial to a leader because it enables his or her accurate assessment of the stage where a group or organization is currently functioning. It also facilitates clear planning for the next steps of development that need attention. Without the ability to assess stages of development, you could commit often-made mistakes such as these.
1. Trying to build teams before goals are clarified
2. Setting goals and attempting strategic planning before there is a clear purpose in the minds of the people involved
3. Specifying programs to achieve results before identifying specific goals to be accomplished

To be a leader who can demonstrate versatility, it is useful for you to use some kind of model to understand the development of groups and organizations. There are various models for assessing the levels of development of a group or organization: some are complex and others are relatively simple. Of course, in reality, events overlap in each stage, but the details of the five-stage model presented below will be useful to help you map the territory of group and organization development and thereby respond more effectively as a leader.

Introduction to the Five Stages of Group and Organization Development

Stage One: Design, Orientation, and Commitment
This stage complements what Adizes describes as the Courtship Stage in his book, *Corporate Life Cycles* (1988). Orienting people to the entrepreneurial, inspiring, or ennobling vision, values, and goals of the organization inspires them to commit themselves to the task of achieving the vision, all critical factors in *Transforming Leadership*.

Informal introduction and orientation processes are appropriate at this stage. These can involve retreats, the "whisper in the ear" approach where successful group members act as ongoing mentors in the orientation or coaching or training processes. Usually, people want to know how they can succeed in the organization or group when they first enter it. Those who meet this prime need are likely to be heard most thoroughly. Often some kind of emotional experience needs to occur for an orientation "courtship" to be effective. Some companies have effectively created their corporate cultures with their executives at retreats in remote places where the company's norms, values, beliefs, and philosophy were introduced in both a formal and informal fashion.

Commitment by a member to a group or organization is achieved to the extent to which the neophyte "buys into" the stated purpose, philosophy, and goals of the organization in a genuine way. The closer the new member's position is to the group's values and beliefs prior to joining, the more likely there will be a "locking in" or bonding effect. Just prior to commitment, there is often an experience on the part of the new member of, "I feel like I belong here." This sense of belonging would appear to be a critical factor in achieving the level of commitment required for the achievement of highly developed corporate culture that leads to exceptional achievements.

Stage Two: Making the Transition—Overcoming Resistance and Obstacles
This stage is similar to what Adizes calls the infancy stage. Even though a person has psychologically "bought into" the group or organization at the end of Stage One, there has not yet been a real investment of self, time, energy, planning, envisioning of achievements, and sweat to match dreams. In making the transition to full involvement, group members need to be personally involved in formulating some of the general goals and action plans that will later result in programs that will be implemented and evaluated. People need to be recognized and rewarded in ways that are personally meaningful.

It is during this transition stage—where general goal setting and specific objectives are committed to by each member—that resistance and obstacles often rear their heads. Many people will commit themselves to lofty goals and agree to achieve objectives, but when they show up at the next meeting, often they have not achieved what they intended. The way people are handled by leaders during this critical stage can set the tone for the failure or success of a group.

It is also at this stage that the distracting or withdrawn group or team member will often surface. This is the time when some of the individuals who said they "bought in" to the purpose and philosophy of the group or organization often unwittingly reveal feathers of a different color. Conflict ensues, feet drag, and some members just can't seem to "get with it." Resentment can develop on the part of the group members who are with it. If the leader does not facilitate the group or organization through this stage, it is likely it will never move on to accomplishments that fulfill the vision thought to be shared, but that may limp along acceptably, minimally, for a time.

At this stage—when goals are set and objectives cast as commitments—

leaders who facilitate further development will take actions such as confronting and coaching (or dismissing) poor performers, resolving group member conflict, working through intergroup clash or confusion, and refusing to tolerate opposition to or undermining of valued corporate culture. If the leader allows conflict and tension to continue to the point of undermining the potential effectiveness of the group or organization, then he or she is either knowingly or unwittingly participating in its demise. If leaders intervene swiftly and effectively at this time, however, great potential lies ahead in the working stage of the group.

Stage Three: Doing the Work of the Group

Adizes calls this stage the "Go-Go" stage. When individual resistance, group-member conflict, and intergroup clashes are for the most part handled, then the group members can get on with achieving the vision with a simultaneous sense of relief and enthusiasm. When this stage begins, people often sense it! It is a pleasure to work at a place—with a group—in an organization where the "unfinished business" doesn't pile up under the carpet. Leaders are respected when things can move to this working stage; when energy is released, learning and creativity are unleashed. When problems are encountered at this stage, the group or organization has already developed systems and approaches to deal with many of them effectively. New products get launched, new systems are put into place, and there is a fresh sense of being a part of a "going concern."

In addition, several other important things occur during this stage. Members have become acquainted with one another; they are more familiar with one another's personal and workstyles, strengths, difficult areas, reactions to stress and pressure, and tendencies to lead or follow. This familiarity can breed performance and fine-tuning of the team's efforts. Job descriptions can also be renegotiated and rewritten into working agreements—based on expressed needs for change or newly recognized talents of group members in areas of specialty previously unknown in Stage Two.

Stage Four: Making the Transition from an Entrepreneurial Run Firm to a Professionally Run Firm

This stage is similar to what Adizes calls the Adolescent Stage. Typically, this is the most difficult transition to make because the senior leader or owner has to make great changes to establish financial, information, marketing, sales, and quality improvement systems that tax him or her to current knowledge and skills limits. This is where the senior leader must learn to work more on the organization and not so much in it. Teams get developed and learn to function well, cross-functionally. They also learn to communicate with customers so that they can answer concerns enough to demonstrate that they care and will deliver what the customer wants, fast. So many companies fail at this stage because of what Adizes calls the "founder trap"—where the owner cannot delegate or accept input from others, and is often unwilling to do the proper planning and implementation that must pave the way to larger-scale success. Where the leader does make it through this stage, the organization becomes what we call a leadership organization.

Stage Five: The Mature, Flourishing Organization
Adizes calls this stage the Prime Stage. There is a balance with innovation, planning, operational implementation, and integration of systems. The ability to learn from mistakes quickly and to correct course based on facts is greatly enhanced. A key feature of the mature company is that it is wise, anticipates and tests the accuracy of predictions regarding future trends, and is on the growing edge of creating and responding to new markets and providing new services. This stage represents a fully functioning learning organization.

Learning from feedback, both positive and negative, celebrating success, and planning for new levels of achievement can all have a powerful impact on how people experience their membership in organizations and groups. If developing a leadership organization is such an important preparation for building a learning organization, let's look at the ten steps involved in developing teams and organizations.

TL Skill #55: Facilitation of the Stages of Organizational Development

Ten Steps in the Process of Developing a Team or Organization

We will now, in detail, examine ten steps in developing a team or organization so that you can gain further insight into the nature of the process of the way groups and organizations develop, and how you can act as a catalytic agent to make this development occur.

Step One: Solidifying and Communicating the Mandate This step of team or organization development requires that the leader have a mandate or some authority to proceed with a position of power to decide, power to move in certain directions, or a vision or mission that has the sanction of an official body. For example, only when a college president has a mandate from the board or other governing agency to provide a certain level of quality and scope of instruction may he or she proceed with clarity and authority. Furthermore, if an entrepreneur were to start his or her own company, then the government of most free-world states would give that person the right to exercise a self-decreed mandate: to make money by engaging in free enterprise.

It is often necessary and many times desirable that there is a clear mandate (from "on high," as it were) to proceed without coming into conflict with the purpose of the organization or authorities in charge of its overall direction or operation. Volunteer organizations are famous for "splintering" when a "leader" decides he or she needs to achieve a personal purpose not in harmony with the larger (officially) "mandated" vision of the organization according to its constitution. It is desirable to prevent this splintering effect whenever possible by making the mandate clear in the minds of everyone in the group or organization.

Clarity is made possible by publishing the mandate in writing and by initiating an orientation process whereby people understand that going against the mandate will result in their losing membership in the group or organization. One delivery company has issued a mandate of safety at all levels of the organization. Irresponsibility toward the safety of anyone is not tolerated. If, for example, an employee of the company is caught speeding while driving a company delivery vehicle on the freeway, the result is known in advance to be immediate dismissal.

In summary then, the mandate makes explicit what the purpose of an organization or group can and cannot be. It specifies what is acceptable and what is not. It spells out in no uncertain terms how things will be, and often remains quite stable and inflexible throughout the life of the organization, as in the constitutions of various government bodies. The mandate comprises the assumptions, fundamental definitions, and rules that everyone is required to know and follow when dealing with one another and with the organization. Some organizations or groups call the mandate its "terms of reference."

Many individuals resist creating, publishing, communicating, or standing up for a mandate because it seems to be "authoritarian" or rigid to some people. It does not have to be, however, as in the case of a constitution founded upon the democratic principles of freedom of speech, freedom of worship, freedom from discrimination, etc. A humane mandate—is built upon the assumption people are valuable—will be a solid foundation on which to build a group or organization.

Example Mandate Statement of A to Z Community Services Agency: "Our Mandate is to provide support and develop community-based social services mostly to needy members of the community. We cannot compete with existing government or private agencies, but will supplement their services to fulfill unmet needs where such government services fall short due to funding, staff shortages, or people's inabilities to pay for such services."

If you can assist a group or organization to clarify and communicate its mandate effectively to its members, you will likely prevent all sorts of misunderstandings, misdirection, and conflict from emerging to destroy the integrity and cohesion needed for further development. After achieving this first step, the next one is assisting in the clarification of the organization's purpose, vision, or mission.

Step Two: Clarifying Purpose, Mission, or Vision As a next step in this first stage, a purpose statement is a further specification and extension of the mandate statement. The terms purpose, mission, and vision are used synonymously to refer to a group or organization's reason for being. Some leaders, such as Dr. Martin Luther King, have a "dream"—in his case, it was an inner vision driven with passion and commitment—that they communicate to their group members. Others have a purpose statement that is perhaps less fiery, but that nevertheless provides overall direction and reason for being to the members of a group or organization.

Assisting group members to achieve understanding of and consensus around a purpose statement, and what the statement means, is a critical prerequisite to "gelling" the group into one functional entity. If you can get people to "buy in" to the organization's reason for existence as a part of their own reason for being, then you have instant commitment! For example, it wasn't hard for Douglas Aircraft plant workers to arrive at workgroup consensus about what their purpose was at the beginning of the Second World War! The employees realized they were an absolutely necessary part of a war machine that, if they built it fast and well, had the potential to save their own lives and also the lives of their children.

Example Purpose Statement of A to Z Community Services Agency:

> *Our purpose is to enrich the lives of community members—especially the poor, provide for their basic material needs, and offer them personal development opportunities they otherwise would not receive, and provide training and avenues for the expression of volunteer services and financial contributions.*

Step Three: Specifying and Gaining Consensus about Philosophy, Values, Beliefs, and Norms This next step in the First Stage of developing a group or organization is also very important. Without a similar philosophical orientation, there really cannot be a cohesive group or organization. A group's philosophy is comprised of values (priorities and importances) and beliefs (assumptions about what is true, good, false, bad, etc.). In addition, without agreed-upon norms (extension of values and beliefs—agreements about ways of treating people and solving problems), people may find they have frequent clashes with one another, and the group or organization will likely either live in disharmony and lose productive energies, or may fall apart.

In one organization where I was acting as an external consultant, staff were working with a base of conflicting values, beliefs, and assumptions. They certainly were at odds with one another—with resultant harm to young people in the organization where a mandate was in place to rehabilitate them.

In this example, about half of the correctional officers in the juvenile correctional facility honestly believed their purpose was to attempt to facilitate the development of juveniles with the eventual hope of rehabilitating them as self-respecting citizens of the community. The other half of the staff referred to the residents as "slugs who'll never amount to anything," and they treated them with strong disrespect. The staff fought bitterly with one another and were in conflict daily about this issue of the worth of the offenders in custody. Staff turnover was high as management was blamed by both sides (!) for "hiring a bunch of idiots."

The leaders of the juvenile facility did not attend to this issue of specifying and communicating purpose when they hired the correctional officers. They didn't even ask them or their previous employers their purpose for working with juveniles! The juveniles received these two conflicting messages on a daily basis. As a result, program efforts were undermined and discipline procedures were implemented with entirely opposite spirits—one with a spirit of discipline and the other with a spirit of punishment. The end results were disastrously in favor of the punishing officers' predictions.

At a point of crisis—after a riot where the youth damaged the facilities extensively—management asked me to facilitate a team-development process with the management group first, then with the whole staff. We started with an examination of the mandate that was in the contract the agency had signed with the government funding body. Then we moved on to creating purpose statements on "flip-charts" on the walls until we had as much consensus as possible among the group of twenty-eight staff. It became clear it was going to be difficult to move ahead with the next step of specifying philosophy because the conflict in the air was so thick that it turned everyone to ice.

When we moved into clarifying the organization's philosophy about how to treat kids and staff, the worth of kids, the approach to discipline and control, etc., the frustration was so great among those with a punitive attitude, that eight of the "old school, old guard" staff quit within days. New staff were soon hired—individuals who "bought in" to the juvenile center's philosophy—and stress and conflict levels decreased immediately. The organization began to "gel" into a cohesive group of people "of the same mind." Within a few weeks they observed consistent evidence of positive impact on the juveniles in their care. They were then in a position to reevaluate the general goals of their organization.

Step Four: Formulating General Goals that Meet Needs or Solve Problems
Motivating goals can be effectively formulated only upon a foundation of clear and agreed-upon mandate, purpose, and philosophy statements that are real to those in a group or organization. Perhaps it is true that a band is no better than its worst player—that a band with a drummer who plays to a different beat should suggest the drummer go play jazz fusion somewhere else (unless the band's purpose is to play jazz fusion). If there is no agreement on the

general direction and hoped-for accomplishments of a group, then it will not achieve much of what it intends to achieve. If there is agreement on general goals, it will be possible to achieve higher levels of success. The transforming leader's job is to assist—in the consulting mode—to articulate and translate the aspirations of group members or the needs of a group whom they serve (or sell) into goal statements that are motivating, realistic, achievable, worthwhile, and adequate to solve problems or meet needs.

In the case of the juvenile correctional facility, a subsequent consulting intervention resulted in writing down and implementing the following goal and objectives statements.

Goal #1. We will provide a clean, colorful, and socially supportive environment that will encourage the development of residents at the spiritual, intellectual, physical, social, emotional, and creative arts levels.

> **Objective A:** Staff Team E (educators) will implement the Skills for Living Program for life-skills development from January through April of this year.
>
> **Objective B:** Staff Team P (physical plant maintenance staff) will paint this ugly place during the next month in colors that the kids have a say in choosing.

You can see from the above results that from the general goal flows specific objectives. Clear general goal statements are the soil from which grow specific implementation plans and commitments.

Step Five: Specifying Objectives Objectives are statements of commitment with a name and a date attached. They are highly specific in terms of defining what will be accomplished by a certain date. They are based on general goals that reflect known and felt needs or problems.

To facilitate the achievement of specified objectives, each objective can be recorded on simple sheets during staff or planning meetings. These sheets can become the "minutes" for any meeting, and they can, in turn, be reviewed and evaluated at the next scheduled meeting. Each team member with an objective to achieve can set up a program of steps to achieve it and can get ideas from team members for the effective implementation of the program plan. An example format of a sheet we used in objective-setting meetings with the correctional staff is outlined on the following page.

As you can see from the format of the overly simplified version of the staff-meeting minutes, each person at the meeting eventually committed him or herself to accomplishing a specific objective by a specific date, and agreed to give a report on that date about the results incurred from his or her effort. This kind of specific planning and recording by each member of a group or organization has the effect of enlivening meetings, setting up achievable targets, and it meets the needs of staff members to be recognized for their accomplishments. It also allows them to gain assistance and support when their efforts fail.

Step 6: Planning Action Steps Programs are objectives translated into the smaller, logical, more realistic steps required to achieve the desired objectives within certain timeframes. Planning requires experience in the area of expertise being exercised. This is true because if the steps are too large to be achieved, people will become discouraged by failure. If the steps are too small, they will become bored or fatigued with meaningless repetition. Steps in programs need to be large enough to be challenging but small enough to be realistically achieved. Failing to plan realistic but challenging steps is the main reason many objectives fail to materialize into action. Unless these steps are accomplished thoroughly and carefully, individual or group objectives may never be translated into achievements.

Step 7: Implementing Plans Effective program implementation by a group or organization requires a follow-through on the leader's part to monitor, recognize achievement, encourage commitment, and reward performance in both formal and informal ways. The consistently successful implementation of a sales program, for example, could likely depend upon the long-term follow-through of a good sales manager who realizes that the power of his sales force resides within the skills, attitudes, and motivations of the people who sell. This sales manager will plan regular and meaningful sales feedback, training, motivational incentives, and various types of ongoing recognition.

Step 8: Learning from the Past: Evaluation Honest and valid feedback to members of a group or organization can be extremely valuable or destructive. Regular performance reviews can be conducted by leaders in touch enough to actually observe performance. Obtaining an agreement in advance of such an assessment—so that it will occur on a regular, formal basis as well as on an ongoing informal basis—can alleviate much of the anxiety often associated with such evaluations. One method of beginning the performance review process is to ask group members to critique the performance of their own work team during team development or planning sessions. People in leadership positions can also give and receive feedback about positive and negative impacts that occurred as a result of their actions or practices. One company gave weekly feedback to assemblyline employees about how their performance compared with the competition's performance. They were embarrassed to the point of increasing their productivity more than 15 percent in the following weeks—6 percent on average over the competition's.

Planning for improved future performance is another event that can occur on a regular basis as a part of Step Eight. This step often has to be leader-induced because work teams may be resistant to improving their performance when it means they have to work harder. If planning for improved performance will result, however, in an increase in meaningful rewards and recognition, we can expect there will be more enthusiasm for such activities.

Step 9: Celebrating and Enjoying the Rewards If genuine celebration can be fostered and allowed to occur, it can seal a group together for long periods of time. Genuine celebration can only occur, however, when there has been some kind of dramatic and hoped-for achievement beyond the commonplace. If leaders can challenge exceptional performance in only one area and provide opportunity for valued recognition and rewards to come back to group members, there will likely be further commitment to the achievement of other challenging objectives. Rewarding innovation and creativity is another way to promote celebration and recurring high performances.

Step 10: Recycling the Ten Steps It is important to recycle group or organization members through any or all the steps in the process of developing a group or organization, as often as is needed. Sometimes it

> **If genuine celebration can be fostered and allowed to occur, it can seal a group together for long periods of time.**

is critical to reexamine the mandate. It may need to be adjusted to respond to changing markets, changing needs of people being served, changing priorities, or the shifting values of those in positions to set the course or fate of an organization. Mandates, however, are perhaps the most stable of all the steps in the process. I have found it most useful to insure that the value of the vision is renewed in the minds of group and organization members regularly. I have also found it especially helpful to reassess needs and problems to insure that our goals are in line with what is truly important. When failure occurs, it is especially important to examine the appropriateness and workability of objectives and programs.

"Well Functioning" Is Not Enough: Pressing Toward Transformation

Ackerman (1986) describes the essence of what she calls "flow state leadership in action"—a nontraditional view of organizations as bundles of energy-in-motion.

In Ackerman's words, "To increase performance, leaders must be able to release energy that is blocked, to free untapped potential, and to organize in ways that facilitate rather than impede energy flow (Ackerman, p. 245)."

The basics of Flow State leadership are in sync with *Transforming Leadership*. The ideas that blocks must be removed, a vision created and communicated, that people must be empowered and enlisted, and that performance factors must be enhanced are key to *Transforming Leadership*.

Teams, companies, or organizations that merely run smoothly often fail to grow and creatively adapt to changing demands and opportunities. They often become boring and generally lack an innovative spirit which, if its potential were released, could generate enthusiasm and energy capable of propelling even higher, more interesting, and more rewarding achievements. Therefore, we will conclude this book with an examination of the nature of the transforming process and begin to explore this relatively new field of how we can transform organizations or groups into dynamic high-performers (such as Federal Express, People Express, and Microsoft).

After you have practiced the skills and awareness you have assessed in this book as needing further development, you will have an opportunity to creatively apply the *Transforming Leadership* approaches in your own groups or organizations.

The development and transformation of a group or organization into a dynamic and high-performance entity is an inspiring phenomenon to observe and be actively involved in.

An Illustration of Organization Development and Transformation

There were five of us at Manuel's place on a hot July evening in Southern California, practicing rock and roll numbers for a dance scheduled for the following Saturday night. We had been playing together for only about two years, but were good enough that we enjoyed playing about twenty-five different numbers (albeit somewhat mechanically). Our "organization" had developed to a point that we were a solid group of musicians who had enough talent to contract to play-for-pay at some local dances, schools, and fairs. Together, we had agreed on a vision of becoming the best band in Southern California—and of winning the upcoming "battle of the bands" at the San Bernardino County Fair (our competition, little did we know, would be The Beach Boys).

That evening, after about two hours of practice, something new happened that began the process of transforming our group into an exciting and dynamic performing group. We were so competent at playing a particular song that we **Groups, companies, or organizations that merely run smoothly often fail to grow and creatively adapt to changing demands and opportunities.** simultaneously forgot to "try"—there was a feeling of effortless "flowing," of "having it made." Mutual glances and grins spread from member to member, as a fine, clean sound emerged that most other sixteen-year-old band members would have been "green with envy" to have achieved.

In jazz slang, we had finally started to "cook." Prior to that, all we had been doing was cutting the tomatoes and the celery on the cutting board. It wasn't a bad salad, but boring after a while. But when our performance "heated up" to the point of excellence, more than twenty of the neighborhood kids often dropped in to listen to our practices (eighteen of them were girls!)—then we knew we had transcended the "beginner" phase. Our band (organization) had become transformed to a new level of creativity and expression of "spirit"—a spirit of success and freedom that went beyond the commonplace novice performances of our past.

As a result of this new "flowing" sound, an unexpected mystique developed around our band; we were among the first to achieve enough recognition to have "groupies" follow us around to our dances (groups of girls who admired and wanted to date us). We used our profits to buy the best Fender guitars, Showman amplifiers, French Selmer Saxophones, a '55 Chevy, a T-Bird, a street rod, a '57 Chevy, and a VW van. A "cool" young culture of dancers and other young musicians developed around us and regularly attended the dances where we played.

As our excitement and confidence continued to build, we learned to trust that we could practice nearly any song and "glide" (or transcend) into that same clean, crisp, competent sound that moved people to dance and even return to our next performance. As a result, bigger dance promoters began to book us for the dances where more than 1,000 kids—and on several occasions even over 2,000 kids—would turn up. We added some rather simple choreography to our stage presentations (rare in 1963) and became one of Southern California's five most popular bands (known as Manuel and The Renegades).

As a result of all these factors, we earned exciting new jobs at the Cinnamon Cinder Teen Nightclub, came in second at the "battle of the bands" at the San Bernardino County Fair (yes, the Beach Boys won!), and cut several "surfing" style records that unfortunately, only sold well in Chicago.

> **Perhaps the "trick" of releasing the transforming "spirit" in other settings is to learn to transfer the same principles and practices learned in the "hotter" settings to the more mundane ones.**

Those of us in The Renegades went through the design, development, and transformation stages of a group without any awareness of what was happening to us. Our experience was so rich and powerful that nearly all of the groups and organizations we have encountered since those days have been pale (and some have been grim) by comparison. For years after we disbanded, we felt a sense of disillusionment with the other groups and organizations to which we belonged, including some band members' marriages and certain colleges and universities because none of them ever "transcended" the ordinary, "heated up," or creatively "cooked" to the same extent the Renegades had. To my great relief, I finally found another "hot" band with which to play music (The Reactions) during my college years, and to this day, I still find myself playing the audio tape recordings we made at the dances at Running Springs Lodge near Big Bear Lake, California.

The significant thing about this story is, at that time in my life, I first realized that the same type of experiences and performances of being "on a roll," "really high," "on," or "in the groove" can be achieved inside of myself first, then to an increasing extent in family, group, and other organizational settings.

Perhaps the "trick" of releasing the transforming "spirit" in other settings is to learn to transfer the same principles and practices—learned in the "hotter" settings—to the more mundane ones.

> **The endeavor of creating and managing positive change is really just emerging as a science and an art.**

1. Set up the group or organization properly at its inception—with enthusiasm about a clear vision, a worthy purpose, adequate goals, and shared beliefs, values, and norms.
2. Select competent members who genuinely share and "buy into" the foregoing vision.
3. Gain a refined consensus and commitment among the members about the specific purpose, goals, values, and norms of the group, company, or organization.
4. Learn to play a series of "numbers" well together.
5. Practice until you begin to "cook" with spontaneous creativity.
6. Apply that creative style-shifting power and "flow" you have developed to any number of other emerging situations or problems.
7. Stay open to the potential of positive change and a diversity of approaches that demonstrate themselves as appropriately viable—as long as they are consistent with number 1, above.
8. Play "numbers" or create products or services that meet the emerging needs or challenges of the times.
9. Stay alert to changes in the environment that require a response so that adjustments and developments can be made in a timely fashion.
10. Celebrate the achievement of goals, recognize the unique contributions of each member, share in the "take" so that each member receives a portion of the profits from the endeavor, and look to the future for new opportunities.

IN CONCLUSION

The endeavor of creating and managing positive change is really just emerging as a science and an art. This book has been a starting place from which to collect what in the past might be effectively transported into what I believe in the future will become a new kind of practice of leadership—a constantly adaptive and evolving leadership.

Many books describe transformation in organizations and illustrate how excellence has been achieved. They do not, however, offer a comprehensive, integrated, competency-based working model that reveals and develops within you the knowledge, skills, and tools for transforming yourself and your organization into a more powerful one—one that can produce both business and human development results simultaneously. There is a wealth of additional ideas regarding the nature of the transformation process and how leadership can have positive impact (see Albrecht, K. (1987); Bass, B. C. (1985); Bennis, W. G. (1966); Beckhard, R. and Harris, R. T.(1987); Brandt, S. C. (1986); Kirkpatrick, D. L. (1984); LeBoeuf, M. (1980); Martel, L. (1986); Tichy, N. M. (1983); Tichy, N. M. and Devanna, M. A. (1986). For those serious about reviewing some of the critical works that have come before this, you can read any one or all of these books.

To conclude this chapter, we turn to the words of John Kotter (1990), Professor of Organizational Behavior at the Harvard Business School. He writes:

> Some people have the capacity to become excellent managers but not very strong leaders. Others have great leadership potential but, for a variety of reasons, have great difficulty becoming strong managers. Smart companies value both kinds of individuals and work hard to make them a part of the overall team. But when it comes to grooming people for executive jobs, such firms ignore the recent literature that says people cannot manage and lead, and focus their efforts on individuals that seem to have the potential to do both. That is, they try to develop more leader-managers than managers and leaders, and for one very important reason.
>
> Leadership and management are sufficiently different that they can easily conflict. A firm made up mostly of leaders and managers often polarizes into two warring camps—eventually resulting in one side winning (usually the managerial camp because it is bigger) and then in the purging of the other side. In firms with a large contingent of leader-managers, this rarely happens.
>
> Developing enough leader-managers to help run the huge number of complex organizations that dominate our society today is a great challenge. But it is a challenge we must accept. The more pessimistic individuals among us think this is hopeless. Some people argue there is no such thing as a leader-

> *manager. They are clearly wrong; most of the individuals discussed in this book both lead and manage. At this point, it is simply not clear how many more of these people would emerge if circumstances were right. The only way to find out is to try.*

The *Transforming Leadership* approach asserts confidently that any manager who wants to become a better leader can learn to do so! *Transforming Leadership* is an attempt to provide these "right circumstances" Kotter suggests. This book, combined with a program of formalized mentoring or coaching, could be a next step for many who would stretch themselves from the limitations of management into the exciting challenges of leadership. This new development and growth can have positive impact at every level of society: at home, at work, and in our other systems.

Now you can turn to Chapter 9 to formulate your own Personal Leadership Development Plan.

References

L. **Ackerman** in *Transforming Leadership: From Vision to Results.* Ed. by John D. Adams. (Alexandria, VA: Miles River Press, 1986.)

I. **Adizes**, *Corporate Life Cycles.* (Englewood Cliffs, NJ: Prentice Hall, 1988.)

K. **Albrecht**, *The Creative Corporation.* (Homewood, IL: Dow Jones-Irwin, 1987.)

T. **Anderson** and **Robinson**, E. T., *The Leader's Manual for the Personal Style Indicator and Job Style Indicator: A Guide to Their Significance, Development, Administration, and Practical Applications.* (Abbotsford, BC Canada: Consulting Resource Group International, Inc., 1988.)

T. D. **Anderson** and **Robinson**, E. T., *The Personal Style Indicator.* 3rd ed. (Abbotsford, BC Canada: Consulting Resource Group, Inc., 1988. pp. 4, 6, 14-15.)

M. **DePree**, *Leadership Is An Art.* (New York: Dell Publishing, 1989.)

B. **Bass**, *Leadership and Performance Beyond Expectations.* (New York: The Free Press, 1985. p. 201.)

R. **Beckhard** and **Harris**, R. T. Organizational Transitions. (2nd ed.) (Reading, MA: Addison-Wesley, 1987.)

W. G. **Bennis**, *Changing Organizations.* (New York: McGraw-Hill, 1966.)

S. C. **Brandt,** *Entrepreneuring in Established Companies. Managing Toward the Year 2000.* (New York: Mentor, 1986.)

D. L. **Kirkpatrick**, *How to Manage Change Effectively: Approaches, Methods, and Case Examples.* (San Francisco: Jossey-Bass, 1984.)

J. A **Kotter**, *Force for Change: How Leadership Differs from Management.* (New York: The Free Press, 1990. pp. 125,126.)

M. **LeBoeuf,** *Imagineering: How to Profit from Your Creative Powers.* (New York: Berkeley Book, 1980.)

M. **Lombardo**, *Looking At Leadership: Some Neglected Issues. Center for Creative Leadership, Technical Report Number 6, January, 1978.* Research sponsored by: Organizational Effectiveness Research Program, Office of Naval Research (Code 452), under contract No. N00014-76-C-0870;NR 170-825.

L. **Martel,** *Mastering Change: The Key to Business Success.* (New York: Simon & Shuster; 1986.)

D. **Merrill** and **Reid**, R., *Personal Styles and Effective Performance.*(Radnor, PA: Chilton Book Company, 1981.)

R. E. **Quinn**, *Beyond Rational Management: Mastering the Paradoxes and Competing Demands of High Performance.* (San Francisco: Jossey-Bass, 1988. p. 51.)

E. T. **Robinson**, *Why Aren't You More Like Me?* (St. Lucie Press, Delray Beach, FL: 1997.)

N.M. **Tichy,** *Managing Strategic Change: Organization Development Redefined.* (New York: Wiley, 1983)

N.M. **Tichy** and Devanna, M.A. *The Transformational Leader.* (New York: Wiley, 1986.)

Part Three

Chapter 9

BUILDING YOUR PERSONAL LEADERSHIP DEVELOPMENT PLAN

Introduction

In Chapter 2, you completed a personal assessment and developed a profile of your relative strengths and weaknesses in the five *Transforming Leadership* skill sets.

The following diagram was introduced in Chapter 2. It illustrates the dynamic relationship between the leadership skills measured in the *LSI* with the job of translating your vision, insight, or strategy as a leader into influence. It is a leader's influence that moves and leads individuals, groups, and organizations.

The real potential for change and growth through using the *LSI* is realized only when you take action based upon what you have learned.

Using the results of this assessment

The insights you gain from completing this *LSI* assessment can be used to develop a plan for your growth and development as a leader. There are different ways to benefit from the results of the *LSI*.

1. Based upon what you have learned, you can begin to target resources, training events, or classes that would help you to increase your understanding and practice in these various skill areas. You will benefit from paying attention to skills where you already have a degree of strength so you can enhance your leadership influence and effectiveness. You will also benefit from working on skills that are weak. You begin to capture lost opportunities and potential.

2. Share the results of this *LSI* assessment with someone you consider a coach or mentor in leadership, someone more experienced and effective as a leader than you are. This individual can use these insights as a basis for giving you input, direction, and coaching in key skill areas where he or she can help you.

3. Begin to take note of leaders around you in your environment and observe their practice of these various skills in their leadership roles. While this is a common way to learn to do what we do anyway, you will be amazed at how much more you will see and benefit, with this set of skill categories in mind.

Fewer than one in ten professionals have been observed, in video-taped assessment sessions, to use the whole range of skills (to at least Level Four competency) outlined in this *LSI* assessment. Yet, these skills are critical for success and effectiveness.

Fortunately, effective leadership behaviors can be observed, learned, and transferred to others. These behaviors can be broken down into microskills and can be demonstrated, practiced, and refined, and competency can be developed. But microskills are not wisdom. How you go about integrating the various skills into your personal leadership style is a matter of your individual creativity and requires much intentional practice and development.

Realistic expectations: how quickly can you develop your leadership skills?

Most people who aspire to be effective in leadership, and who realize the complexity of the task (and the preparations needed), understand that development does not come primarily because of a course or a book. Usually people have to go through the following levels in developing competency and the advanced ability to pass the "torch" along to others.

1. Knowledge about concepts and skills take a few hours to a few weeks to internalize.
2. Gaining understanding and working knowledge (ability to try the skill on one's own without supervision) can take up to a month or two.
3. Competency (the ability to perform reliably well) is learned through mentoring, training, coaching, and through making unpleasant mistakes as well as having successes. This stage may take from six months to two years for some of the more complex skills.
4. Dynamic creativity in the application of skills comes after many years of practice and experience.
5. Ability to mentor and train others comes easier when your own skill sets are well established and you are able to be unconsciously competent in a wide range of skills.

Skills Development Plan Worksheet:
The Skills of Personal Mastery

Review the results of this *LSI* assessment for this skill set on page 27 in Chapter 2 and fill out the worksheet on this and the next page. In this way, you will develop an overview of the key skills in this skill set that would benefit from additional focus.

1.   **What are your three strongest skills in this skill set?**

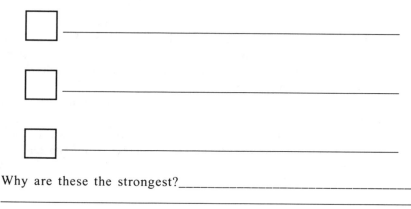

    \#   Skill Name

Why are these the strongest?_____
_____
_____

2.   **What are your three weakest skills in this skill set?**

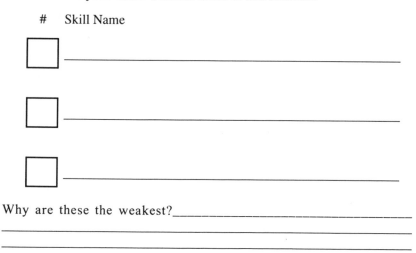

    \#   Skill Name

Why are these the weakest?_____
_____
_____

Can you identify any next steps that can be taken to maximize these skills of Personal Mastery in your leadership role?

Skill #	Action Step #	Action Item	Coach/Mentor/ Target Date
☐	1.	_____	_____ ___/___/___
☐	2.	_____	_____ ___/___/___
☐	3.	_____	_____ ___/___/___
☐	4.	_____	_____ ___/___/___
☐	5.	_____	_____ ___/___/___
☐	6.	_____	_____ ___/___/___
☐	7.	_____	_____ ___/___/___
☐	8.	_____	_____ ___/___/___
☐	9.	_____	_____ ___/___/___
☐	10.	_____	_____ ___/___/___

Skills Development Plan Worksheet:
The Skills of Interpersonal Communication

Review the results of this *LSI* assessment for this skill set on page 29 in Chapter 2 and fill out the worksheet on this and the next page. In this way you will develop an overview of the key skills in this skill set that would benefit from additional focus.

1.   **What are your three strongest skills in this skill set?**

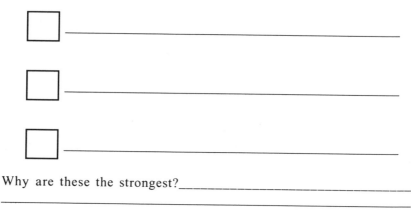

   \#   Skill Name

Why are these the strongest?_____
_____
_____

2.   **What are your three weakest skills in this skill set?**

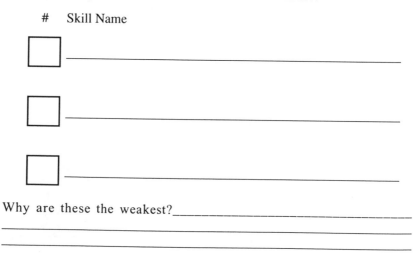

   \#   Skill Name

Why are these the weakest?_____
_____
_____

Can you identify any next steps that can be taken to maximize these skills of Interpersonal Communication in your leadership role?

Skill #	Action Step #	Action Item	Coach/Mentor/ Target Date
☐	1.	_____	_____ ___/___/___
☐	2.	_____	_____ ___/___/___
☐	3.	_____	_____ ___/___/___
☐	4.	_____	_____ ___/___/___
☐	5.	_____	_____ ___/___/___
☐	6.	_____	_____ ___/___/___
☐	7.	_____	_____ ___/___/___
☐	8.	_____	_____ ___/___/___
☐	9.	_____	_____ ___/___/___
☐	10.	_____	_____ ___/___/___

Skills Development Plan Worksheet:
The Skills of Counseling and Problem-Management

Review the results of this *LSI* assessment for this skill set on page 31 in Chapter 2 and fill out the worksheet on this and the next page. In this way, you will develop an overview of the key skills in this skill set that would benefit from additional focus.

1. What are your three strongest skills in this skill set?

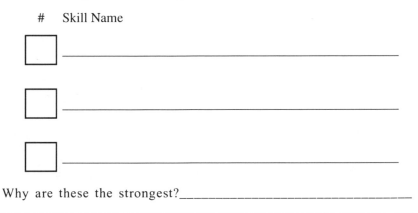

    #   Skill Name

Why are these the strongest?_____
_____
_____

2. What are your three weakest skills in this skill set?

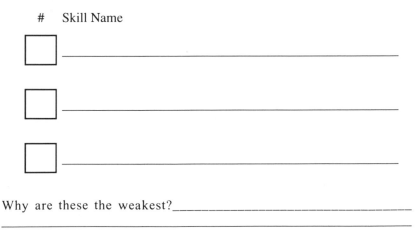

    #   Skill Name

Why are these the weakest?_____
_____
_____

Can you identify any next steps that can be taken to maximize these skills of Counseling and Problem Management in your leadership role?

Skill #	Action Step #	Action Item	Coach/Mentor/ Target Date
	1.	_____	_____ ___/___/___
	2.	_____	_____ ___/___/___
	3.	_____	_____ ___/___/___
	4.	_____	_____ ___/___/___
	5.	_____	_____ ___/___/___
	6.	_____	_____ ___/___/___
	7.	_____	_____ ___/___/___
	8.	_____	_____ ___/___/___
	9.	_____	_____ ___/___/___
	10.	_____	_____ ___/___/___

Skills Development Plan Worksheet:
The Skills of Team and Organizational Development

Review the results of this *LSI* assessment for this skill set on page 33 in Chapter 2 and fill out the worksheet on this and the next page. In this way, you will develop an overview of the key skills in this skill set that would benefit from additional focus.

1. **What are your three strongest skills in this skill set?**

     #   Skill Name

Why are these the strongest?_____
_____
_____

2. **What are your three weakest skills in this skill set?**

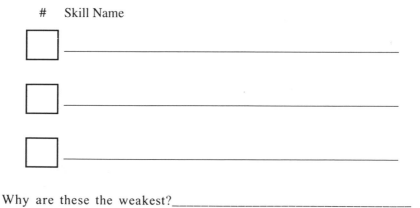

     #   Skill Name

Why are these the weakest?_____
_____

_____

Can you identify any next steps that can be taken to maximize these skills of Consulting in your leadership role?

Skill #	Action Step #	Action Item	Coach/Mentor/ Target Date
☐	1.	_____	_____ __/__/__
☐	2.	_____	_____ __/__/__
☐	3.	_____	_____ __/__/__
☐	4.	_____	_____ __/__/__
☐	5.	_____	_____ __/__/__
☐	6.	_____	_____ __/__/__
☐	7.	_____	_____ __/__/__
☐	8.	_____	_____ __/__/__
☐	9.	_____	_____ __/__/__
☐	10.	_____	_____ __/__/__

Skills Development Plan Worksheet:
The Skills of Versatility in Style, Role, and Skill-Shifting

Review the results of this *LSI* assessment for this skill set on page 35 in Chapter 2 and fill out the worksheet on this and the next page. In this way, you will develop an overview of the key skills in this skill set that would benefit from additional focus.

1. **What are your three strongest skills in this skill set?**

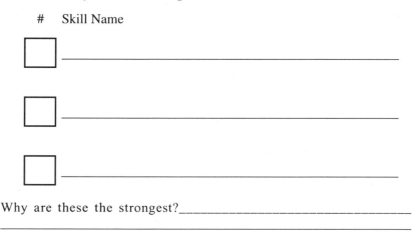

       \#   Skill Name

Why are these the strongest?_____
_____
_____

2. **What are your three weakest skills in this skill set?**

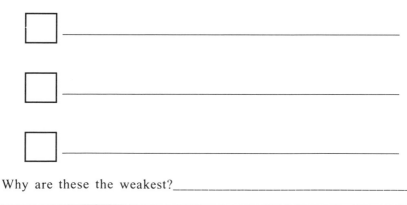

       \#   Skill Name

Why are these the weakest?_____
_____
_____

Can you identify any next steps that can be taken to maximize these skills of Versatility in your leadership role?

Skill #	Action Step #	Action Item	Coach/Mentor/ Target Date
☐	1.	_____	_____ ___/___/___
☐	2.	_____	_____ ___/___/___
☐	3.	_____	_____ ___/___/___
☐	4.	_____	_____ ___/___/___
☐	5.	_____	_____ ___/___/___
☐	6.	_____	_____ ___/___/___
☐	7.	_____	_____ ___/___/___
☐	8.	_____	_____ ___/___/___
☐	9.	_____	_____ ___/___/___
☐	10.	_____	_____ ___/___/___

Part Four

Chapter 10

LEADERSHIP THEORIES OVERVIEW: The Nature of Leadership

During the 1980s, people and organizations pursued "excellence" with great vigor and determination. And, while creating excellence will probably continue as a mainstay during the 1990s, a new quest has clearly emerged: the pursuit of integration and balance. Individuals, families, organizations, and society in general increasingly see the need for greater harmony among professional career and personal relationships, worldly success and spiritual fulfillment, economic prosperity and environmental protection, accomplishment and peace of mind, tough-mindedness and gentleness, immediate gratification and enduring joy, for this generation and future generations.

Craig Hickman

Introduction

The goals of this chapter involve your gaining perspective on the nature of leadership, comparing traditional vs. transformational views on leadership, and understanding the Transforming Leadership Model.
1. Philosophies of Leadership
2. Definitions of Leadership
3. Theories of Leadership

Comparing Traditional and Modern Philosophies of Leadership

This chapter will be theoretical in nature, and because of this, you may find the application of the contents of any one approach somewhat challenging. Most people have had difficulty applying leadership theory and, in part, this is why the nature of leadership keeps changing. The many possible ways of viewing leadership can be confusing and overwhelming. Rather than my recommending any one approach, I believe it will be helpful for you to review a number of the philosophies of leadership to compare one with another. You will find that their fundamental assumptions and the consequences that flow from these assumptions differ significantly from one another.

As a first step toward understanding various perspectives of leadership, it is important for you to grasp the basic assumptions that have guided various leaders in the past, and consciously formulate more encompassing assumptions to guide you as a leader into the future. This first step of achieving a more balanced understanding can be achieved by looking at some definitions.

Webster's New World Dictionary (1984) defines philosophy as: "A study of the principles underlying conduct and thought." It is valuable to compare the traditional with the more modern assumptions (principles) because we can then better see the value of them both. Gaining a basic understanding of leadership philosophies will assist you to formulate your own integrated philosophy of leadership.

The Operating Assumptions Behind Theories X, Y, Z, and R

The first philosophy of leadership we will look into is outlined in Douglas McGregor's work (McGregor, 1960). After studying a number of organizations and the operating assumptions of those with decision-making authority, he identified a set of beliefs that summarize this early view. He called this first view Theory X. Here it is called a philosophy, not a theory, because it is really a set of beliefs about the nature of work and the nature of workers. McGregor based his work on the work of Maslow. Like Maslow, he was interested in what motivated people toward greater personal development and improved performance. McGregor argued that traditional leader behavior was inappropriate since it was based on questionable assumptions about employees. These assumptions are outlined below.

Theory X Assumptions

1. Employees are inherently lazy and will avoid work unless forced to do it.
2. Employees have no ambition or desire for responsibility; instead they prefer to be directed and controlled.
3. Employees have no motivation to achieve organizational objectives.
4. Employees are motivated only by physiological and safety needs.

These assumptions form the basis of a philosophy that can be very dehumanizing to others, and even to self as a leader. McGregor believed that Theory X assumptions were outdated, and that employees would perform better if treated with a very different set of assumptions he called Theory Y. This is the second philosophy, or set of operating assumptions, we will look into.

Theory Y Assumptions

1. Employees find work as natural as play if organizational conditions are appropriate. People appear adverse to work only because their past work experiences have been unsatisfactory.
2. Employees can be motivated by higher-order needs such as ego, autonomy, and self-actualization.
3. Employees seek responsibility since it allows them to satisfy higher-order needs.

Autocratic philosophy is at the root of Theory X, with the leader initiating all the structure, and where the central focus is on production, not on people. In Theory Y, there is a more democratic philosophy where leaders "believe the best" about employees, and treat them more as "people who work" rather than as "workers who also happen to be people."

Even today, McGregor's work stands as a breakthrough in identifying basic operating assumptions of leaders and the impact those assumptions can have on morale and organizational effectiveness. Much development has taken place, however, since McGregor's findings regarding basic assumptions or philosophies about leadership.

Theory Z Assumptions

In 1981, Ouchi presented a clear set of operating assumptions that have impacted the functioning of a number of companies in the Fortune 500 cadre.

1. Offer people long-term employment, a positive "family" of coworkers and leaders, and clear objectives and they will stick around, do a good job, and have a sense of pride in the work done.
2. Offer people a piece of the pie when it comes to making decisions that will affect their work and they will understand and support the decisions more often and more wholeheartedly.
3. Expect people to take individual responsibility for their own performances as an important part of a bigger "team," and they will fulfill that expectation.
4. Evaluate people over the long-term rather than frequently because this gives them opportunity to develop, based upon their inner sense of integrity, rather than on outward pressure.
5. Build trust and integrity into all interactions between managerial and nonmanagerial personnel to develop a sense of the importance of individual contributions to the group effort.
6. Maintain few levels of authority in the organization and emphasize work groups to get jobs done because this maximizes an individual's sense of belonging to his or her group, and to the organization as a whole. It also increases individual and group accountability and performance.
7. Use informal rules and regulations, with formalized measures of performance to further encourage individual workers to internalize personal responsibility for achieving group and organizational objectives.

Theory Z takes the spotlight off the individual and puts each person in the context of the group, the organization, and the culture in which he or she is living. This gives the individual a sense of value and importance based upon the accomplishments of the overall organization, and takes some of the heavy pressure off each individual in each moment to perform all out. In Japan, this has created personal and corporate determination to succeed at functioning in groups to reach departmental, organizational, and even national cultural goals.

Critics of the Theory Z philosophy claim that it will not really work in North America because of cultural differences between here and Japan (Biggs,

1982). Some of the assumptions have been, however, successfully implemented, especially in some small family businesses, and in larger corporate structures like IBM, Hewlett-Packard, GM, and others (see Ouchi, 1981).

It is ironic to consider that North America, previously driven by predominantly Judeo-Christian historical and cultural roots, has found or would find the values of cooperation, support, loyalty, family closeness, intimacy, and caring so foreign to its way of leading businesses and organizations. Individual accomplishment, competition with others, confrontation between labor and management, and an emphasis on self in general have come to the forefront of the value structure of so many people since the 1950s. One important reason could be that the reward system of the company is usually skewed to individual performance and is not connected to group achievement.

The Assumptions of Theory R: A Relational Approach

Alderson (1985) has introduced a unique set of assumptions into the arena of leadership philosophies. Given the name of Theory R, the guiding assumptions underlying this philosophy are as follows.
1. That all people need love (affirmation), a sense of dignity (appreciation), and need to be treated with respect (recognition that they are of intrinsic value, and that their work is a valued contribution) in the workplace—not just at home, or in other environments.
2. That the building of a person's sense of self-esteem through meeting the foregoing three key needs will have a positive impact on worker morale, quality of work, and productivity.
3. That reconciliation, not confrontation, in leader-follower relations will help to create the needed sense of mutual respect, dignity, and unconditional concern for one another as human beings.
4. That relationships between leaders and followers are the keys to productivity, morale, and quality concerns.
5. That people have the desire to work hard and take pride in what they accomplish.
6. That when people are placed in an environment sensitive to the "Value of the Person," they will be cooperative, creative, and productive.
7. That treating people "right" is the right thing to do, and that is reason enough to actively value people.

At first glance, these ideas seem too simplistic to have much credence in the "real," complex world. But, at least in the hands of Alderson, they worked stunningly well in a steel foundry in Pennsylvania called Pittron. Alderson found something that both labor and management could agree upon. Every man and woman in the entire operation had something in common: each wanted to be valued.

Two years after the Value of the Person approach was implemented, the plant went from a six-million-dollar loss to a six-million-dollar profit; from 300 to 1,100 employees; from 600 grievances per year to one grievance per year; from 20 percent absenteeism to 1 percent; from poor-quality production to high-quality production; and productivity was up 64 percent! Such dramatic changes warrant our attention. Anyone wishing to read the published story, which outlines the whole case study of Pittron's turnaround, should see Sproul, 1980.

Thus, we see a dramatic shift in the evolution of the guiding assumptions of leadership theories from the autocratic sweat shops of Theory X, to the humanistic Theory Y, to the group emphasis of Theory Z—to the value of people theory of Theory R. But there are more questions we must ask. In the next section, we will compare these more traditional definitions of leadership with new insights into the nature of transformational leadership.

Comparing Traditional and Transformational Definitions of Leadership

Traditional Definitions

Leadership has been defined in many ways by people of varying perspectives over the years. Indeed, there are so many definitions that vagueness and confusion seem to prevail in the many minds about the whole issue. It is not surprising then that many leaders question their roles, their effectiveness, even their importance, and are questioned by those around them. Below you will see a brief summary of many definitions of leadership, most of which are traditional in nature; some, however, lead toward the more transformative (adapted from Stogdill, 1974) and then give a specific definition of transforming leadership.

1. Definitions and aspects of leadership: a potpourri
2. Determining group structure, ideology, and activities
3. Coupling leader behavior with the meeting of group needs
4. Keeping one step ahead of the group
5. Innovation in accomplishment of tasks
6. Achieving the most with the least friction
7. Inducing compliance, respect, and cooperation
8. Goal-directed communication that gets positive results
9. Serving others and meeting their needs
10. Persuading others to accept a particular view or strategy
11. Exercising positive power to get desired results

12. Making the most of individual differences to reach goals
13. Being perceived as legitimate, expert, trustworthy

As you can see by the range of definitions above, there are considerable differences among these various views of leadership. Few individuals bother to search the literature to discover alternative views. This lack of a working definition of leadership can be a problem for someone who wants to develop leadership potential and become more effective and successful in achieving goals.

In contrast, you will see below a focused definition of leadership that can assist you to develop a more integrated and applicable understanding of leadership and its more transformative nature.

Transforming Leadership: A Definition

Transforming Leadership is vision, planning, communication, and creative action that has a positive unifying effect on a group of people around a set of clear values and beliefs, to accomplish a clear set of measurable goals. This transforming approach simultaneously impacts the personal development and corporate productivity of all involved.

The transforming leader also transforms self and the nature of leadership itself in a continuing process of learning to lead better. Therefore, everything is affected by a transforming, developing leader who is, by definition, an active agent of positive change: the environment is affected; organizations are affected; groups are affected; interpersonal interchanges are affected; the character of leadership becomes more mature throughout the organization; others are developed; and the leader's understanding is developed in the process. The transforming leader is no "super person," but the subtle, ripple effect of positive leadership can affect all parts of an organization and all the people in it. As a "spin-off," their families at home can be positively affected, and this can even impact the tone of the communities in which people live.

Transforming leaders could be people who are administrators, managers, supervisors, educators, health and medical professionals, counselors, clergy, criminal justice workers, parents, and others who might have the knowledge, skills, tools, and abilities to impact and develop both an organization and the people in it at the same time. This is the case when a father or mother (the transforming leaders) in a family (the organization) facilitate themselves and their children to grow by combining structuring and nurturing behaviors. It is also the case when an executive structures an organization through long-range planning and policy development, and develops teams of people who grow toward increased morale and productivity. How many organizations do strategic planning to increase productivity? Quite a number. How many of those organizations also do strategic planning and budgeting to increase the quality of the work and interpersonal lives for the people who produce that hoped for productivity? Not nearly as many. Therefore, you can see the potential importance of defining leadership in terms of people who are the producers— rather than producers who also happen to be people instead of robots.

Traditional Theories of Leadership: An Overview

Now that we have reviewed some general definitions of leadership and have compared them to the working definition of transforming leadership, it will be useful to review some general theories of leadership and compare them with transforming leadership theory. A theory is defined by *Webster* as: "A formulation of underlying principles of certain observed phenomena which have been verified to some degree." Important aspects of leadership are contained in many of the traditional views of leadership, and some important lessons can be learned by identifying some of their limitations.

Biological—Personality Theories

The Great Man Theory: In 1960, Jennings presented a comprehensive survey and analysis of the "great man" theory of leadership. In summary, this earlier theory advances the idea that certain people are born stronger, more intelligent, more able to lead. Heroes, royalty, and the more successful people in general were thought to have inborn talent and ability that enabled them to stand out from among the masses and achieve unusual successes. This idea that born leaders had certain characteristics gave rise to the related trait theory of leadership, studied and popularized in the 1920s and 1930s by Bernard (1926), Bingham (1927), Tead (1929), and Kilbourne (1935).

Trait Theories: These theories were sometimes intermixed with racial, sexual, and class discrimination to promote supremacy of one race over another, one sex over another, or one social or economic class over another. A king would have his brother or son (or at least a daughter) succeed his throne because of the "good stock" inherent in the blood. Though it is possible that some strengths are hereditary (as revealed in medical research), it is clear there are too many surprising exceptions to this theory for us to give it significant credence.

Environmental Theories

Leader-Behavior Theory: This position suggests that circumstances themselves cause a great leader to rise to the occasion. Under the "right" conditions, a leader will emerge as if by nature's necessity or invention. Bogardus (1918) suggested that the type of leadership that a group will develop or accept will be determined by the nature of the group and the problems it must solve. Victor Frankl, in his book, *Man's Search for Meaning,* cites examples of leadership emerging from the most frail of beings in the terrible conditions of a concentration camp. There have, however, been many crises that have not produced a person equal to the occasion. Therefore, we cannot necessarily give great credence to this theory of leadership either.

Personal-Situational Theory: This theory is the first to propose a complex set of factors involved in the shaping and development of leadership, and is the first to be scrutinized by serious research efforts. Westburg (1931) proposed that the critical factors involved in leadership were a combination of the "affective, intellectual, and action traits of the individual as well as the specific conditions under which the individual operates." The idea here is that success in leadership is dependent upon a leader's ability to understand the followers and the surrounding environment, and then react appropriately to those people and situations as they change.

Bennis (1961) recommended that theory on leadership should consider the measurement of rationality; the impact of informal organization and interpersonal relations; the positive influence of a benevolent autocracy because it structures relationships between superiors and subordinates; job enlargement and employee-centered supervision that permit individual self-development; and participative management and joint consultation that allow the integration of individual and organizational goals. Bennis emphasized the importance of interpersonal dimension in determining the quality of the work life in an organization. He also emphasized the value of the person in relation to productivity.

Interaction-Expectation Theory: In this theoretical orientation, leadership is the act of initiating structure supported by group members because such structure solves mutual problems, conforms or positively transforms group norms, and causes members to expect that success will come from following a leader of such initiative. Leadership, according to this theory, involves both initiating and fulfilling the expectations of followers. Leader credibility is based upon the ability to fulfill expectations generated by the leader (Homans, 1950; Stogdill, 1959).

Humanistic Theories of Leadership

The theories of Argyris (1964), Blake and Mouton (1964), Likert (1967), and McGregor (1960, 1966) are focused on the development of effective organizations through a "humanizing" process of structuring the work or living environment so that individuals can meet personal needs and organizational objectives at the same time. This theory attempts to balance the needs of the individual with the goals of the organization, but has been accused at times of sacrificing organizational "bottomline" results for the sake of realizing human values such as employee morale, worth of the individual, quality of the work life, meaning and purpose in work, mutual trust, and productivity based upon the internal motivation of workers.

This approach can contribute much to our understanding of human needs in the workplace, and can cause us to be more cognizant of the "people" side of enterprise, the importance and dignity of human life, and the importance of personal meaning and purpose in work. It has also revolutionized thinking about productivity and performance; basically, it has clarified that people— who like what they do, feel respected and valued, and are involved—will perform better. Here are some major contributions from the these authors.

Argyris: Pointed out the inevitable conflict between the individual and the organization. He claimed that organizations are most effective when leaders provide avenues for workers to make valuable contributions and be recognized for their efforts in reaching organizational objectives. He also explained how most organizations overplay the rational and underemphasize the emotional—especially the negative emotions (1982). In his opinion, the best organizations recognize and process negative emotions until resolution, or at least compromise, is achieved.

Blake and Mouton: Presented a grid to illustrate the relationship between concern for people and concern for production. They created one of the first leadership-style assessment instruments, and formulated a theory that suggested that a leader who scored high on both people and production concerns was most effective.

Likert: Suggested that leaders need to seriously consider the values, expectations, and interpersonal skill competencies of others with whom they work. The positive leader, as defined by Likert, is one who appreciates an employee's efforts and builds self-esteem in others. Task and relationship factors are both important and interrelated.

McGregor: I include McGregor in this section because some of his assumptions have been verified through observation and research over the years. He developed a theory of understanding leadership behavior along a continuum from "Theory X" to "Theory Y." The leader with a Theory X orientation is thought to be "old school," believing that followers are self-oriented and uncaring about the needs of the organization, and so attempts are made to directly influence and motivate them in the direction of accomplishing organizational goals—without much regard for their own feelings or motives. A leader with a Theory Y orientation is thought to be "new school," believing people are self-motivated and self-actualizing by nature, and that leaders should arrange the organizational environment to capitalize on those internal motivations to help employees reach organizational goals.

All of these humanistic theories suggest a single path for leader behavior, and are considered today to be somewhat narrow. It has become increasingly clear that no one theory or approach really works best. Depending upon a host of variables, a wide range of interventions may work. This is not to say there are not some key principles that can be applied throughout the leadership process, but for now we will examine the more situational approaches.

Situational or "Contingency" Approaches to Leadership

These approaches reflect important advances over the more simplistic "one best way" methods-to-lead models. Contingency models suggest more complex diagnosis of the situation at hand, and more complex leadership interventions. Situational or contingency approaches reflect the belief that there is a relationship between employees' satisfaction and performance, and their environments. The basic premise of these approaches is that if we understand the factors that impact employee morale and performance, and apply that understanding successfully, we can have more direct influence and control over morale, and—the belief of many—productivity.

Fiedler (1967) advanced a theory called The Leadership Contingency Model, which serves at least three main purposes. First, it supports the idea that effective leadership is situational in nature, that a leader has to attend to a wide range of situational variables to make a wise choice of leader behavior. Second, Fiedler found that more-directive leaders were effective in certain situations, and this finding was contrary to the philosophies of the 1950s and 1960s, dominated by human relations theories. Fiedler also opened up the issue of leader versatility, and the placement of a leader in a situation where he or she can capitalize on his or her strengths, i.e., "engineer the environment to fit the manager."

A second theory that suggests leader behaviors can influence worker performance and satisfaction is the Path-Goal Model formulated by House (1971). This approach suggests that the leader's job is to increase the pay-offs to workers for achieving work goals. The leader does this by clarifying the path to these goals, by reducing blockages that prevent workers from reaching the goals, and by behaving in a way that will increase worker satisfaction while workers are achieving those goals. If workers feel they are capable of doing a good job without direction from the boss, they will be dissatisfied with—and even resent—directive leadership behavior. House's model is important because it gives us insight into some ways leaders can increase employee satisfaction.

A third type of situational or contingency theory of leadership is contained in Vroom and Yetton's (1973) Decision-Making Model. According to this theory, it is critical for the leader to decide on how much participation subordinates should have when making decisions. They provide guidelines for leaders to decide how much participation is appropriate in each situation. They stress the importance of decisions and information availability, and show that acceptance of decisions by subordinates is an important issue in regard to their productivity.

Finally, Situational Leadership was developed and popularized more recently by Blanchard and Hersey (1977, 1982). Even though the roots of this approach go back to Westburg (in Stogdill, 1974), it is fair to mention the impact and importance of this work as a major voice in communicating to many leaders (and trainers/educators of leaders) the value of carefully considering the developmental level of a follower or group of followers, and matching the leadership style to the ability of the follower to perform a particular task.

A concern for follower development is clearly voiced and this approach is continuing to be influential in shaping thinking and training in leadership flexibility for greater appropriateness, and, therefore, greater effectiveness in face-to-face leadership situations.

Summary

As you can see, leadership theory has become more and more complex as time has moved on. The simple authority relationship of boss/employee has shifted greatly toward a realization of the importance of the people factors— factors in each situation that affect overall outcomes, and people and situational factors that interact to affect one another.

Only a few people in a situation rise to the top for a number of complex reasons, and succeed or fail for a number of complex reasons. Theories of leadership are each limited, none of them metatheoretical (integrating and including many useful theories into one), and have been based upon interesting academic or valuable research trends, and upon the philosophical beliefs of a particular decade or era.

For a more complete account of the development of leadership theory, see Stogdill (1974). It is useful to see the historical development of leadership to note the direction in which it has moved in past years, and to thereby gain a sense of where it is likely to move in the next decade. Leadership, at all levels, from family to government, will have great impact on how we move into the next century.

A Price to Pay for Complexity

Theories of leadership are moving from simple to the more complex as we move through time. There comes a time, however, when the richness can become clutter—a time when the complexity goes beyond what is applicable by the average leader. This is the price we pay for more complex theories. They are more difficult to learn, more complicated in their applications, and require more sophisticated training methods. More intricate research methodologies are needed to study their effectiveness.

A Pay-Off for Integrating the Logically Useful Parts of Various Theories

As we develop more intricate but integrated models of leadership, there is a greater likelihood these models will represent guidelines that can work in the real world. The challenge is to state them clearly enough so they become tools that can be tested and used. Research on leadership effectiveness reveals that at this point, we are still groping for the "magic formula," that there is some conflicting evidence about the effectiveness of leadership training (Fiedler, 1972), and that each leader is still basically out there on her or his own to make a positive difference using the talents, knowledge, and skills he or she has.

Hickman (1990) does an excellent job of contrasting, comparing, and integrating traditional and transformational definitions, roles, and functions of management and leadership. In the preface of his new book, he states:

> *In organizations, this gravitation toward balance has encouraged business people to begin integrating incremental strategies with innovative breakthroughs; cultural values with corporate policies; stability and security with change and opportunity; flexible processes with structured systems; and short-term gains with long-term progress. The complex global business environment of the 1990s demands that we go much further in this direction. Given the growing pressures, complexity, change, and competition facing business organizations today, most executives find themselves confronted with an escalating conflict and schism between the managerial and leadership requirements of organizations. An "either-or" mentality dominates at a time when organizations most desperately need the best of both.*

Transforming Leadership is an emerging assessment and training model with promise for providing a clearer vision of how powerful and enlivening leadership can be integrated with the wisdom of traditional management, and offers concrete ways we can grow into becoming better "leading managers" through expanding awareness and receiving training in deficit areas.

References

D. **Guralnik** (ed.), *Webster's New World Dictionary of the American Language*. (New York: Warner, 1984).

D. **McGregor**, *The Human Side of Enterprise.* ⁻(New York: McGraw-Hill, 1960).

W. **Ouchi**, *Theory Z: How American Business Can Meet the Japanese Challenge*. (Reading, MA: Addison-Wesley, 1981).

B. **Biggs**, "The Dangerous Folly Called Theory Z," *Fortune* (17 May, 1982): 48-53.

W. **Alderson**, *Value of the Person: Theory R Concept*. (Pittsburgh: Value of the Person, 1985).

R. **Sproul**, *Stronger Than Steel*. (New York: Harper and Row, 1980).

R. M. **Stogdill**, *Handbook of Leadership*. (New York: The Free Press, 1974).

E. E. **Jennings**, *An Anatomy of Leadership: Princes, Heroes, and Supermen*. (New York: Harper, 1960).

L. L. **Bernard**, *An Introduction to Social Psychology*. (New York: Holt, 1926).

W. V. **Bingham**, "Leadership," In H. C. Metcalf's *The Psychological Foundations of Management* (New York: Shaw, 1927).

O. **Tead**, "The Technique of Leadership," *In Human Nature and Management* (New York: McGraw-Hill, 1929).

C. E. **Kilbourne**, "The Elements of Leadership," *Journal of Applied Psychology*, 43, (1959): 209-211.

E. S. **Bogardus**, *Essentials of Social Psychology*. (Los Angeles: University of Southern California Press, 1918).

E. M. **Westburg**, "A Point of View: Studies in Leadership." J. *Abnorm. Soc. Psychol.*, 25, (1931): 418-423.

W. G. **Bennis**, "Revisionist Theory of Leadership." *Harvard Bus. Rev.*, 39(1), (1961): 26-36, 146-150.

G. C. **Homans**, *The Human Group*. (New York: Harcourt, Brace, 1950).

R. M. **Stogdill**, *Individual Behavior and Group Achievement.* (New York: Oxford University Press, 1959).

C. **Argyris**, *Integrating the Individual and the Organization.* (New York: Wiley, 1964).

R. R. **Blake** and J. S. **Mouton**, *The Managerial Grid.* (Houston: Gulf, 1964).

R. **Likert**. *The Human Organization.* (New York: McGraw-Hill, 1967).

D. **McGregor**, *The Human Side of Enterprise.* (New York: McGraw-Hill, 1960).

D. **McGregor**, *Leadership and Motivation.* (Cambridge, MA: MIT Press, 1966).

C. **Argyris**, *Reasoning, Learning and Action: Individual and Organizational.* (San Francisco: Jossey-Bass, 1982).

F. E. **Fiedler**, *A Theory of Leadership Effectiveness.* (New York: McGraw-Hill, 1967).

R. **House**, "A Path-Goal Model of Leader Effectiveness," *Administrative Science Quarterly* 16 (September, 1971): 312-338.

V. **Vroom** and P. **Yetton**, *Leadership and Decision Making.* (Pittsburg: University of Pittsburgh Press, 1973).

K. **Blanchard** and P. **Hersey**, *Management of Organizational Behavior: Utilizing Human Resources.* (New Jersey: Prentice-Hall, 1982).

Ralph M. **Stogdill**, *Handbook of Leadership.* (New York: The Free Press, 1974).

F. **Fiedler**, "How Do You Make Leaders More Effective: New Answers to an Old Puzzle," *Organizational Dynamics* (Autumn, 1972): 3-18.

Craig R. **Hickman**, *Mind of a Manager, Soul of a Leader.* (New York: John Wiley & Sons, 1990).

Chapter 11

HOW BUILDING A LEADERSHIP ORGANIZATION PREPARES THE WAY FOR LEARNING

by Marilyn Hamilton, Ph.D. (Cand.)

Now that we have reviewed previous theories of leadership, we will examine how *Transforming Leadership* can prepare you to build a leadership organization—one ready to become a learning organization. You will see where the skills become so very important in the development of an organization, its people, and how the skills also enrich the relationships with the customers who drive the business.

What is a Leadership Organization?

A Leadership Organization creates and sustains a leadership-centered culture where leaders develop leaders from the top down and the inside out.

Organizations not led by Transforming Leaders look a lot like a cart with square wheels. The leader is out front alone, head down, pulling and straining to move the organization forward. Meanwhile the other members of the organization who may well be at the back of the cart pushing (or sometimes pulling in the opposite direction to the leader) exert a tremendous effort—without even seeing the destination, let alone the view ahead. The people at the back of the cart have little to no communication with the leader.

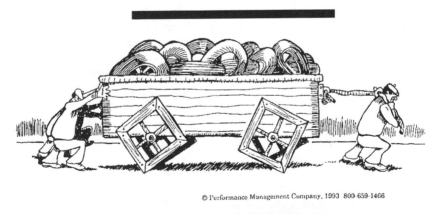

© Performance Management Company, 1993 800-659-1466

In organizations without Transforming Leaders, the square wheels on the cart too often represent ineffective operations, inappropriate methods, resistance to change, no flexibility, lack of innovation, lack of creativity, dead weight, unwillingness, and a lack of readiness for change.

An organization that looks and functions like a cart with square wheels needs to replace its square wheels with round wheels. Otherwise, this organization cannot create an environment where it is natural, normal, and easy for leaders to create and sustain a leadership-centered culture.

There is an answer for organizations with this dilemma. Most probably it is contained in the very cart the leaders are lugging behind them. If they only looked inside the cart, they would probably find more than enough round wheels to put on the axles to create a Leadership Organization. These round wheels are not only new ideas, other options, unused assets—they are also the potential capabilities for every person in the organization to become a Transforming Leader.

What would a Leadership Organization look like?

For starters, it would maximize the potential of both people and technical systems by developing them in a balanced way. Instead of just concentrating on placing round wheels (technical systems) on the organizational cart, key leaders would develop a team of people with leadership skills who could work together. It would require that leaders provide inspiration, plan strategic direction, make effective operational decisions, work as a team to implement strategies, evaluate accomplishments, and enjoy (and celebrate) the process and results of working together.

I would not only optimize the current operations, but would prepare for a preferred future, based on vigilantly crafted forecasts of current trends that develop into the waves of change. Doing the same old thing, selling the same old product, treating customers the same old way just won't work any more. The luxury of staying the same for most services and products is over.

A Leadership Organization views people as a vital—and at least equal—part of the system along with its technical strengths. For organizations with a high technical component, this is often a challenge. We have worked with manufacturers, hospitals, construction firms, security advisors, computer hardware suppliers, chemical testing laboratories, agricultural associations, engineering groups, and resource management firms where the traditional concentration on technical solutions makes it very difficult for these organizations to redefine themselves with an equal emphasis on *Transforming Leadership* skills. In the past, these organizations have often been at the forefront of their sector because of technical excellence. With the rapid spread and assimilation of technical competencies, however, the only way for these organizations to differentiate themselves is to develop the people side of their systems.

Leadership Organizations equip and develop leaders, not just to optimize their technical capacities, but to optimize individual, team, and organizational performance while they develop other leaders. Leadership Organizations recognize that they create a synergy by connecting the development of individuals, teams, and organizations. This synergy has a permanent, long-term multiplier effect on satisfaction and performance at every level.

Without this approach, organizations develop in a lopsided way. They reengineer, restructure, implement TQM, obtain ISO9000 accreditation, or simply upgrade technology. They obtain early returns from these sound and practical new systems. But unless the organizations invest the resources to develop leadership skills—or carefully select new and skilled leaders from the outside—the demands of these new structures and methodologies will likely break down. They often fail because of lack of communication, lack of commitments to accountability, and lack of skills to implement the underlying assumption of most of these revised work practices—namely, that everyone is someone else's customer.

A Leadership Organization with a people-development culture at all levels can avoid the problems of such costly mistakes. From a technical point of view, these mistakes are little more than the equivalent of harnessing the cart with square wheels to a bulldozer or replacing an intelligent living system (people) with brute force (such as a horse). Neither solution maximizes the potential of the whole organization. Moreover, both approaches discourage, anger, demoralize, and disrespect potential leaders.

So why is Leadership Development so Important?

The amount and pace of change we have experienced in our lifetime is only the beginning of an exponential change growth curve. For organizations to survive in these circumstances, such change must be anticipated and led. Recently, two women explained to me exactly how this truth was affecting their lives.

One, a Canadian travel agent, had known for months that the airlines were going to "cap" their commission structures (i.e., limit how much they paid per ticket). This change was going to seriously affect the revenue structure of every travel agent. She had seen it coming (it had been implemented in the U.S. last year) and so she had been restructuring her business, retraining her staff, and reeducating her customers in anticipation of this change. Instead of cutting back services, she added new ones and discovered customers were willing to pay for them. Her first efforts were rewarded with significant revenues, happier team members and new customers—from other travel agents who had no plan to face these changes in the supplier environment.

The other woman, Margaret Wheatley—author of *Leadership and the New Science* and coauthor of *The Simpler Way*—admits that everything she ever learned about managing and leading organizations must now be reevaluated, relearned, and reframed in the light of new scientific discoveries. Concepts from quantum physics, mathematics, biology, and meteorology have changed her perceptions of how people relate with one another and to their organizations.

Change on the magnitude we witness around us every day is stressful. Stress is at an all-time high. Without *Transforming Leadership* skills, organizations suffer the deficiencies that stress can cause. People become unavailable because of physical, psychological, emotional, and spiritual suffering. When people are absent in body and/or mind, it creates more stress on the people who are present. Many of the downsizing efforts have backfired because the people who remained to do the work burned out from overload because they were now doing the tasks two people used to do.

In many workplaces, people are expected to work in teams without a traditional leader (so-called self-directed teams). Flattened organizations and self-directed work teams need more leadership skills in all team members so that they can perform effectively. When everyone has leadership skills, he or she can assume leadership roles as and when required. This kind of just-in-time availability of leadership skills makes individuals, teams, and organizations more flexible. It also prepares them to respond to global quality standards, and is the key to balancing people with technical issues.

If the Value of *Transforming Leadership* Skills is so High, what is Blocking Leaders from Developing them?

The answer must be examined in the light of the readiness and willingness of leaders to develop themselves and create a leadership-development culture. The concept of readiness and willingness has been discussed previously. Transforming Leaders develop when individuals have Level Three and Four readiness and willingness levels. So the question then becomes—why are many leaders at a Level One or Two resistant or only thinking about change?

Leaders are often justifiably proud of their accomplishments, position, and recognition. They fear being exposed as inadequate. Many leaders have struggled throughout their careers to work their way up the technical and administrative ladder. It is often a shock for them to learn they need to learn additional skills—some of which may take years to develop—at a point in their careers when they thought they had completed their learning. An interesting example of this is evident in the health care system. Many women physicians are the most resistant to change in hospitals wanting to restructure around program management and patient-focused care. At first blush, this seems difficult to explain until we learn that their success in the "traditional health care system" has been obtained by overcoming many odds along the career path—from simply getting into medical school to attaining departmental leadership status. When these women are asked to give up power and status to share it with others, in newly reengineered organizations, they are often quite unwilling.

Many leaders also fear they do not or will not have credibility when they develop and practice new leadership skills. They have depended for their recognition and credibility on their technical competence in the past. If *Transforming Leadership* skills are new to them, at first they do not feel on certain ground. They fear they will lose credibility in the eyes of others (peers, subordinates, outsiders, colleagues, spouses, children). Adults do not like to be made to feel uncertain or incompetent.

Many of these feelings result from simply a lack of preparation, training, and coaching for new learners. Lifelong learning is still a new paradigm for many people. Most baby boomers still live with the image that their career education was completed before they turned age thirty. Few of us have had the benefits of coaching or mentoring relationships or programs to assist us to learn and to develop our *Transforming Leadership* skills on a regular basis. Many men who have chosen technical careers have shared with me that they never expected to need these skills so they never learned them—or valued them. A new consultant in the north recently shared with me that her clients who work in the resource-based industries still do not understand how these skills would relate in any way to the work they do.

Traditional organizations and traditional managers often have a false trust in the old ways of management. I have been told more than once in my career "If it ain't broke, don't fix it." Managing without leadership skills can be a dangerous job these days. It allows managers to be blindsided by the behaviors of valuable employees—which may have expensive legal implications, the actions of competition on the other side of the world, or the reactions of community activists.

The other side of this "trust" coin is management's failure to trust people's potential. One retail owner has told me more than once, " It is easier to do it myself than to train someone else to do it. They never do it the "right" way, anyway." This attitude is self-defeating for the organization as well as the leader. The complexity of our world today means that leaders with this expectation will shoulder an ever-increasing load and innovation will be stymied in the organization. Recent scientific discoveries teach us that diversity and innovation are the keys to transformation. They confirm the old saying that "if we always do what we've always done, we'll always get what we've always got."

Finally, a major block to learning *Transforming Leadership* skills arises because of personal difficulties and/or internal emotional problems. Stress can originate at home and be imported into the workplace and vice versa. If this happens and is not addressed, it can become a self-perpetuating cycle. Leaders need TL skills so that they know how to manage this kind of stress for themselves, recognize and assist others who are suffering from it, and keep the round wheels on the organizational cart. Organizations cannot create a leadership-centered culture that promotes learning unless addressing the causes of stress is supported and accepted.

Leadership Organizations Benefit from Transforming Leaders.

Transforming Leaders prevent and solve people and organizational problems. They develop the perspective of not just working IN the organization but working ON the organization. They see the organization as a whole, not just an assembly of parts. They are caring and committed to individuals, teams, and the organization as an integral system. They demonstrate a wide range of competencies, including both technical and people skills. They are forward-looking visionaries, anticipating possibilities for the organization.

"Make no small plans, for they do not have the power to move men's souls." A successful entrepreneur coached a class that I attended of developing business owners, with that challenge. It speaks loudly to developing a vision for a positive future and linking it with the ability to communicate and energize this vision to others. A Leadership Organization doesn't have just one person who can "move souls" but a group of people who have the skills and willingness to energize each other on a continuous basis. They have found ways to capture hearts that are tied to a common vision. This moves the exercise of strategic planning onto a completely different plane. It creates an expectation that individuals and teams will act, and that success is inevitable.

In fact, "the moving of souls" can produce long-term practical benefits that go far beyond simply celebrating targeted successes. One of the best examples of how practical this can be is told by Bill Gibson. Bill told us about Dunsmuir Shell, a gas station in Victoria, BC, owned by Bob Dunsmuir. In the 1970s and 1980s, Bob looked for ways to differentiate his gas station from others, many of which became self-serve operations. He focused on providing not simply personal service, but exceptional service.

As a Transforming Leader, he engaged his young staff in deciding how to demonstrate exceptional service to their customers. They invented many ways that have since been adopted by others—such as running to the pumps, giving flowers away, and vacuuming cars while the owner waited. These services did win the operation a large and loyal following, and impressed the staff with the impact of their decisions.

Bob knew that was important because gas jockeys are typically young people, often struggling students, or even school dropouts. Bob wanted to keep his staff highly motivated and involved, so he took the unusual step of teaching them how to read Dunsmuir's financial statements, and he shared the results on a regular basis with them. He also set up profit-sharing opportunities for them.

Bob continued to look for ways to create a Leadership Organization and even taught his staff to consider the next customer as potentially their next boss—as he encouraged his staff to move on to better opportunities. With a highly dependable crew in place, it was not difficult for Bob to take a vacation and know operations would run smoothly. At one point, he found out exactly how fine a job he had done. Bob decided to take a holiday on his motorbike in the southern U.S. Unfortunately, he ended up in an accident that put him in the hospital with amnesia—he couldn't remember who he was, or where he came from. After some months, Bob recovered health and memory, but had been a long time away without any contact with the business. Because of the Leadership Organization culture he had created, Bob returned home to find the whole operation running as smoothly and even more profitably than when he had left it.

The Dunsmuir Shell story is a classic example of the mutual benefits that exist for Transforming Leaders in Leadership Organizations. It demonstrates that Management and Leadership are both necessary. They both help to manage change. They are both needed to balance technical and people issues, the present operational and future change issues. If Bob hadn't developed leadership skills in his management staff, he would have found a floundering operation on his return; if he hadn't developed management skills along with leadership skill, she would have found an injured or dead business. Leadership Organizations need more managers like Bob who don't over-manage and under-lead.

Leadership Organizations need Transforming Leaders who can even go beyond management and leadership. Leadership Organizations really need leaders who can focus on development and not just the status quo. Development of people is the secret to transforming the culture of the organization. It has been my experience with all the leaders with whom I have worked that when they develop, the organization develops—and as the organization develops, leaders develop. Development is a bridge that opens new possibilities for everyone.

Leadership Organizations are concerned even with the opportunity to transform people along with the organization. Transformation happens when the whole system—person, team, or organization—develops to a new level of performance. A Transforming Leader demonstrates a wholeness of mind, body, emotions, spirit, and interpersonal relationships that becomes the foundation for organizational transformation. Such leaders not only know they can't lead everyone directly—they know they need help to lead an organization. They are the leaders who create and develop teams of leaders able to move mountains.

Summary

The greatest satisfaction for Transforming Leaders is to ask the protégés they are coaching to describe the benefits—to themselves and the organization—

of their new *Transforming Leadership* skills. Here is a collection of comments others have shared when asked to identify the benefits of learning *Transforming Leadership* skills.

Benefits of *Transforming Leadership* Skills to Individuals and Organizations

TL Skill Set	Benefits to Individual	Benefits to Organization
Self-Management Skills	Has control over his/her life Competent in basics Reduces stress self-respect Has personal "act" together	Can inspire others Positive model to others More effective Better use of resources
Interpersonal Skills	Can communicate with others Can express needs Credibility Values self/others Can listen and hear	Communicates others needs Can influence others Two-way communication Able to work with others
Counseling & Problem-Management Skills	Can manage work/life Manages others Evaluates options Self/other understanding Effective with staff and family	Can coach others Can help others Can solve problems Can develop ideas Trusts others Works with people and technical issues
Consulting Skills	Can plan forward Feels in control Evaluates options Has insight, honesty, truth, confidence	Can give direction Can lead Proactive Confident Develops teamwork Serves others
Versatility Skills	Can assess styles, skills, roles Can understand others Credibility Open to change Effective Tolerant, patient Empathic Can assess, suspend, shift Versatile, flexible	Manages change Works with teams Organizational development Future-oriented Able to change fast Effective

In the next chapter, we will examine the components of our Comprehensive Personnel System and how it works to accelerate the organization's performance. Part of what Transforming Leaders do is transform the whole human resource area of their organization so it has a systems approach to finding, selecting, placing, orienting, coaching, and reviewing the performance of people and teams.

Chapter 12

TRANSFORMATION THROUGH PERSONNEL SYSTEMS

If organizations wish to be successful in managing the turbulence of the modern world...they will view their people as a key resource and value knowledge, information, creativity, interpersonal skills, and entrepreneurship as much as land, labor, and capital have been valued in the past.

Gareth Morgan

Introduction

One of the most important aspects of leadership where a transformative effect can be realized is in the careful assessment, selection, and development of people. Finding and retaining high-quality, committed employees or followers is absolutely critical to the success of any leader and any organization.

This book has, to this point, introduced you to knowledge and skills that can assist you to improve your effectiveness as a leader. But tools are important, as well. I could not fulfill my original vision for this book without including a system and some tools that can be implemented to improve the quality, productivity, and profitability of organizations.

Therefore, this chapter will introduce you to the concepts, steps, and practices originally introduced in the Comprehensive Personnel System (CPS) (Anderson and Zeiner, 1989).

First, a brief history of the CPS. It was originally designed in 1986 as a paper-based introductory seminar program entitled: Selecting and Developing Exceptional Employees. It was field tested between 1987 and 1991 with over 400 small-to-medium-sized companies. The program was evaluated very positively, and many of the companies have implemented parts or all of the CPS in their day-to-day operations. They did so in some cases on their own, and in other cases with the assistance of CRG Associate Company Principals, who are business consultants. Most of the company owners and personnel managers who attended the one or two day sessions either had not taken a course in personnel management or had not implemented the principles they were introduced to in such courses. Therefore, to their satisfaction, many of the staff problems they encountered on a day-to-day basis were addressed in the seminar.

As a group, they reported that the following fifteen of their most frequently encountered problems were causing them moderate to serious concern, from time to time.

1. Not hiring the right person for a job
2. Failing to communicate clear performance expectations
3. Fear of telling employees what they honestly think
4. Forgetting to reward or recognize positive performance
5. Losing track of personnel information
6. Failing to collect personnel information

7. Seeing employees make the same mistakes repeatedly
8. Fearing legal repercussions when firing low-performers
9. Misplacing files or information in files
10. Seeing their people not motivated to perform well
11. Seeing employees not doing what I want them to
12. Failing to capitalize on strengths and talents
13. Noting that absenteeism rates are too high
14. Believing employees can't problem-solve on their own
15. Feeling that training takes too much time, or is ineffective

Selecting and Developing Exceptional Employees

The CPS is a time and cost-effective communication system where employers and applicants or employees share a common language to discuss performance expectations and review progress on the job with those who manage or supervise them. It is not a substitute for careful decision-making or testing (when appropriate), but a vehicle for enhancing the specific description, communication, and recording of information about jobs and people in the workplace.

Often we are "caught" without a key person in a given position—and there is very little time to establish a comprehensive system to fulfill our immediate needs. Therefore, to reduce frustration and save time and costs, this system is presented in a practical and easy-to-use format.

There are twelve key things you can do to select and develop the people critical to the performance and productivity of your organization:
1. Screen applicants more accurately and efficiently
2. Build a data base of applicant and employee information
3. Create target interview questions and use them
4. Assess work behavioral style of applicant or employee
5. Assess work behavioral style of each job
6. Assess past work-performance history
7. Match knowledge and skills of employees with jobs
8. Contract for employee performance enhancement
9. Conduct and record performance reviews
10. Create and record an employee career plan
11. Reward and recognize employee performance
12. Communicate on a regular basis, using a shared language

The CPS can assist you to assess, record, or report all these things in a time and cost-effective manner.

Results You Can Expect When Using CPS Concepts

CPS adds productivity, efficiency, and profits to your organization or company by assisting you to more carefully manage how you:
1. Select, orient, place, train, and evaluate people.
2. Organize things and people in the work environment in order to make best use of people's talents.
3. Record and track all personnel data.
4. Use ideas to improve performance and morale on the job.

The primary aim of the CPS is to provide you with the knowledge and tools needed to lead others effectively toward increased productivity, efficiency, and profitability. Because employees differ in regard to motivation, age, maturity, experience, competence, and styles of approaching people and tasks, it is important to understand each employee or applicant on an individual basis. The CPS will assist you—or those in your organization who are responsible for developing human resources—to get to know each applicant or employee more quickly and carefully, and to have a record of this information that can be accessed instantly. Thus, you will be able to make more effective personnel and leadership decisions.

Dispel Employee Fears, Suspicions, and Anxieties

Clear expectations and feedback provided by the CPS relieve anxiety and promote positive motivation. Once people understand the system and know it will be used to help them do a better job, they will see how they can benefit from it personally. It is relatively easy to dispel suspicions and fears that can crop up when managers attempt to be careful and accountable in personnel practices, if the information that goes into the system is understood by the employee. If your policy is to give employees access to viewing their own files, and gain their consent prior to adding "soft" information to their files, you will find that trust levels will increase between employees and management.

Nine Steps in the Personnel Assessment and Development Process

Some people may already be familiar with the personnel process and the steps involved in it. The following page, entitled The Comprehensive Personnel Process, will assist you to do an assessment of the areas you think need attention in your organization. Simply highlight the area(s) you would like to see developed further.

The Comprehensive Personnel Process

Job Analysis—Job Specification—Screening

1. Job Analysis	2. Job Description	3. Screening Process
Identify Required:	*Specify in Writing:*	*Rate Applicant's:*
• Results	• Results expected	• Skills
• Job tasks	• Specify tasks	• Knowledge
• Job skills	• Specify roles	• Work history
• Social skills	• Extent of authority	• Extent of training
• Behavioral styles	• Job-style pattern	• Extent of education
• Difficulty level	• Performance criteria	• Application form
• Training requirements	• Progress evaluation date	• Decide on short list

Selection—Placement—Orientation

4. Application Review	5. Applicant—Job Fit	6. Orientation Process
Assess Applicant's:	*Rate Applicant's:*	*Contract for, or Inform re.:*
• Skills	• Skills	• Work tasks
• Knowledge	• Knowledge	• Expected results
• Work style (i.e., *PSI*)	• Training Required	• Work behavioral style
• Perception of job (i.e., *JSI*)	• Work/job style fit (*PSI/ JSI*)	• Appraisal criteria
• Past work experiences	• Interview performance	• Appraisal dates
• Interview Impressions	• Past work performance	• Workteam placement
• Testing results	• General suitability	• Length of probation

Performance Appraisal—Career Path Planning—Research

7. Performance Review	8. Develop Plans	9. Career Path Plan
Give Feedback about:	*Facilitate Agreement re.:*	*Specify Agreements re.:*
• Results achieved	• Present strengths	• Future job potentials
• Problem areas	• Past successes	• Plans for development
• Performance of tasks	• Areas to develop	• Completion dates
• Relationship factors	• Plans to develop	• Lateral transfrer options
• Work style/job fit	• Plans for training	• Research to validate selection criteria
• Performance goals	• On-the-job coaching	
• Probationary status	• Date of next review	

1. Specify Knowledge and Skills Required in a Position

Both skills and knowledge areas need to be delineated for each position. Relationship, task, and leadership factors also need to be specified. *The Job Knowledge and Skills Inventory* is used to specify all of the skill areas required by an employee so that he or she will be most effective in a given job. The more carefully the job analysis is done, the more accurately the requirements for that job will be understood and communicated to those doing the interviewing to select new personnel. Follow the instructions on-screen to analyze a particular job—this analysis leads to the production of a job description that can be attached to each employee's file. This job description can be easily edited as changes may be required from time to time.

2. Specify Appropriate Work-Style Behaviors in Each Job

By seeking agreement on a range of *Job Style Indicator (JSI)* scores on each style dimension of the *JSI*, managers and supervisors can agree upon an appropriate work style for each position in the organization. Asking employees who do a particular job to complete the *Job Style Indicator* is also useful in arriving at their understanding of the job they do.

This style (or range of acceptable behaviors) can be included as a part of each job description if you want to print or view the *JSI* scores for a job role. This agreement can be achieved by using the *Job Style Indicator* to define the appropriate work style for each position in the organization, as above. Those employees assessed as being very successful in their positions should have input into describing the requirements of each position so that managers who have never done that job can appreciate and consider their successful workers' points of view.

Doing a good job analysis requires a careful assessment of all of the dimensions of the job. An annual (or even more frequent) review of the job requirements often reveals that jobs change over time.

3. Specify a Job Description

Each position needs to have a clear job description, which attaches all of the above information plus the following.
1. Any objectives and timeline performance requirements
2. A clarification description of roles in relation to other positions—how this job fits in with other jobs
3. A clarification of extent and limits of authority in the position
4. A clear line of authority (who is above and below)
5. Information on how problems can best get solved
5. Progress evaluation criteria (how the employee will be evaluated)

6. Incentives or rewards that will be given if goals and performance criteria are reached
7. First and second performance evaluation dates, and who is to conduct them
8. Terms of probationary appointment
9. Conditions of termination (behaviors that will definitely cause the employee to be fired)

A good job description can be created from the information gathered from the above two steps. CPS automatically prints all such information when you ask for a particular job description on file.

4. Screen Applicants on Paper Qualifications First

Using the *Applicant Job Knowledge and Skills Inventory*, evaluate each applicant's extent of training and experience. Arrive at a short list based on close examination of paper applications, letters of reference, and resumes.

5. Assess Work Styles and Prepare for the Interview

Use the *Job Style Indicator* and the *Personal Style Indicator* to arrive at a clear summary of an applicant's perception of his/her work style and his/her perception of the work style thought to be appropriate for the job. If an applicant is not familiar with computers, a receptionist can assist to get people started—the rest is easy! Sometimes instead of using the computer, you may wish to use the paper-based response sheets available from Consulting Resource Group or a CRG Associate Company. In these cases, the *PSI* audio tape and *Living and Working with Style* (Anderson, Clark, & Clark) administration program can save staff administrative time. Some employers simply give the paper-based *PSI* and *JSI* to an applicant to complete at home, offering to answer questions about the instruments on the phone or in person, if needed.

Assess Other Relevant Factors: various other factors can be assessed at this time and entered into the applicant's data base such as typing speed, other task competencies, intellectual abilities, knowledge or personality tests, etc., appropriate and directly related to the requirements of the job.

Preparation for the Interview: applicants are instructed prior to the interview to come ready to talk openly about how they would personally approach the tasks and the people in the job for which they are applying. Make sure applicants have completed the *Personal Style Indicator* and *Job Style Indicator* before the interview and that they have read the interpretive comments appropriate to their profile pattern. In this way, applicants will be prepared to specifically answer the following eight (among other) key questions.

1. How do you treat people while you get your tasks done?
2. How much of a "fit" is there between how you see your own nature and the nature of the job?
3. How much style flexibility are you able and willing to demonstrate in your approach to tasks and people in this job?
4. What strengths would you bring to this job?
5. What difficulties might you have in this job?
6. How do you react under increased stress?
7. Do you have leadership inclinations or preferences? What kind of boss are you likely to follow?
8. What training do you think you might need in order to do the job better?

In the CPS system, applicants are given a copy of the appropriate *In-depth Interpretation* from the *PSI* (and instructions about how to prepare for the interview) to take home with them. They are instructed to highlight those statements in the interpretation with which they agree, and expand upon the interpretation in their own words in preparation for discussion during the interview. They are told they will be required to answer the above eight questions, as well as other questions deemed important.

It is made clear to all applicants in these instructions that neither the *Job Style Indicator* nor the *Personal Style Indicator* results will form the primary basis of any decision to hire them or not to hire them, but that their responses to the questions asked in the interview will partially determine the outcome. The instructions inform them they are being assessed on a number of measures, all of which will be included in the final decision to hire or not to hire. They are also informed prior to the interview that they will be encouraged to clarify their approach to the job in their own words during the interview.

Below is a sample of the one-page letter from CPS that you could use to assist the applicant to understand the interview and selection process you will be implementing:

To the Applicant: Preparing For Your Job Interview

Dear candidate,

Congratulations! You are among several candidates being given a final interview for the position you are seeking. Before you arrive for your interview, it is requested that you complete the *Personal Style Indicator* and the *Job Style Indicator*. Preparing to discuss your styles in the interview will take about one hour of your time at home, using the materials below. These indicators are not tests—but tools we use to help us communicate about the requirements of the job, and to help you communicate clearly to us about your style of getting the job done. You will not be selected or rejected on the basis of your responses to these indicators, but only on the basis of your qualifications and your performance in the interview. The *Indicators* are used as communication vehicles only.

You may take home the interpretation booklet or computer printout to assist in your understanding of your work style and the style you think is appropriate on the job.

You will be asked to talk about your work style in the job interview. Your understanding of the attached materials will assist you in interpreting your style indicators and in speaking clearly about how you would react to certain people or certain situations on the job.

Be ready to answer the following eight questions.

1. How do you treat people while you get your tasks done?
2. How much of a "fit" is there between how you see your own nature and the nature of the job?
3. How much style flexibility are you able and willing to demonstrate in your approach to tasks and people in this job?
4. What strengths would you bring to this job?
5. What difficulties might you have in this job?
6. How do you react under increased stress?
7. Do you have leadership inclinations or preferences?
8. What training do you think you might need in order to do the job better?

General Instructions: With the *Personal Style Indicator*, you will describe your work style. With the *Job Style Indicator*, you will describe the style you think is important in the job you seek. Follow the instructions in the *Personal Style Indicator* booklet and *Job Style Indicator* booklet. Complete both booklets. Please ask for assistance if you need further clarification, or use the *Personal Style Indicator Audio Tape Seminar* for clear instructions.

6. Interview Short-Listed Applicants

During this interview, the interviewer would have a similar set of questions (prepared in advance) to ask each interviewee to have some continuity between each interview session. These questions can be generated or read from the Job Description. This makes it possible to compare the way each applicant answers the same or similar questions. Mostly open questions should be asked (questions that require elaboration by the applicants, rather than closed questions requiring a "yes" or "no" answer) so that there can be depth in key areas of focus.

7. Hire, Orient, and Train New Employees

After hire, the new employee will likely have many questions about the manner in which he or she was hired, and will have a new appreciation for the issue of STYLE and its impact on job performance. Some companies have provided each new employee a copy of the *Personal Style Indicator* package to go through at home—most employees become extremely curious about such instruments and want to use them with their family members. This is a positive step because they are likely to learn to use the knowledge for their own personal development. When this occurs, they will bring this learning back into the workplace.

If groups of employees are hired at the same time, then they could all take a *Personal Style Indicator* workshop to orient them to the whole area of personal style, understanding and working with others' styles, and developing style flexibility to build effective workteams and improve performance and harmony in the workplace. For this, they could use the paper-based *PSI* rather than the computer-based assessment.

Most new employees will see quickly why you have used the CPS in the process of hiring them and will see the sense of it all in clarifying the requirements of their new jobs. Most will appreciate your taking the time to clarify how they can be more successful and how to be successful is often uppermost in the minds of new employees. They will also be able to understand the styles of their new supervisors, and how to work with them more effectively.

During the orientation process, you can provide your new employees with the following information if you want to get maximum performance with a minimum of confusion.

1. The purpose, philosophy, and goals of your organization (you obviously want your new employees to "buy into" how and why you want them to accomplish things)
2. The policies, practices, and procedures the new employees will need to know to be most effective and least confused (ideally you would already have prepared a staff manual with all this information in it)

3. The job descriptions of their new positions, which will include everything (mentioned above) that is needed to understand what is required of them
4. A formal letter describing the terms of their appointments, including length of probationary periods, amounts of pay, etc.
5. How the performance review and promotion system works in your organization, and when the first performance review will occur

Check to see that all new employees actually have the opportunity to talk about each item on their job descriptions. New employees may be so disoriented that they tend to assume they understand everything in their job descriptions. They often do not.

All of this information can be included in the Personnel Manual contained in the CPS, which can be edited and tailored to fit nearly any organization. This manual could be given to all new and existing employees to help them understand and gain a sense of accord with your organization.

8. Conduct Performance Reviews

For Employees Who Are Being Taken Off Probation We have found that employees will, when given a chance, do their own performance reviews. They can do this review on-screen within CPS themselves, if you give them access to the computer and to the CPS program for that purpose. If you do not want to do this, you can ask them to write one out that can later be inputted into CPS.

In the performance review, make sure feedback is tied to some kind of (preferably recent) behaviors the employee can recall. Give positive feedback first, then feedback regarding areas in need of improvement.

Respond to the employee with some understanding of how he or she is feeling and thinking about the items in the appraisal, and about the appraisal process itself. It is important that two-way, encouraging communication take place, and that the interview is seen as focused on how you appreciate that the employee has done well—and second, what the employee can do to improve. Get commitments on paper about improved performance in a maximum of three areas (a long list doesn't work as well). Then give the employee his or her copy of the performance review printout and Performance Enhancement Guidelines, and set a date for the next review.

Performance Review: For Employees Who Will Stay but Will Require Further Documentation These employee appraisal interviews are more difficult because you are giving a double message: You are saying their performance is not satisfactory, but you are going to continue employment anyway, at least for a specified period of time.

It is especially important with these employees that the positive things they have done are highlighted, and that agreements for specific changes are identified, written down, and committed to. Supervisors also need to commit to giving the necessary coaching and support to get the desired results. Then, later, if the employee meets the specified requirements, he or she will have hope of being taken off probation.

To develop morale and encourage minimal performers, you have to communicate to them that you believe their developing into good employees is a real possibility; otherwise, their next three to six months will be too stressful (or boring) and will add to their anxiety—or to their low performance, while they find another job at your expense. Give them support and feedback every week or two for awhile, until progress is sure.

If you have serious doubts, tell the employee this in no uncertain terms, using the approach outlined below.

Exit Review: For Employees Who are Being Let Go If during the specified probationary period the employee is identified as a high-risk low performer, you will find it necessary to inform him or her of your decision to terminate employment. You can explain that job performance has not been to the standard specified on the job description, and/or that the style of treating people (which you have described in the Performance Enhancement Guidelines: Performance Planning Agreement) while getting the job done is not acceptable. If all this information is specified on the job description and your warnings have been entered into CPS, you have covered your bases and are increasing your insurance against wrongful dismissal charges.

A letter of dismissal is appropriate at this time, and some outplacement service and direction regarding where to go from here may be appropriate. This is an important service to provide to the workforce and to society in general—particularly if you see strengths in the employee that might be better exercised in a different work environment.

You are unlikely to see grievances from legal or union sources when you have fairly told the employee ahead of time that certain tasks had to be performed to specific standards for him or her to remain in the position, and if there is documentation on paper that he or she, in fact, did not do so. Most employees will not argue with facts stated in terms of behaviors that they agree they have done or failed to do adequately. When in doubt, however, you should always refer to legal counsel and to the labor laws in your jurisdiction.

9. Career Path Planning

For those employees demonstrating leadership or managerial potential or some other needed expertise in the workplace, a career path can be identified and discussed with them in advance of an opportunity or job opening. They still need to know there will be competition for the position, but that you see them as having some potential for gaining it.

This must be sincere, and you can't do this with very many employees because usually only a few can move up the organization's ladder. You can sometimes lose some really good employees with real potential because you fail to help them see they have real possibilities for promotion or lateral transfer. Help them articulate what they would need to do to get ready for a job competition. Encourage them to take courses, do readings, take workshops, etc., that would increase their likelihood of being promoted.

Use the *Job Style Indicator* and *Personal Style Indicator* to help the employee understand the style behaviors appropriate for the available position. This can help the employee formulate a motivating internal career plan and a personal development plan, feel more challenged by the work, and assume more responsibility. This combination of factors will likely motivate him or her to seek the position even more strongly.

People Information is Performance Information!

By using the CPS, I have come to know those who work for me better. I also work with over 200 university students each year. I have found that if I know them well enough, I come to understand what challenges them as individuals. If I can come to know what areas of responsibility they want to assume, then I have incredibly motivating information! People information is leadership information!

Frederick Herzberg (1989) asserts that we cannot do it by improving work conditions, raising salaries, or shuffling tasks. He asserts:

> KITA—the externally imposed attempt by management to "install generators" in employees—has been demonstrated to be a total failure. The absence of such "hygiene" factors as good supervisor-employee relations and liberal fringe benefits can make workers unhappy, but the presence of these factors will not make employees want to work harder. Essentially meaningless changes in the tasks that workers are assigned to do have not accomplished the desired objective either. The only way to motivate employees is to give them challenging work for which they can assume responsibility.

If we can communicate with followers clearly enough to understand and appreciate the desires of their hearts—and provide opportunities for them to find the realization of them to some extent—we will likely find increased performance, loyalty, and longevity as a result. In achieving this result, we will have been transforming leaders.

Appendices

STAGES IN THE DEVELOPMENT OF A PERSONAL FAITH POSITION

Introduction to the Seven Cornerstone Principles

There are cornerstone principles that can make an important difference in our lives. Before we look more in-depth at the stages of faith development, I will present, discuss, and explore these principles. If these cornerstones are not used to build teams, organizations, families, and individual clarity, then the consequences can be serious. Briefly, these are the cornerstone principles.

1. Individual clarity precedes commitment
2. Individual commitment precedes motivation
3. Motivation precedes individual high performance
4. Individual performance precedes team performance
5. Team values alignment precedes high performance.
6. Goal clarity precedes team high performance
7. Higher performance is important in a competitive world

An Example from Sweden

A year after we published the First Edition of *Transforming Leadership*, I went to Stockholm to conduct a seminar for Swedish executives. Many of them had recently read the Swedish translation of my book, *Transforming Leadership: New Skills for an Extraordinary Future*.

For the past few decades, the Swedes have been ahead of much of the rest of the world in their innovative approach to team management. Even so, they were interested in hearing more about how the principles and practices in *Transforming Leadership* could help them strengthen team leaders to build world-class teams that could better compete with the pressures of global competition that we all face.

They also sought answers to some other problems they see as unique to their culture. Problems such as individual identity and motivation in a previously affluent society and a commitment to a vision of the common good through individual effort have pressed upon the Swedes. These problems are similar in nature, but perhaps more intense and obvious than those of the seventeen-to-thirty age group in North America (called "baby busters" by sociologists and marketing specialists).

I trust they gained some useful ideas from my seminar, but I was the one who left Sweden with some useful insights about how incredibly important managing the future with clarity and meaning is. If you are like me, you will be able to immediately apply these insights into creating and managing your own future by considering the Swedish experience.

Learning about Clarity from Sweden's Unique Experience

Sweden has produced an economy and form of government that is socialistic in the extreme.
1. If you want to go to college or university, it is all government-funded, as long as you want to go.
2. If you are unemployed (by choice or not), you are likely to earn as much as if you were employed.
3. If you have a medical problem, your medical fees are paid by the socialized medical plan.
4. If you are absent from work, you are paid anyway.

As a consequence of these and other forces, a number of companies, like Volvo, have to hire 30 percent more employees than they need to get the work done. On the average day, 30 percent of the employees are absent! In some ways, this can seem like a kind of utopia from the employees' perspective. I overheard one of them say, "I owe it to myself to take one or two days off per week; I'm paying for it in my taxes—and if I didn't take the time off, my fellow workers would hassle me!" When you listen to executives talk about the negative consequences of these conditions, you don't get the impression of utopia at all.

Please, Come to Work!

What some of these executives told me is that they have a hard time finding employees who want to work hard when they are at work, and an even more difficult time finding employees who will come to work at all on a regular basis. This disruption of the work environment due to absence and low motivation has eroded team synergy, quality, performance, and morale in many companies. Many people, both young and old, have lost their inner desire to work. Why is this?

At first, I thought this was the same problem many companies in North America have, especially among younger-generation employees who seem to lack commitment to the work ethic and who have lower motivation and morale—unless they get to do what they want to do. Then, as I listened more carefully, I heard things that revealed deeper causes.

1. "Our people have become used to being taken care of, from the 1970s until recently, having all the opportunities laid out for them, and now that things have changed and they have to take initiative on their own, they just don't feel like it—they don't believe they have to."
2. "They have lost a sense of reliance upon themselves and have become dependent upon 'government' to get their basic needs met. As a result, their souls have gone dry."
3. "We have lost our spiritual roots. We have become 'secularized' to the point that individuals have no life stance, and as a people we have no common world view—this has weakened our ability to act as a nation. For example, even though 95 percent of us claim to be Lutheran, less than 10 percent really believe in Christ and practice the Christian lifestyle."
4. "Some cling to the cultural and social history of our royalty but no longer acknowledge or seek to understand the deeper mysteries of life. We don't like anything that smells of religiosity (which we have experienced in the past as social control)—so we avoid spirituality altogether. This is a form of throwing the baby, as it were, out with the bath water. But we haven't found anything to replace what we have rejected. Perhaps some of us have even forgotten that we need to have deeper meaning in our lives in order to be inwardly motivated?"
5. "I find that we no longer have beliefs in ultimate things. In fact, I suspect that we are even curiously lacking in a definition of what the word 'belief' means—there is no directly translated word for it in Swedish. I have heard a number of executives saying that this is the single most interesting aspect of your book and your seminar presentation. We want to know what you mean by the word 'belief.' "

As I reflected on these comments, I found they aren't very different from those of our colleagues here in North America. The problem is perhaps more intense, and possibly more clearly articulated by our Swedish friends: people without a vision, without foundational assumptions, are vulnerable to a whole host of difficulties, and experience an inner emptiness. Lack of clarity breeds lower motivation; lower motivation results in lower performance and morale. Less optimism and hope are the end result—a downward spiraling of individual lives, corporate life, and family life.

Personal and Corporate Issues of Spirit

Many key leaders are keenly interested in looking into deeper personal and corporate issues of spirit—spirit in self and spirit in the workplace. Spirit is that innermost part of us that—while remaining somewhat of a mystery over our lifetimes—can be fathomed more and more as we grow.

It is that part of us that wants to know answers to ultimate questions, that wants to find some kind of relatedness to the ultimate, to grasp what we cannot see. It is that quiet center that can experience peace, joy, clear vision, and assurance of truth. It has been called, "The still, small voice within." It is the part beyond the psychological—the mysterious consciousness part that cannot be explained by psychology. It is in the spirit of a person that clarity can come. I offer the following learnings that have, in part, emerged from extended conversations with my Swedish friends.

Clarity of Beliefs, Identity, and Purpose is the Foundation of All Commitment and Action

Beliefs, identity, and purpose: They are intertwined, but beliefs are the foundation of the three. To become a motivated person who loves your work, I suggest that if you haven't done so, you seriously consider embarking on an exciting lifelong journey to seek clarity about why you really want to do anything.

This journey involves an exciting venture to seek greater truth about what life means, who you are, and what your purpose is. Vision, values, and goals are surely important but have much more power when they are based on inspiring and motivating beliefs, identity, and purpose.

In more detail, actions you can take to delve into these three parts are outlined:

1. Clarify options for your belief stance and choose one to test the reality of it—this involves studying the belief options and acting from a clear foundation of belief.
2. Clarify who and what you are as a person—with an inner life that gives you guidance and direction for personal and career life. This involves being authentic with others about who you are (your beliefs, strengths, preferences, purpose, values, goals, etc.) in ways that respect them rather than preach at or judge them.
3. Clarify a primary purpose for your life by writing it, speaking it, and living it—this involves pinpointing what sets you on fire, what could be a lifelong mission that you can feel wholehearted about, and getting into action to realize it.

If you are already well along on this "road less traveled," I encourage you to continue traveling it to gain more depth. If you are just beginning your conscious journey toward clarity, I encourage you to move ahead boldly for very good reasons.

These three primary issues—clarity about beliefs, identity, and purpose—are at the heart of what motivates individuals, allows groups to commit to common goals, and results in increased organizational performance. If neither the leaders nor their constituents have clarity about these critical issues, we can't reasonably expect them to be motivated about getting everyday work done. Moreover, if they have conflicting beliefs, identities, and purposes, they will work in a house divided against itself, and this house will likely fall. Clarity and consensus are critical if people are to feel they belong and want to perform well.

Therefore, to become more clear about what you believe, who you are, what you want, and why is to become free of vagueness, confusion, and lack of direction. The added clarity will give you a laser-beam focus that will fuel your motivational system.

The more clear it is, and the more sure you are of it, the more it will remind you of your commitment to bring it into reality. Going through this clarification process consciously—rather than unconsciously—is what gets people moving forward to realize their visions and dreams—because they have them clearly in mind.

If some things do not become clear to you at first, that's to be expected. Clarity comes as time goes by, as you study and meditatively focus, as you talk with others, and as you continue to seek it. As your beliefs, identity, and purpose become more clear, your vision of an ennobling future, values, and priorities will also become more focused. Then goals and plans more easily crystallize, as well.

Clarity as a Foundation for Leadership

In a complex and quickly accelerating world, we cannot afford to be without clarity in the center of the storm. We can choose to be clear. From this base of clarity, we can more consciously choose those with whom we wish to work, marry, partner, team, and live. Watch for the next article entitled, Clarifying the Muddy Waters to Build Strong People, Groups, and Organizations. That article will expand on the main points here and provide operating definitions of the key terms outlined in this article.

Like our Swedish friends, perhaps everyone—no matter how much we think we know now—can take a positive step forward toward greater clarity, commitment, and fulfillment of our mission in life. I invite you to begin or continue your journey of intentional living now. Those you love and serve will be the direct benefactors.

To develop this clarity, let us first examine my summaries of the developmental stages of belief delineated by Fowler (1981).

Clarification: A Developmental Process

Fowler describes the clarification and development of clear beliefs from a developmental perspective, by outlining what he calls "stages of faith."

Stage 0: This is a prestage called UNDIFFERENTIATED faith. The seeds of trust, courage, hope, and love are sown here during infancy and correspond somewhat to Erikson's psychosocial stage of Trust vs. Mistrust. When thought and language begin to converge, then the child moves through the transition to Stage 1.

Stage 1: This first stage is called the INTUITIVE-PROJECTIVE faith stage. Between ages three to seven, fantasy and imitation powerfully and possibly permanently form some basics of a belief system. Fluid thinking, the beginnings of self-awareness, and the verbalization of learned doctrines and concepts (mixed with imagination) are expressed, and the child begins to become more concrete in thought, separating fantasy from "doctrine," and getting ready to move into Stage 2.

Stage 2: MYTHICAL-LITERAL faith is characterized by the emergence of concrete, causal thinking, which is able to separate fantasy from the stories, doctrines, beliefs, and observances that have been taught in order to belong to the family or surrounding community. Symbols are taken literally, as are moral rules and attitudes. This is the faith stage of the school child (age seven to twelve), though this stage is found in many adolescents and adults.

People at this stage are able to be deeply affected by stories and dramatic presentations (highly vulnerable to influence, therefore) but are not yet able to consciously reflect on the meaning or possible errancy of such presentations (TV included). Because of a lack of reflective or relative-thinking capacity, they may seem to be "legalistic," black-and-white thinkers.

The transition to Stage 3 is marked with a breakdown of literalism. Contradictions in stories or reflective logic can cause disillusionment with previous teachers or teachings (including parental influences and early religious training). Formal operational thought makes such reflection possible and necessary.

Stage 3: This stage is called SYNTHETIC-CONVENTIONAL faith. It emerges most often in adolescence, but for many adults, becomes a place of nonresponsible comfort, fun, or avoidance of further development. This is a "conformist" stage because a person's security and identity are defined and dependent upon others. It does not have enough inner—and autonomous—judgment or solid faith to build and maintain an inner resolution about beliefs. The Stage 3 person believes, but often not in a wholehearted, well-examined manner, and constantly scans the environment (especially the social environment) to see if what is believed is popular and accepted.

The adolescent is using the beliefs and assumptions acquired in childhood in a sense to "get by" during the turbulent and insecure teenage years—until full formal operational thinking capacity develops; then, a full and thorough examination regarding the source, validity, and utility of a belief system (and therefore an inner identity) can be independently begun. Quite often crises occur (such as the failure of a love relationship, the parents' marriage, or leaving home), which precipitate the breakdown of Stage 3 and the need to move into the "crisis of the deeper life," which can prove to be the most critical, but also most rewarding, transition.

Stage 4: Stage 4 is called INDIVIDUATIVE-REFLECTIVE faith. At this time, a person realizes how alone he or she really is in deciding everything, even if there has been relegation of that responsibility to others, a person's self-awareness causes a painful realization that "my decisions are in my own hands." Many adults do not reach this stage, perhaps because they are, for a number of reasons, unable—or if they do, they turn away from the burden of responsibility for their own consciously chosen life, and turn to the age-old philosophy of Numbism, supported in full force by the increasingly available forms of "soma" (alcohol, drugs, eating, TV, and other "give up" paraphernalia described by Glasser, 1984).

This level is extremely difficult to face, and especially difficult to face alone. There are fewer and fewer people more developed than you are to give you help as you move up the stages of development! If the call to higher belief definition is heeded, the reward is a sense of one's own being beyond the definitions others give us, and beyond the roles one happens to be in at the time. For many people in this stage, a certain sense of the reality of a "higher being" has been reported to be especially strong and clear in a personal way.

At this level, the ability to critically reflect on one's own self-identity and upon various outlooks or ideologies is greatly enhanced. The ability to be increasingly objective is a danger, however, in that there can come a kind of cognitive self-assurance that closes off a continuing deeper search, and trades it in for "settling for security." For many people, however, there creeps in a certain restlessness, a sense of flatness, or sterility to life that prompts or even urges a higher search for greater meaning and intimacy with what ultimately is to be discovered. This stage has been called by many the "mid-life crisis," and seems to often occur for many people in their early to mid-forties.

Stage 5: Stage 5 is called CONJUNCTIVE faith. Often the potential power in symbolic meanings comes alive for people in this stage. Ricoeur calls it a "second naivete" ACCENT where the emotional and/or spiritual impact of one's beliefs becomes quickened, or alive in each moment—"becoming as a little child," if you will. A reworking of the fabric of one's past into the garment of the future must be attended to. In mid-life, when this stage usually occurs, there is a seriousness that emerges and it knows the realities of defeat, the irrevocability of certain commitments and acts, and it is in full appreciation that life is more than half-over (at best).

This is the sobering, deepening time when the search for inner resolve and resolution is contrasted with a curious openness to new depths of spirituality and the possibility of personal revelations. A sense of the ironic—the paradoxes of life, the unsolvable mysteries—makes life both more magical and the individual more able to be in a state of wonder and awe. On the other hand, some people become bitter or get into a state of complacency or cynical withdrawal if the power of faith is not sufficient to withstand a more full awareness of the inescapable presence of death and the unknown.

While many people in this stage report deep peace, inner resolution, and interrelatedness to their supreme being and loved ones, others report a sense of hopelessness and futility and excruciating hollowness when they arrive near the top of this developmental climb. In only a few cases, people who arrive at this stage are moved or committed to move on to the stage of radical actualization called Universalizing Faith (Stage 6).

Stage 6: UNIVERSALIZING FAITH is characterized by the person's radical commitment to the sanctity of all being, all life, justice, love, and of selfless passion for a transformed world. They aren't pushing what they personally wish to see happen (as Hitler or the Reverend Jim Jones), but are committed to a transcendent vision as were Gandhi and Martin Luther King, Jr., and as is Mother Theresa— and many others who had "no greater love than this, than to lay down their lives for their friends" (Jesus, approximately 33 AD). They seem to have a "subversive" character that challenges the status quo, governments, and/or individuals to reach past their own usual patterns of self-orientation to the higher path of love for others.

Fowler states of these Stage 6 people:

> It is my conviction that persons who come to embody Universalizing faith are drawn into those patterns of commitment and leadership by the providence of God and the exigencies of history, heated in the fires of turmoil and trouble, and then hammered into usable shape on the hard anvil of conflict and struggle (Fowler, p. 202).

These people in Stage 6 have a clear vision of what life is "meant to be," are able to feel the injustice and suffering imposed on others, are nearly always heralded for their uncommon courage and faith, and are willing to die for the cause of justice and the liberation of any and all people. Not many of us are able or perhaps willing to take the full leap into Universalizing faith.

Admittedly, the six steps outlined above are "Western" in their orientation, much as are the developmental stages of Piaget. These stage-specific theories do not seem true to some people in other cultures. Fowler, however, has at least given us a starting place in understanding the development of what many people would call the spiritual part of people.

Steps in the Process of Clarification of Your Belief Stance

The process of clarifying your beliefs involves several steps. By following these steps, your own belief stance will become more clear as time passes. The steps for clarifying beliefs can be done with your own self, or you can help an individual or group of people to gain resolution by coaching them through the following steps.

1. As best you can, specify in writing your present answers to life's major questions as outlined in Chapter 4 (or attempt to answer your own problem questions).
2. Search out the sources of your beliefs and write down these sources for later comparison.
3. Examine your criteria for accepting these beliefs as true, and write down the various validations for your beliefs that you accept.
4. Write a clear and concise position paper about your stance on life's major questions and issues.
5. Read this paper over once a week while you consistently attempt to take on this position in a real way, living it out on a daily basis as congruently as you are able.
6. Review your position statements every three to six months, and examine how your position helps you to deal with problems or better appreciate the joys of life.
7. Note any "holes" or inconsistencies in your belief positions that you think may be invalid, incomplete, or problematic.
8. Examine other differing belief positions (ones you think are incomplete, or false, if any) that validate how true your position is for you. Or note how there are parts of other positions that seem to have truth in them on the premise that "truth is truth wherever it is found." To assist you to get started with this step, I suggest that you consider reading Chapter 9 in Naisbitt and Aburdene's book, *Megatrends 2000*. This book will give you a factual overview of what is occurring in the world of beliefs. Using this chapter as an introduction, you could move ahead with a more thorough study of each of the various philosophical or religious belief positions.

Students who have generally followed this series of steps in my courses on self-awareness and interpersonal communication have reported in course evaluations that this exercise was the most challenging and meaningful of their semester. Some of them even reported it was the most important step in their whole lives.

The Downside of Failing to Clarify a Lifestance

People who avoid this whole issue of belief clarification—or give up on its resolution—perhaps are less deeply "rooted" in a life position. They may be more easily influenced to move in a number of directions, depending upon which way a personal, social, political, or economic "wind" is blowing at the time; they often claim that "flexible" tendency to be a strength—that they are "open minded," willing to "change with the times." They also often say that they have little inner peace, that decision-making is difficult without a clear reference point, and that their relationships suffer because they often clash with people who have clear beliefs.

I believe those who have a metaphysical understanding of and orientation to life (answers to the "why" questions) have a distinct advantage—even if their orientation may ultimately be incorrect in the end. I believe they are more solid, act more consistently, can get feedback from the environment as to the validity and workability of their actions (because they have a position as a reference point), and many times, are better able to understand others' positions—a "tolerance" skill important when leading people.

Beliefs form the solid foundation of a clear purpose in life; clear values are structures upon which to build goals, strategies, and actions. With only values to live by, the "why" of life is not addressed, explored, or resolved in the least. Beliefs directly address the "why" and "what" questions of life.

When people can share some basic beliefs, they are more likely to join together to create something productive. This is true for marriage partners or any other type of endeavor in business, health, education, community development, or human services—where team effort is required.

Furthermore, if you understand others' beliefs, you are more likely to comprehend why they have given their "hearts" to their beliefs, why they feel they need them, why they need to keep their own beliefs, and you can become even be more tolerant.

If you want to move ahead toward greater clarity, you could turn to the last chapter in this book and complete the process called "Deep Structure Strategic Planning."

DEEP STRUCTURE STRATEGIC PLANNING

A Process to Optimize Personal, Team, and Organizational Clarity and Performance

"Sharpening the Inner Edge" for Morale and Performance Improvement

A great number of strategic planning programs deal with strengths, weaknesses, opportunities, threats, vision, and goals. These aspects of planning are inadequate by themselves. There are important, deeper issues that need to be included in personal and organizational strategic planning if extraordinary and lasting results are to be achieved.

First, we need to clarify the murky waters of the many critical concepts in strategic planning to identify the important differences among them. These are the critical concepts: **beliefs, identity, vision, mission, purpose, values, ethics, and goals.** Most individuals do not have clear definitions or descriptions of these separate and important parts of their inner lives. Neither do most organizations. This vagueness is demoralizing and undermines meaning, strong motivation, and performance.

For example, leaders often express their values as though they were their beliefs. They state their missions as though they were their visions or values. This murky, but likely unintentional practice, prevents visions from solidifying, blocks consensus for team development, and thereby undermines performance improvement. In an attempt to dispel this confusion, I will provide you, in the paragraphs that follow, with the most discrete operating definitions of these transforming concepts I have seen anywhere.

Once you understand the differences among these concepts—and see that you can use each concept to gain important life-changing insights—you will want to go through a process of becoming clear at each level. We should have had the opportunity to do this on an ongoing basis since our school years, but who had the know-how to assist us?

First, let's get a visual picture of the components that form a strong inner architecture. You will see below that each component forms a solid foundation for the next.

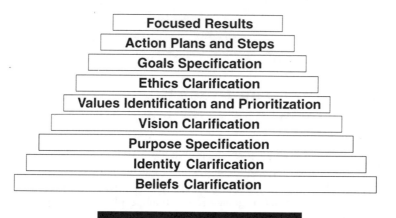

Focused Results
Action Plans and Steps
Goals Specification
Ethics Clarification
Values Identification and Prioritization
Vision Clarification
Purpose Specification
Identity Clarification
Beliefs Clarification

Developing Inner Clarity to Achieve External Results

The process of inner development and formation of internal "architecture" is not entirely linear (as illustrated above). It seems to develop rather organically—sometimes with unexpected bursts of clarity at various levels. It does make sense, however, to pay attention to the more foundational matters like beliefs, identity, purpose, or vision before attempting to formulate our goals or plans. Most people, without realizing it, start with goals and omit clarifying the motivating reasons of beliefs, purpose, vision, or mission that could jump-start and sustain their performance.

It also helpful to understand there is a process for building strength and clarity inside individuals, within groups, and in organizations. This process can be step-by-step, as indicated above in the **Hierarchy of Key Success Factors**. It is even more helpful to put this process into action by focusing separately to gain clarity at each level. This process is what I call **Deep Structure Strategic Planning**. This kind of deeper structure strategic planning involves considering the nearest and dearest motivations of each individual and blends these into a team and corporate culture that results in exceptional morale and performance. The literature on high-performance teams and companies attests to the fact that clarity and consensus get results.

It is most difficult, but most fruitful, to begin at the foundation with beliefs and purpose. People often fail to adequately attend to "why" issues (beliefs and purpose) because they are more difficult to articulate and express. Most people have general goals but don't know WHY they might want to be a police officer, business manager, school teacher, nurse, or bike technician and they do not consider what **consequences** might follow (personally, for their family or financially), or what deeper or higher purpose a particular personal vocation or corporate strategic plan might fulfill.

If you leave out or skip over one of the building blocks, your "building" will not have the strength it needs to withstand the storms of change, or the power it needs to push ahead with vision toward an ennobling future. Investing the time to make each block strong, clear, and solid builds confidence, and this confidence increases your morale and performance. Outlined below are the explanations of the main building blocks, with some suggestions about how you can gain clarity to strengthen them. Consider this outline an introduction to the concepts that will be covered in depth should you participate in a **Deep Structure Strategic Planning** workshop-seminar or individual coaching session.

Beliefs are Your Assumptions about these Concepts:

1. WHAT is going on here in this universe?
2. What is true, real, false, unreal, good, and bad?
3. How can I validate what is true? What criteria are reliable?
4. What is the origin, source, and purpose of life?
5. What is at the foundations of life?
6. Why does life exist? My life?
7. How should I conduct my life and how should I love?
8. Should I even concern myself with these types of questions?
9. How do I know my life has meaning?

These are, of course, tough questions. Your beliefs are the foundation cornerstones of **everything** you think, judge, plan, hope for, and seek to achieve. They form the basis for all moral and ethical decisions. They are the screen through which you filter and interpret your world. Your beliefs also determine your mental attitude to some extent—in terms of your being basically hopeful, neutral, or pessimistic about life.

Some people have very clearly defined assumptions about what they believe, but most people are just not clear. Others dismiss the issue as "philosophic fuzzy stuff" that they don't want to deal with right now. The caution is, **be careful how you assume things to be because for you, that's how they are right now!**

I should say here that I believe that some beliefs are in error. For example, I cannot subscribe to fascism or any type of authoritarian rule that overrides individual free will because I BELIEVE that free will is integral to commitment, motivation, morale, and performance. You can continue to clarify your beliefs over time and, as you do so, you will discover greater depth of meaning in life and work.

In the Space Below, Write a Point-Form Summary of Your Key Beliefs:

-
-
-
-
-
-
-
-
-
-
-
-
-
-
-
-
-
-

Your Identity is Based on:

1. WHO and WHAT you *believe* you are
2. Experiences with family
3. Experiences with social groups and school
4. Success, failure, and traumatic experiences
5. A vision of what could be possible for you
6. An internal image of how you think others see you

Your identity is shaped and limited by the boundaries of your beliefs. You can only think of yourself in ways you assume are true about the nature of people and the nature of life itself. For example, if you assume, as the existential philosophers do, that life is absurd and has no meaning, then you will consider you are nothing but a speck of sand on the shore of a drifting, chaotic universe that may be washed away at any moment. The consequences of such a belief system are that people often adopt a philosophy of, "Carpe Diem" (seize life!)—or translated into "baby buster's" language (age seventeen to thirty): "Party on dude, for tomorrow we may die!"

If, on the other hand, you assume you are a created spirit of an intentional Being who knows and cares for you and all people, then your view of your identity will be that you and all people are extremely precious—the most valuable of all life forms and more valuable than the most expensive crown jewel. Would you trade someone you love for such a gemstone? This is just an example of how our beliefs shape what we can conceive ourselves and others to be. This conception, therefore, shapes our beliefs about our own and others' worth.

If you want to gain clarity about how you see yourself now, you can list words or phrases that describe **who** and **what** you believe you are (such as "visionary leader," "protector of the people," "cool dude," "great musician," "serious scholar," "child of God," etc.). These phrases can help you to remain conscious of how you see yourself. How you see yourself limits or expands what you will do with your life in a serious way.

In the Space Below, Write a Point-Form Summary to Describe Your Identity:

What is Important and Exciting to You?

1. List the 7 most important events in your life:

    .

    .

    .

    .

    .

    .

    .

2. List the 7 most exciting events of your life:

    .

    .

    .

    .

    .

    .

    .

3. List 7 phrases that describe who and what you are:

    .

    .

    .

    .

    .

    .

    .

4. Complete the sentence, "I am a person who..." _____

_____

_____

Now look over your list and identify what it was about these events that made them important or exciting.* This will assist you in painting your future vision. You do not need to know why they are important, only that they are.

> * For example:
> Exciting Event   Presented to 5,000 people
>
> Excitement was: Speaking to a large group of people; preparing the presentation; telling people about the event

This process will assist you to gain greater clarity about the kind of person you are—in terms of your interests, abilities, and the significant life experiences that have shaped your current understanding of your identity to this point in your life.

Vision is a Mental Picture of What You Believe to Be Possible for Your Future:

1. For a preferred future
2. To inspire and motivate self and others
3. Regarding dreams that could come true

We can only envision what we can conceive to be possible because of our beliefs and our identity. If we believe we are "stupid" because of previous negative experiences at school, we won't envision ourselves receiving a Ph.D. years down the road! If we do envision ourselves as having a Ph.D. years hence, **it is possible** that this could occur! If we don't, it surely will not. So, vision is at the beginning of most things we end up doing, **whether we are conscious of our vision or not.**

Consciously held visions often take on power and energy and come into being, but if visions are not consciously in focus, they tend to lie somewhat dormant. If you want to get a start on clarifying your vision, write a brief statement that outlines what your life will be like, what you will be doing, where you will be living, and with whom you will be living and working in five years, and in ten years. Revise your vision as time goes by and as your understanding increases. This is a powerful exercise that gets results!

In the Space Below, Write a Point-Form Vision of Your Future:

In Five Years

•

•

•

•

In Ten Years

•

•

•

•

Purpose is a Public Statement:

1. Of WHY you intend to move ahead toward your vision
2. Of what you intend to accomplish
3. That sets you on fire
4. That could be lifelong, but is updated often
5. That emerges from a deep and clear sense of vision

Purpose cuts to the chase, goes to the jugular vein of our lives, and helps us to get in touch with what truly moves us in our hearts and guts. Having a clear sense of purpose is to *understand the reason that underlies what you want to do with your life—and with your career.*

So many people do not search for and find a sense of clear purpose. They do not find because they do not search. As a result, their lives are hollow and they feel they are stuck on treadmills over which they have no control. Over 80 percent of workers in one survey report not finding satisfaction in their work. More than 80 percent express confusion about where they would go and what they would do if their present career were to come to an end.

Life does not have to be that way. It is possible to gain a clearer sense of purpose **by continuing to consciously seek for greater clarity**, the same way as outlined in the beliefs and vision sections above.

Sometimes it is difficult to get in touch with this issue of purpose within ourselves. It is very important to do so, however, because that can build your motivation level.

1. The greater the clarity of purpose, the more intense the "laser beam" motivation.
2. The greater your motivation, the easier it is to concentrate.
3. The easier it is to concentrate, the greater your success.

As an example of a purpose statement, one person who wants to become a leader wrote this:

> *"It is my purpose to lead people toward realizing their talents, interests, identities and sense of purpose. My leadership of their personal development will positively influence their loyalty to my company, will enhance their performance, and we will all move ahead toward success together.*

If you want to make an attempt toward additional clarity of purpose, you could write a first draft of your own purpose statement and continue to revise it as time goes by. Post it in a place where you can review it each morning and evening. It will become emblazoned in the forefront of your mind and will drive your motivation and accomplishments.

In the Space Below, Write a First-Draft Summary of Your Purpose Statement:

Values are Personal Priorities about What's Important To You:

1. They determine HOW you go about getting things done.
2. They determine how you treat people.
3. They determine your real priorities.
4. How you spend your *time* is a true measure of values.

Once we have a clearer sense of beliefs, vision, and purpose it is easier to sort through all the possible values priorities we could embrace in life, and begin to limit ourselves to focus on the ones that are ***most important*** to us. This process of narrowing down our options is called **values clarification or specification,** and is difficult but rewarding to do.

Most people do not really think seriously about this issue. As a result, they set goals, get jobs, and wonder why five years later they are caught in a job that doesn't fit their interests, abilities, and purpose. Now they have kids, a mortgage, a car payment, and credit card bills, and find it difficult to find time to seriously search—let alone go back to school or start a new business.

This pattern is scary and far too common. The value priorities they unconsciously held when they laid the foundations of their adult lives were fun, money, relationships, etc. But, because many people don't do these kinds of things for a higher purpose, they lose a sense of deeper meaning in their work. Or, they base their lives on their career goals, rather than base their career goals on their plan for living a purposeful, value-ordered life. The unexamined life can feel like it may not be worth living, if it goes to the extreme.

In the Space Below, Write a Point-Form Summary of Your Operating Values:

• Example: Honesty and integrity

•

•

•

•

•

•

•

•

•

•

•

•

•

•

•

•

•

Ethics are Formal Codes of Conduct

They are:
1. Based on values
2. Agreed-upon between parties
3. Shared by an association of people
4. Breakable, and penalties are often imposed for ethical breaches (Dishonesty and manipulative gain are two examples.)

Ethics are ways of acting that conform to the agreements between people who belong to certain groups or associations. For example, psychologists, doctors, lawyers, and accountants all have professional codes of ethical conduct—confidentiality, for example—that they must follow if they want to continue to practice. If they breach their ethical oaths, they can be prevented from working for a period of time, and for serious enough offences and breaches of ethics, they can lose their licenses to practice.

In the Space Below, Write a Point-Form Summary of Your Ethics:

-
-
-
-
-
-
-
-
-
-

Goals that Lead to Success Are:

1. Set after beliefs, vision, purpose, and values are specified
2. Well-defined targets for accomplishment
3. Concrete and specific
4. Bound by timelines
5. Worthwhile achieving
6. Realistic and achievable
7. Committed to wholeheartedly

Goals help bring substance to your vision of your future. When you write out a goal statement, it is far more likely to get accomplished than if you just think about it. If you post your goals in a place where you see them regularly, check your progress, and reward yourself for achievement—your list of accomplishments will be increased. A written goal becomes a commitment to get results by a specific date. The more specific and well defined your goals are, the more enhanced your chances of reaching them will be. Goals, once they are translated into accomplishment statements, become achievable as a part of a step-by-step plan. These goals can be personal growth goals, educational goals, career goals, spiritual goals, and/or physical goals.

In the Space Below, Write a Point-Form Summary of Your Personal Goals

-
-
-
-
-
-
-
-

Action Plans and Strategic Steps Are:

1. Agreed-upon by individuals
2. Supported by team consensus
3. Challenging enough to stretch performance
4. Realistic enough to be achievable
5. Defined in concrete, actionable terms
6. Accountable on a schedule for review
7. On someone's job descriptions
8. In your or someone's time schedules

This step is critical to the implementation of your plan. This is really the most important step of all, because it is the one that will result in achievement of your goals. It is on this page(s) that you want to summarize action steps for the achievement of each of your goals. These action steps get translated to your schedule or to another team member's schedule for implementation. You will meet with yourself or others for a review and celebration of the accomplishments, analyze failures, and plan for further success.

In the Space Below, Write a Point-Form Summary of Action Steps and Strategies for the Achievement of Your Goals:

Action Steps   Completion Target Dates

-   __ / __ / __

-   __ / __ / __

-   __ / __ / __

-   __ / __ / __

-   __ / __ / __

-   __ / __ / __

-   __ / __ / __

-   __ / __ / __

-   __ / __ / __

Index

T

V

W